MW01201621

Sustainable Online Library Services and Resources

SUSTAINABLE ONLINE LIBRARY SERVICES AND RESOURCES

Learning from the Pandemic

Mou Chakraborty,
Samantha Harlow, and
Heather Moorefield-Lang, Editors

An Imprint of ABC-CLIO, LLC

Santa Barbara, California • Denver, Colorado

Copyright © 2023 by ABC-CLIO, LLC

All rights reserved. No part of this publication may be reproduced, stored in a retrieval system, or transmitted, in any form or by any means, electronic, mechanical, photocopying, recording, or otherwise, except for the inclusion of brief quotations in a review, without prior permission in writing from the publisher.

Library of Congress Cataloging-in-Publication Data

Names: Chakraborty, Mou, editor. | Harlow, Samantha, editor. |
    Moorefield-Lang, Heather, editor.
Title: Sustainable online library services and resources : learning from
    the pandemic / Mou Chakraborty, Samantha Harlow, Heather
    Moorefield-Lang, editors.
Description: Santa Barbara, California : Libraries Unlimited, [2023] |
    Includes bibliographical references and index.
Identifiers: LCCN 2022027127 (print) | LCCN 2022027128 (ebook) | ISBN
    9781440879258 (paperback ; acid-free paper) | ISBN 9781440879265 (ebook)
Subjects: LCSH: Electronic reference services (Libraries) | Electronic
    information resources. | Electronic information resource literacy. |
    Libraries and public health. | COVID-19 Pandemic, 2020–
Classification: LCC Z711.15 .S87 2023 (print) | LCC Z711.15 (ebook) | DDC
    025.5/24—dc23/eng/20220701
LC record available at https://lccn.loc.gov/2022027127
LC ebook record available at https://lccn.loc.gov/2022027128

ISBN: 978-1-4408-7925-8 (print)
        978-1-4408-7926-5 (ebook)

27 26 25 24 23   1 2 3 4 5

This book is also available as an eBook.

Libraries Unlimited
An Imprint of ABC-CLIO, LLC

ABC-CLIO, LLC
147 Castilian Drive
Santa Barbara, California 93117
www.abc-clio.com

This book is printed on acid-free paper ∞

Manufactured in the United States of America

Contents

Introduction

There are few moments in life permanently etched in our minds—"flashbulb memories" that highlight where we were at the time of a chaotic event. The modern "shot heard 'round the world" happened on March 13, 2020, when the landscape of the world shifted with the onset of a global pandemic. The COVID-19 pandemic's effect on the health care industry was glaring, but what about the changes in education, particularly for libraries? A silver lining of this historic turbulence was the newfound accessibility of education through distance learning, but the transition to an online learning environment was challenging for patrons, staff, and teachers at all institutions and libraries, including university, special, school, and public systems. But service institutions tend to persevere; in this book, we showcase the experiences of diverse librarians who were and are facilitating a helpful and inclusive online learning environment.

Changes are inevitable—the switch to primarily online learning would likely have occurred eventually as we accelerate into a fully digital age—but the COVID-19 pandemic hastened this change, adding a new layer of challenges to student-faculty relationships. It prompted the utilization of digital learning platforms, which created a learning atmosphere previously unfamiliar to a majority of teachers, faculty, and librarians. This book highlights the ever-changing roles of librarians during this unprecedented time of monumental change in library infrastructures, partnerships, and access to materials. The weight of the pandemic on all populations was a heavy one, with many concerned about loved ones while dealing with job loss and an uncertain economy. Many people also were deprived of the typical school, college, or work experience. Despite all of the challenges posed by COVID-19, libraries found ways to connect patrons to services and helped foster communities of compassion. With the promise of vaccines and an ongoing search for a cure, educators armed themselves with masks and Zoom to give patrons the resources they deserve, for after all, "there is no pleasure more complex than that of thought."

As we returned to a sense of normalcy, or embarked on a new normal, we (the editors) wanted to hear from different kinds of libraries, particularly what they have been doing to adjust and what ideas are sustainable for the future. COVID-19 has impacted and shifted how all libraries and public institutions provide services and resources; the future of libraries will depend on the ability of librarians, teachers, and designers to learn and grow from these transitions. Different types of libraries were impacted by the pandemic in different ways, but librarians at each learned valuable lessons on how to shift and transition in a challenging time. The chapters in this book chronicle how they pivoted services and resources online to continue to serve patrons during the pandemic and beyond, and we discuss which services and programs will be sustainable and scalable to continue to best help patrons.

This book will serve as a road map of what library assistance can be implemented in a post-pandemic world and of challenges that might arise in the future. The chapter topics include instruction strategies, asynchronous online design and creation, accessibility and equity issues, collection management, public service techniques, programming, and more. Online learning in the delivery of programs and services can prepare librarians for many different situations, emergencies, or challenges that might arise and provide lessons that libraries will keep and implement from their experiences during the pandemic.

The sudden pivot to virtual learning was not anything new to many librarians; they were already providing instruction and support to distance students using a variety of modalities. In fact, as libraries and educators grappled with paradigm shifts during the pandemic, librarians and online resources quickly became more vital than ever. The pandemic initiated a surge of "other online duties as assigned" for librarians who otherwise would not have considered themselves distance or online learning librarians. The chapter "Other Duties (and Places) as Assigned: How Analog Approaches Are Impeding Progress in Online Librarianship" acknowledges these temporary "other online duties" and notes that this cannot be a sustainable option in the long run, as we now know that the shift toward online learning is permanent.

A somewhat related note is echoed in the chapter "The Impact of the COVID-19 Pandemic on Hiring and Onboarding in Academic Libraries," in which the authors describe the struggles and successes in job searching, interviewing, relocating, and ultimately beginning new librarian positions just prior to or during the COVID-19 pandemic. Similar sentiments are noted from a special library perspective in the chapter "Retooling the Academic Librarian Hiring Process."

Several chapters discuss new and creative ways of pivoting to virtual services and instruction. "Chatting into the Void: Scaling and Assessing

Chat Reference Services for Effectiveness" tells about a library team analyzing chat data to ensure online resources contain essential information. "The Archive Is Temporarily Closed: Teaching Students Alternative Methods for Finding Archival Materials Online" provides an overview of traditional archival literacy practices and challenges, analysis of effective strategies, and sustainable solutions to conducting primary source research in an online environment.

A focal issue for reference and instruction librarians during the pandemic was to decide how to most efficiently cater to user needs during this ongoing crisis through flexibility, creativity, and adaptability. This theme resonates in several chapters dealing with online instruction. In the chapter "Leverage from the Lockdown: Transitioning Information Literacy Instruction during the COVID-19 Pandemic: A Case Study," we learn about information literacy and instruction strategies deployed at the University of the West Indies in the developing country of Barbados. "The Virtual Graduate Research Marathon: Remote Library Instruction for Doctoral Candidates" shows us strategies for the specific audience of graduate students. Similarly, in "Converting In-Person Library Instruction for an Introductory Communication Studies Course into an Online Asynchronous Module: One Team's Experiences," we see a librarian instruction team's strategy of working asynchronously with first-year students at a mid-sized, public university. Instruction within the learning management system and creating and maintaining online learning objects about information literacy is vital to helping students, and this is portrayed in the chapter "Keeping Instruction Sustainable Post-COVID-19 with a Learning Objects Repository." And in "Exploring the Feasibility of a Hybrid Approach to a Post-pandemic Information Literacy Lesson," a science and technology (STEM) college takes a hybrid approach to help students with research assignments, which is showcased in this case study.

Assisting employees and colleagues during challenging times is also crucial for the success of any institution, and this book contains case studies on different techniques of different library departments, as well as chapters on training and professional development strategies. Describing the shift toward online training, the chapter "Building the Train as We Chug Along the Tracks: A Reimagined Staff Training Model" presents a description of the tools used to provide high-quality virtual professional development to all employees within the library. The chapter "Keeping the Focus on Patrons at the Salisbury University Libraries" is about how one university library system navigated the pandemic to provide the best service possible in all of their departments and incorporated takeaways and lessons learned into their permanent workflows to promote greater access for all patrons. And in the chapter "Library Workers' Well-Being during a Pandemic," there is information on library directors', supervisors', and managers' experience with training employees for virtual work, and it showcases what was done for library workers' well-being during a crisis.

Both academic and public libraries struggled to connect with their communities, and most took this as an opportunity to develop virtual programming options to promote various services and resources. In the chapter "Data: How Do You Drink from a Waterfall?," we get a global perspective in which the authors discuss open educational resources (OER) and data from Latin American repositories as a potential solution for integrating and democratizing access to health knowledge for professionals. "Finding New Ways to Support Social Connections for Older Adults: Rural Public Libraries Innovate during the Pandemic" provides information to public librarians and anyone working with older adults about the innovations rural librarians pioneered as they sought to support social connectedness for the elderly, as well as the implications of these experiments for public library services going forward. The chapter "Maintaining Comics and Gaming Programming during Institutional Change" delineates how the university library explored creative alternative solutions to gaming services and pop culture events in response to COVID-19 with the closure of the library. This chapter also shows how the experience provided insights into establishing a sustainable game library collection while maintaining relationships remotely with various stakeholders.

The recent pandemic changed all of society and induced a definite shift in the collective mindset. Libraries are vital services that help with a diverse set of information literacy needs, and they encountered many different challenges throughout the COVID-19 pandemic. But ultimately, librarians are adaptable and flexible, and this book was created to showcase the resiliency of educators and librarians during the global crisis. The editors wanted to show a wide range of perspectives on how online learning has changed and grown over the last couple years, with a focus on what services and resources are here to stay for libraries across the globe. We hope that readers can connect the many lessons learned in these chapters to some part of their job or life, no matter what library they come from or are heading to, and find their own sustainable path forward in this brave new world.

Building the Train as We Chug Along the Tracks: A Reimagined Staff Training Model

Emily Leachman and A. Garrison Libby

INTRODUCTION

When the COVID-19 pandemic hit in March 2020, it caused disruptions across libraries. Classes, events, and services that were in-person had to quickly be transformed so that they could instead be delivered remotely. As services changed, it became especially important to train staff so that the transition could be as seamless as possible to ensure continued library operations and service to patrons.

For Central Piedmont Community College, this meant reconsidering how to conduct training for a library with staff at seven different locations. Although the transition to working remotely was abrupt, it also provided a chance to reevaluate how trainings were delivered. These changes would ultimately be beneficial for the continued development of library staff and would provide a new model for training even as the college returned to in-person work.

OVERVIEW OF THE COLLEGE

Central Piedmont Community College is a multi-campus community college in Mecklenburg County, North Carolina. Mecklenburg County has a population of 1.1 million people and includes the city of Charlotte as well as six other cities and towns (United States Census Bureau, n.d.). Central Piedmont is one of the two largest community colleges in North Carolina and is one of the fifteen largest employers in Mecklenburg County (Charlotte Regional Business Alliance, 2018).

Central Piedmont offers almost 300 programs of study, including associate's degrees, middle college for high school students, and GED. It also offers robust corporate and continuing education programs. Each year, about 43,000 students are enrolled in college-credit programs, with an additional 12,500 enrolled in continuing education courses. Student demographics include approximately 3,000 international students representing 152 countries, more than 1,000 military veterans, and 900 middle college high school students (Central Piedmont Community College, n.d.).

Central Piedmont has libraries at six campuses throughout the county. Each library location has at least one full-time librarian. The library department includes a total of 43 employees (30 full-time and 13 part-time). In addition to the six traditional libraries, the paralegal program has a separate law library that is staffed by library personnel. In the spring of 2022, the law library will be absorbed into a brand-new library on the Central campus and will no longer be a separate entity.

HISTORY OF THE TRAINING COMMITTEE AND TRAININGS PRIOR TO COVID-19

The Central Piedmont library system has had a training committee since the summer of 2016. This committee is composed of library employees at the college and includes representatives from multiple campuses as well as both professional and classified (paraprofessional) staff. The training committee originally had three primary charges:

- Creating onboarding processes for full-time and part-time staff
- Creating a cross-training program to allow staff to become familiar with the library at a campus that is not their home campus
- Addressing ongoing training needs of library staff (including topics such as collection development, policy changes, and accessibility tools)

Prior to the pandemic, the majority of training provided by the training committee was in-person training on Fridays at the Central campus. As the slowest day of the workweek, many departmental meetings were scheduled on Fridays, and the full-time staff from other campus locations came to Central. Typically, three Fridays per semester were designated as training days. The training committee determined what trainings were needed and scheduled accordingly, often offering both a morning and an afternoon session to allow for coverage of the service desks. While this worked to an extent, there were challenges. First, there was no great way to record these trainings so that those not able to attend could view them later. Second, part-time staff were frequently not able to attend these trainings, as most of them either were not scheduled to work Fridays or staffed the service desk at their location so that the full-time librarian at their location could attend on-site training at Central.

EARLY DAYS OF COVID-19

Central Piedmont closed all in-person services and shifted to all-remote on March 18, 2020. Library employees had not previously worked from home; this necessitated immediate adjustments to all work. Central Piedmont had started using the Webex platform for staff instant messaging prior to the COVID-19 pandemic, but it had not been rolled out to the entire college community. The first priority of the training committee was to make library staff aware of Webex and get staff comfortable using it. Emails were sent out with the links for downloading Webex. Staff who struggled with installing or using Webex worked one-on-one with training committee members who walked them through the process on the phone. An all-staff meeting was set with the purpose of determining if Webex could support a meeting with 43 participants, establishing which staff had difficulty joining meetings, and getting comfortable with the platform.

Prior to COVID-19, the college had already been using Citrix for remote desktop access. There were two different types of remote access: a generic remote desktop for college employees with the commonly used programs and applications, and remote access to a specific desktop so staff could remotely connect to their own desktop in their offices or workstations. The college stopped offering the possibility to add a specific desktop about a week prior to the shutdown, so only staff members who had already used Citrix had access to their specific desktop. All other staff needed to be trained on how to use the generic employee desktop as well as get used to using a virtual desktop.

On March 13, 2020, just before the college moved to completely online classes and services, library staff had an in-person training day that was previously scheduled. At this retreat, the training committee unveiled a training-specific LibGuide that included short tutorials on basic tools and processes used by library staff. In the early days of working remotely, the training committee created several more tutorials on topics such as using Citrix, accessing the integrated library system (ILS) remotely, and Webex meetings. Additionally, a tab was added to the LibGuide to act as a clearing-house of remote learning opportunities such as webinars, virtual confer-ences, and online classes.

While the training committee had already begun creating tutorials prior to the COVID-19 shutdown, the switch to working from home impacted who could reliably record audio. In some cases, the person with the most knowledge created a script for staff members with a better setup for recording. Staff members were chosen to record the tutorials based on new criteria, such as having a decent microphone at home and limited distracting background noise.

WEB TOOLS

The training committee used several tools to facilitate its work. A mix of technology supported by Central Piedmont and tools purchased independently by the library was used to accomplish its goals. Central Piedmont uses Webex as its primary communication tool. Webex features two main components: discussion channels and video conferencing.

Webex allows users to set up discussion channels called spaces that allow live, real-time communication with fellow staff members. Individual spaces can be set up for a variety of needs: the "All Library Staff" space was the main discussion space for all library staff to talk about current issues, ask questions, and share important information and updates. The training committee also had its own space where members could chat. This space was used to talk through issues outside of regularly scheduled meetings, share in-progress documents and videos for feedback, and keep all members on track. An added benefit of the spaces is that conversation history is maintained, and previous messages can be read and searched for. This allows for easy retrieval of information and for staff to catch up on messages they may have missed while out.

The other major feature of Webex is video conferencing, which was the primary way that the training committee provided live training to all library staff. Webex allows users to share video via webcam and has a screen-sharing feature in order to incorporate slideshow presentations or do live demos of resources. A recording function made it possible to record presentations for later staff review. Although this video conferencing app gave the training committee the ability to implement a variety of trainings over the course of the pandemic, it was not perfect. Unstable Internet connections caused audio and video to drop out, and bandwidth restrictions meant that presenters had to get creative if they wanted to show a video clip, as real-time video did not work well when combined with screen sharing.

Webex is an enterprise-level tool that Central Piedmont purchased in order to facilitate college goals. Many other institutions subscribe to similar platforms, such as Microsoft Teams, Zoom, or Google's software suite. For libraries lacking such tools, other free alternatives might provide similar benefits. Slack is a popular live communication platform used by many organizations. Similar to Webex, it allows discussion to be organized into many different channels for different communication and planning needs. Slack does have a free version, although the free version provides very limited archiving for past messages. The free version also limits video chatting to one-on-one calls only. The paid version allows up to 15 users to be in a single video conference. Discord, a popular chat platform, is another alternative to Webex. Similar to Slack, Discord allows users to set up multiple channels for different needs. Discord also provides support for video chatting with up to 25 participants, allowing more staff to participate in a single video chat. However, it does not have robust administrative controls, limiting how system administrators can set up the program for all users.

While much of the work of the training committee was live presentations, the committee also prerecorded many sessions that contained demos of databases and other tools. In order to facilitate that, the training committee staff primarily used a recording software called Screencast-O-Matic. In addition to recording the visuals from webcams and/or computer screens, it also provides a basic video editor, support for captioning, and automatic cloud hosting of files. The recording and basic video editing features of Screencast-O-Matic are available for free, but more robust editing and hosting features require a paid license. Training committee members recommended it for its ease of use, particularly for editing videos, and its low cost.

The screen recording was combined with a cloud hosting platform provided by Central Piedmont called Panopto. Panopto provides support for both recording and hosting videos. The cloud hosting feature allowed for all training committee videos to be centrally hosted and maintained in one location and provided a set of control options for the videos, including who has administrative permissions for video management and viewing access. Because Panopto is tied to the main Central Piedmont login system, that also gives video creators the option to capture detailed information about which staff watched the videos and for how long. Although the training committee did not make use of this option, it is helpful in case there is ever a need for critical training that all staff will be required to view.

To ensure that all staff members regardless of ability could access and engage with training, all videos and recorded versions of trainings were given closed captioning. Panopto provides support for automatic closed-caption generation, creating captions based on its best guesses for what was being said. While this automatic captioning was not perfect, it produced highly accurate captioning that was easy to edit whenever it made mistakes.

Free alternatives to Screencast-O-Matic and Panopto exist, although free video recording options tend to lack the same power and features. TechSmith Capture is a popular free software, although it limits the amount of time a video can be recorded and does not provide support for captioning. For storage, YouTube is a popular and free hosting service that can store videos and automatically generate captions that can be easily edited.

Lastly, the members of the training committee benefited from having access to remote desktops through Citrix. Despite staff working at home having a variety of setups and software, all staff had access to a Windows desktop with standard software, such as the Microsoft Office suite, as well

Table 1.1 Potential Tools to Support Training

Product	Usage	Benefits	Drawbacks
Webex www.webex.com	Messaging and video conferencing	Can support large numbers of staff members in multiple discussion spaces and video conferences, complete archive of past messages	Enterprise-level software that may be cost prohibitive for some libraries
Slack www.slack.com	Messaging and video chat	Free option available with limited features, allows for multiple discussion spaces	Free option has limited message archiving and limits video chats to one-on-one. Paid version is required for video conferencing, with a maximum of 15 users in a call
Discord www.discord.com	Messaging and video conferencing	Free and allows for multiple discussion spaces	Video conferencing is limited to up to 25 participants. Does not have robust administrative tools
Screencast-O-Matic www.screencast-o -matic.com/	Screen recording and video editing	Affordable option with robust features, support for automatic captioning	Advanced editing tools and video hosting cost extra
Panopto www.panopto.com	Screen recording and video editing	Robust video recording and hosting platform, support for automatic captioning	Enterprise-level software that may be cost prohibitive for some libraries
TechSmith Capture www.techsmith .com/jing-tool.html	Screen recording	Free video recording software	Limited recording time, no editing, does not host videos
YouTube www.youtube.com	Video hosting	Free video hosting, support for captioning	Does not offer screen recording capability
Citrix www.citrix.com	Virtual cloud desktop	Allows users to log in to a cloud Windows environment no matter what kind of computer they have at home	Enterprise-level software that may be cost prohibitive for some libraries

as library-specific software and tools like the integrated library system. This meant that trainers and trainees alike could have live access to all the programs they needed for training. The college strived to ensure that all college staff had the equipment needed to do their jobs from home, such as webcams and microphones; all library staff were able to participate fully in training activities.

ADJUSTMENTS TO REMOTE WORK AND EARLY TRAINING NEEDS

In the earliest days of the COVID-19 pandemic, one of the biggest challenges was having enough work to keep all library staff busy when their major task, staffing a service desk, was no longer an option. Just before the pandemic forced staff to work from home, the training committee had unveiled a LibGuide to act as a landing page for all training-related information and links. In trying to come up with things for staff to do from home, a tab for webinars was added to the LibGuide. One committee member kept the guide updated with webinars from vendors, databases, and state-based library organizations. Staff members were regularly reminded that there was a one-stop shop for available online trainings. Many of the part-time staff, especially, who normally work exclusively at the service desk, were able to take advantage of the multitude of virtual offerings that became available.

Addressing changed staff needs also meant that the trainings themselves needed to change. In the pre-pandemic model, the training committee had two to three days per semester set aside for staff training. In talking about what to do for a scheduled date in late April, the committee recognized a need for a refresher on some of the databases. This was needed for several reasons: staff who previously had not staffed library chat were staffing chat while they were remote workers, the number of overall chat hours offered increased from roughly 37 hours per week to 57 hours per week, the volume of chat increased as it became the only way for students to get library help, and students were relying completely on online resources while physical spaces and resources were unavailable. The committee decided that instead of doing a one-time training on the reserved late-April date, they would do weekly sessions for the remainder of the semester, and each session would focus on a different electronic resource.

Previously, while the committee determined and set up trainings and its members were not necessarily the ones giving the training, there was still a fairly limited pool of staff members who actually presented. Moving to weekly trainings meant a need to share the load of work associated with creating and presenting. This provided an opportunity to invite all staff to participate in leading a training session. Using the biweekly emails sent to all library staff by the library director and the weekly all-staff check-in sessions via Webex, the committee put out a call to the entire department for people interested in leading a one-time, one-hour-or-less session on an electronic resource. The committee marketed this opportunity in several ways. First, those interested in presenting could choose lesser-known, lesser-used, or highly specialized databases that perhaps they knew or used or loved but were not widely known. For example, one staff member who started working at the college shortly before the COVID-19 pandemic began had come from a medical library at a hospital. She had in-depth knowledge of the medical databases used by allied health students, a subset of electronic resources that intimidated some library staff. Other examples include a staff member with a background in history who presented on three history resources and a staff member with a personal interest in genealogy who presented on genealogical resources with an emphasis on genealogy for Black/African American individuals.

The second marketing tactic was to provide an opportunity for professional development in a low-stakes, supportive environment. The committee emphasized that if staff members were considering presenting at conferences in the future, these staff trainings were a way to gain experience in all aspects of the process (creating a presentation, doing a presentation, using a virtual environment and sharing the screen, etc.) while presenting in a supportive environment to people they already know. Members of the training committee offered to be a practice audience before a presentation for all staff to help coach and build the confidence of first-time presenters. Several presenters took advantage of this offer and got guidance from one or two training committee members in a practice session. This encouraged several classified staff members and at least one new librarian to present sessions. Overall, 13 different staff members presented sessions between April 24 and July 14, 2020.

The broader variety of staff presenters led to more engagement of staff during trainings. Employees knew these were their colleagues, and in many cases, this was their first presentation of this type, so employees made an effort to be present (virtually) and engaged. This happened naturally, without any involvement from the training committee. Additionally, the feedback from the first round of surveys on training after the work-from-home-transition was very positive; staff really appreciated seeing such a large number of their coworkers presenting trainings and felt that the variety was beneficial. While offering trainings had never been intentionally exclusionary prior to COVID-19, the work-from-home situation caused the committee to actively seek out a variety of presenters on training topics in a way that had not been done before. Going forward, the committee can use the same strategies for recruiting a variety of presenters among library staff.

One full-time staff member created their own training for library staff as a way of keeping busy. A native Spanish speaker, the staff member created a Spanish class for library staff, with an emphasis on phrases used in the library. Through NC LIVE (statewide resource sharing consortium: https://www.nclive.org/), all library staff had access to the language-learning tool Mango Languages. The employee used the existing Spanish language module specifically targeted to library staff and added cultural components, such as football (soccer) culture, differences in phrases from country to country, and music. She offered weekly sessions that started with interactive segments focusing on one or more aspects of Hispanic culture, then moved to language practice based on the Mango lessons that had been assigned for the week. While not all participants kept up with the Mango lessons, attendance and participation in the library class was high and lively. Central Piedmont has a large population of Spanish-speaking students, and having an increase in staff who could use even basic phrases with students was an elevation of library customer service.

TRAINING DESIGN AND DELIVERY

The trainings hosted by the training committee spanned many different topics. The most common area of training was on library resources and databases. These trainings would often spotlight a particular database the library subscribed to. Other times, the trainings focused on common assignments or research questions students have to answer, with the goal of identifying the best tools and approaches to help those students. Some trainings focused on tools or processes used by the wider college, such as an orientation to Brightspace, the college's new learning management system. Another category of trainings was personal and professional development. These trainings were often driven by staff interests, with topics such as genealogy research and mindfulness.

Because the topics were varied and presented by many different staff members, the training committee did not mandate a specific method of delivery. The online format allowed for a greater degree of flexibility compared to traditional, in-person trainings that had typically been held in library classrooms. With a variety of tools available to support their content, presenters got to pick the method that they felt would lead to the best training. The training committee would then take the lead in scheduling a dedicated meeting time for all staff or sending out the content and expectations.

Many trainings were done as live video conferences on Central Piedmont's Webex. This was the format most comparable to traditional in-person sessions, where a presenter could provide a training live as well as ask questions and receive feedback from attendees in real time. This format worked especially well for trainings related to specific assignments and common student questions because the trainers could walk attendees through the process of helping a student step by step.

For others, it made the most sense to record a training video for participants to watch in advance and spend the live session focused on answering questions and providing follow-up. For example, as the library prepared to reopen, staff recorded videos of changes to the physical library spaces to ensure social distancing and make staff aware of the areas of the libraries that would be closed off to students. Prerecording allowed trainers to make videos in the actual space and provided library staff time not just to watch the videos, but also to think through the changes and develop questions. This mode of training was instrumental in the smooth reopening of the library spaces to students.

Delivering training online also spurred the training committee to invite vendors to demonstrate their products. This was a format that worked well and allowed for some useful sessions led by a vendor's internal trainers. An example is a new language-learning database acquired by North Carolina's state library consortium. Because this was a new product for all staff, the training committee invited the vendor rather than trying to present on a product that no one on the library staff had expertise in. This gave all staff the opportunity to learn the ins and outs of the product and ask questions of someone who was already an expert in the platform. And the online format meant it was much easier to coordinate and bring a trainer in, who might otherwise not be able to travel for an in-person session.

The training committee also piloted a "study group," inviting staff members to attend a series of trainings and conversations about topics that could not be covered easily in a single session. Many library staff members expressed an interest in learning more about Oasis, the service tied to the ILS and used by library staff to order books for the collection. Because it is a complex product, two members of the training committee broke it up into several training sessions with brief "homework" assignments every week to help staff members understand how to effectively use it. These trainings were supplemented by a dedicated Webex space for participants to chat and ask questions about the service in between meetings. Although this model required far more time investment from both participants and trainers, feedback was very positive. Time expectations were laid out at the outset, including a commitment that attendees attend every week and do the homework. Because this longer study session was voluntary, the training committee felt comfortable making that requirement of participants. Due to its success, this is a model the training committee plans to use again for topics that require more time and may not be applicable to all staff, such as advanced navigation of the library's ILS or best instruction practices.

Providing online trainings during the work-from-home periods meant that sessions were widely attended, but staff members still missed some trainings due to other obligations. An additional benefit of online trainings, whether premade or live, is that trainings could be recorded and stored online for later viewing. Webex's recording functionality and Central Piedmont's Panopto service allowed for trainings to be easily stored. Access could be restricted to just library staff if necessary or shared with additional partners. This also allowed attendees to revisit trainings for a full review or to rewatch specific parts where they wanted additional clarification. Links to all recordings were maintained in the training committee's LibGuide, which serves as a central repository for training committee materials. In addition to being helpful during work-from-home time in the pandemic, recording trainings in Webex solved a long-standing issue of the training committee. Prior to the pandemic, people who were unable to attend training in person essentially missed the training. Attempts to record sessions were laughably bad. Sessions were recorded in a library classroom, which was not well suited for recording presentations: the audio quality was terrible, there was no good way to see the screen being used in a presentation, and after a few attempts, the committee stopped trying to record, as the recording did not produce a usable product. Webex serves as a marked improvement and will continue to be the preferred method for recording trainings for the foreseeable future.

CHALLENGES

Although remote trainings provided many benefits, there were also hurdles that had to be overcome, particularly for live sessions. Presenters who were sharing their screen often found it difficult to both provide the demonstration and keep an eye on the chat and respond to questions. To solve this problem, the training committee provided a moderator for each session. The moderator was able to field questions from participants and focus on handling any technical challenges, freeing up the trainer to focus on their presentation. The inclusion of a session moderator helped these sessions go smoothly and helped presenters feel more comfortable and confident in their sessions.

Other hurdles included the technical hiccups that should be familiar to anyone who has participated in large online meetings. It was not uncommon for participants to encounter bandwidth issues, audio or video lag, background noise from participants who forgot to unmute themselves, and other similar issues. Although in-person trainings pre-pandemic could have their own share of technological issues, the ones that arose with online trainings were more prevalent. The inclusion of a session moderator helped alleviate these issues. With hosting abilities in Webex, the moderator could mute participants and try to solve any connection issues while the presenter focused on their presentation. Some technical hiccups could not be solved as easily, but the ability to create and host recorded videos provided alternative avenues for participants to engage with the material in the event of glitches on the host or attendee end. And a sense of good humor and understanding from library staff helped keep the mood light and averted any potential stress.

ASSESSMENT

In order to ensure that trainings were serving the needs of library staff members, the training committee conducted assessment surveys to collect feedback and make any adjustments to the trainings, if necessary. Two rounds of assessment were done. The first occurred in late spring of 2020, after the initial round of trainings following the transition to working remotely. The second survey was conducted at the end of the summer session in 2020 to determine whether the trainings were still meeting the needs of library staff members. Copies of the survey questions are included as appendices.

Although developed in Google Forms, much of the survey was inspired by the Association of College and Research Libraries' Project Outcome survey series. The training survey asked respondents questions to determine whether or not they learned new things from the training, whether they felt more confident in using resources, and whether it raised their awareness of library resources and services. Additional questions were added to find out whether or not participants encountered any technical issues and whether the trainings were too long, too short, or just right. Lastly, open-ended questions asked participants what they liked most and what additional trainings they would like to see.

The initial survey yielded 27 responses, a roughly 60 percent response rate from library staff. Overwhelmingly, results were positive: 92 percent of respondents agreed or strongly agreed that they learned new material, 88 percent indicated that they felt more confident using resources, and 85 percent reported more awareness of library resources. In addition, 92 percent of respondents indicated that they had no technical issues, and 100 percent indicated that the length of the training was just right. In response to the question about what participants liked the most, the most common response was learning about different library resources and databases. Additional answers included "use of different presenters and learning from their expertise" and "real world examples from student question[s]."

The second survey yielded similar results, albeit with a lower response rate from staff. Roughly 40 percent of staff responded to the second survey. However, 100 percent of respondents indicated they learned something new and became more aware of library services, and nearly 90 percent indicated that they felt more confident using resources. In response to the open-ended questions, many participants once again reported that they enjoyed hearing from different presenters. However, other responses suggested that the trainings did not need to happen every week.

From those responses, and as the library shifted toward reopening the library, adjustments were made for the fall semester of 2020, which carried over into the spring semester of 2021. Because of the positive response, the training committee continued offering virtual training sessions but reduced the pace, moving from a weekly format to three or four times a semester on designated training days, similar to the pre-pandemic schedule. Also emerging from staff responses was an interest in hearing more about staff interests, which occasionally came up as different staff members provided trainings. This led to the development of Fun Fridays to highlight the talents and hobbies of library staff.

FUN FRIDAYS

One of the suggestions that came out of the first round of assessments in the spring of 2020 was a request for a session on mask making. This was when it was still quite hard to find masks and many of the materials used to make masks. One member of the training committee is a quilter by hobby and had been making masks; it was suggested that she do a session on making masks with easy-to-find materials. This specific session evolved into a series of Fun Friday sessions on topics that were not necessarily work-related.

The training committee saw Fun Fridays as a way to boost morale and create a sense of community at a time when many were struggling with the conditions of the ongoing pandemic. All Fun Friday activities were completely optional and were not recorded. The training committee asked for volunteers to present on any topic they were interested in. In the summer of 2020, there were a total of seven sessions with staff presenting information on topics of their choosing. Sessions in the first round focused on activities that participants might want to engage in during the pandemic. In addition to the original no-sew mask tutorial, topics included baking cupcakes, gardening, light stretching, art journaling, Colombian food, mindfulness, and 3D printing—all presented by staff members from home. While not directly work-related, these sessions were a way to feel and stay connected to coworkers on a personal level. A similar series of non-work-focused presentations by staff was presented in the summer of 2021, which focused on interests of the library staff, such as mantis shrimp or musings on the postal service in J. R. R. Tolkien's Middle-earth.

TAKEAWAYS

In the spring of 2021, Central Piedmont shifted operations back to being fully in-person, bringing an end to the work-from-home environment. Librarians began returning to normal operations, albeit with ongoing safety precautions due to the pandemic.

As in-person operations were restored, the work of the training committee continued. Refreshers on in-person services, the introduction of new tools and databases, and more interest in Fun Fridays meant that there were plenty of opportunities for the training committee to host regular sessions. As the committee strategized, continuing in a virtual format made the most sense. Social distancing requirements meant that gathering all library staff in a single location was difficult, and scheduling times where most staff could come in person would have continued to be a challenge. Consequently, the training committee continued using its set of virtual tools, such as Webex and video hosting, to host further trainings.

Beyond staffing needs, additional factors made the continuation of virtual trainings an obvious choice. It allowed more staff across all campuses, particularly part-time staff, to be involved and engaged, made it possible to record trainings for later review by staff and for archival purposes, allowed more flexibility in scheduling, and continued providing more space for staff to take leadership roles in the training. The decision was popular across both the training committee and wider library staff. Even once the pandemic ends, virtual trainings will still be the default mode.

Additionally, the pandemic reinforced the value of the work of the training committee. Libraries are complex operations with a lot of moving parts. The sudden shift to working remotely and moving all library operations online was a perfect demonstration of what we already know to be true: policies, tools, and services can change rapidly even in "normal" times, and keeping all staff aware of these changes can help provide service to patrons seamlessly. A robust training program, particularly one that can be inclusive of the schedules of all staff, is one of the best ways to ensure the continued smooth operation of the library and maximize use of new tools and services.

The benefits to training do not end with exceptional library service. An added benefit of training is that it supports the growth and development of library staff. Bringing in more participants to conduct the trainings is a great way to help staff grow professionally, building instructional, technological, and public-speaking skills. Hosting trainings provides staff a safe and comforting environment in which to build and showcase their skills, and many staff expressed appreciation for the opportunity and said it helped them feel more comfortable presenting to larger groups.

Building community is an important part of fostering a functional team. Although the Fun Fridays may not be what one would typically consider "training," it was a natural fit for the goals of the training committee. It allowed staff to share information about their interests with their peers, provided a welcome break from the day-to-day work, and built connections among staff. Particularly as a large library system with multiple locations, this was a great way for staff who do not normally interact to get to know one another better.

Libraries have an array of tools, technology, and policies. It can be helpful to embrace the ongoing nature of training by holding periodic sessions to highlight new resources, establish best practices, and refresh staff on procedures. Although in-person training provides many benefits, the shift toward virtual training during the pandemic provided much higher benefits across a large library system. With the right tools, such as video conferencing and screen capture software, virtual training can be a way to include more staff in training sessions, both as trainers and participants, and it can build a stronger, more connected library staff, which ultimately means a library that better serves its community.

REFERENCES

Central Piedmont Community College. (n.d.). About Central Piedmont. Retrieved from https://www.cpcc.edu/about-central-piedmont

Charlotte Regional Business Alliance. (2018). Charlotte area major employers. Retrieved from https://charlotteregion.com/clientuploads/Data/Major-Employers -Q218.pdf

United States Census Bureau. (n.d.). QuickFacts: Mecklenburg County, North Carolina. Retrieved from https://www.census.gov/quickfacts/fact/table/meck lenburgcountynorthcarolina/PST045219

APPENDIX A

Initial Training Survey

1. Did you encounter any technical issues during the training?
   - I could not connect/join the meeting.
   - I had audio issues.
   - I had video issues.
   - Everything worked!

2. The length of the database trainings is
   - Too short
   - Too long
   - Just right, Goldilocks!

3. I learned something new from this training series.
   Strongly Disagree   1   2   3   4   5   Strongly Agree

4. I feel more confident about using what I learned in the training series.
   Strongly Disagree   1   2   3   4   5   Strongly Agree

5. I am more aware of the library's databases.
   Strongly Disagree   1   2   3   4   5   Strongly Agree

6. What have you liked most about this training series?

7. Do you have any specific feedback or questions on any of the three sessions, (1) Finding a Topic, (2) Literary Resources, and (3) Streaming Video Resources, that have been presented so far?

8. What other types of training would you like to see offered in this format (i.e., online via Webex)?

9. Anything else you'd like to tell the training and/or assessment committees about this kind of online training (feedback, suggestions, etc.)?

APPENDIX B

Second Training Survey

1. I learned something new from this training series.
      Strongly Disagree   1   2   3   4   5   Strongly Agree
2. I feel more confident about using what I learned in the training series.
      Strongly Disagree   1   2   3   4   5   Strongly Agree
3. I am more aware of the library's databases.
      Strongly Disagree   1   2   3   4   5   Strongly Agree
4. What have you liked most about this training series?

5. Do you have any specific feedback or questions on any of the sessions since our first survey (medical databases, test prep resources, the stock market assignment, career databases, ILL, history databases, English assignments, mindfulness, and the scavenger hunt)?

6. The training committee is planning to continue offering this training series in the fall. Should we:
    ○ Keep the training sessions on Tuesdays at 2:00, even though some staff will be working on campus at that time?
    ○ Move the training sessions to Fridays, when all physical locations are closed?
    ○ Other (please specify)
7. What types of training would you like to see offered this fall in this format (i.e., online via Webex)?

8. Anything else you'd like to tell the training committee about this kind of online training (feedback, suggestions, etc.)?

2

Chatting into the Void: Scaling and Assessing Chat Reference Services for Effectiveness

Megan Graewingholt, Cotton Coslett, Jonathan Cornforth, David Palmquist, Colleen Robledo Greene, and Eric Karkhoff

INTRODUCTION

While academic libraries have offered virtual reference services for decades, the assessment of these services for effectiveness in meeting patron needs is not always considered standard practice. As libraries everywhere respond to the ongoing effects of the pandemic, now more than ever it is essential to know if virtual reference services are adequately serving users at the point of need. Are information technologies like online messaging services providing the research support patrons require, or are librarians just chatting into the void? In pursuit of discovery toward this end, a group of librarians sought to enhance virtual reference services by implementing a proactive chat pop-up embedded in the library catalog. Following the activation of this feature, interactions were systematically collected and assessed to address the most frequently asked questions from patrons. The data was also reviewed for the purpose of evaluating and revising operator training.

Virtual reference services are an essential way the Paulina June and George Pollak Library serves the California State University, Fullerton campus of more than 41,000 students and 4,000 faculty and staff. This diverse campus community comprises a wide variety of learners, including working professionals, international students, and first-generation college students (Strategic Communications and Brand Management, 2021). One critical goal of the study was to ensure that the online content offered by the library contained the most up-to-date and necessary information sought during the first few months of the pandemic. As libraries respond to all the ways the pandemic influenced campus life, lessons learned reinforce that maintaining online asset accuracy, accessibility, and visibility is in the best interest of users.

LITERATURE REVIEW

Responding strategically and purposefully to reference statistics can lead to lasting and impactful change. The process can alter how data is not only collected, but also identified, analyzed, and meaningfully used. Several studies have examined the impact of COVID-19 on reference services and how data-driven decisions help improve the user experience despite disruption (Flierl, 2019; Garvey, 2021). A widespread survey of libraries performed by Gerbig et al. (2021) captured the experiences of working professionals as changes occurred and what opportunities opened up as a result. Kathuria (2020) suggests the value of performing chat analysis during the closure and how libraries should consider this data in their responses. Similarly, Wilairat et al. (2021) perform a similar analysis while also reconsidering the data collection process itself. Indeed, data resulting from chat analysis has long been used to capture the evolution of this now ubiquitous mode of providing reference.

Recent studies have emphasized the value of machine learning and evaluation, which can work in tandem with manual reviews of data. A comparative analysis can reveal the benefits of either approach (HyunSeung & Fienup, 2021). Taking into consideration various topic modeling algorithms, Ozeran and Martin (2019) reveal the opportunities such approaches can bring to decision making. For instance, manual coding analysis can be used to inform training practices for operators as they relate to user satisfaction during interactions (Barrett et al., 2021; Logan et al., 2019; Pomerantz & Luo, 2006). Conversely, automated topic modeling has been shown to support a data-driven approach to chat analysis (Chen & Wang, 2019). While research points to the value of analyzing chat data using either approach (Jacoby et al., 2016), this analysis can also better inform and improve how services are delivered (Mavodza, 2019; Mungin, 2017).

Several studies suggest that implementing proactive pop-up features significantly increases chat use (Blizzard, 2018; Epstein, 2018; Gardner et al., 2019; Kemp et al., 2015; Rich & Lux, 2018; Wilairat et al., 2021; Zhang & Mayer, 2014), as well as the complexity of chat questions received

(Blizzard, 2018; Kemp et al., 2015; Maloney & Kemp, 2015; Rich & Lux, 2018, Warner et al., 2020). The range of this upsurge can depend on the location and number of proactive widgets employed and whether or not placement is on the website, within discovery tool results, or embedded within database platforms (Fan et al., 2017; Kemp et al., 2015; Hockey, 2016; Warner et al., 2020; Wells, 2003). One clear benefit of proactive features is increased visibility of virtual reference services. In a study by the Penn State University Libraries, 83 percent of survey respondents were more likely to use the chat service due to the presence of the reference widget (Imler et al., 2016). Similarly, a Bowling Green State University library study found that half of the users surveyed would not have sought research help without the presence of the pop-up (Rich & Lux, 2018). This scholarship indicates that libraries should not dismiss the potential of proactively engaging patrons in virtual spaces.

The pandemic increased demand for virtual reference services and engaging self-service resources (Radford et al., 2021; Wilairat et al., 2021). Prior to the pandemic, a 2019 study by the Berkeley College Libraries identified its knowledge base as the most essential tool for their virtual reference services, providing a highly consulted central information point for its campus community (Labrake, 2019). These asynchronous services provide more on-demand research assistance, with librarians and staff regularly reviewing this content for currency and accuracy (Waltman & McGinniss, 2020). As shown in an assessment study of the University of Alberta Libraries' chat service, the single most important suggestion for future decision making was to provide adequate and easily accessible information for non-local staff in the consortium (Meert et al., 2009). Libraries that scaled this type of 24/7 self-service materials were better prepared to respond to closures. This type of investment enables around-the-clock virtual assistance, allows librarians to focus on more in-depth research needs, and provides an invaluable onboarding tool.

PROACTIVE CHAT IMPLEMENTATION

Proactive chat features were activated on June 1, 2020, using the Springshare LibApps suite of tools. In the LibAnswers application, customization options are available for the location, screen placement, language, data fields, and timing of the chat pop-up. There are also options to add stationary widgets that float on web pages, rather than sliding out or popping up into the users' field of vision to prompt them to engage with a librarian. Initially, the pop-up chat widget is positioned at the bottom right of the library's discovery system results page, activating after 60 seconds. The user can choose to chat or decline, and if declined, it will not ask again on that page. Once engaged, the user has the option to provide their name, e-mail address, and question. Though static chat widgets are found throughout the library's website, the library's discovery system results page is the only location where the proactive pop-up is activated.

Anticipating an upsurge in chat usage, virtual reference staffed hours were increased upon proactive chat activation. With the building closed to the public due to COVID-19, library employees were available to staff more virtual reference hours. Reference librarians alone more than doubled virtual reference coverage, with additional shifts added to include earlier hours and extra support during busy times. Following the pop-up widget activation and coordination of staffing, the data collection for the assessment step of the study began.

UNSUPERVISED LEARNING/EXPLORATORY DATA ANALYSIS

Sentiment Analysis

At the outset, sentiment analysis was the machine learning technique the team was most excited about, but in the end, it turned out to be disappointing when applied to the dataset. In examples, the most flattering and least flattering reviews were easily filtered out of a very large corpus. It was hypothesized that identifying similar extremes in the interactions would help target opportunities for improvement in service quality. However, the dataset did not demonstrate such extremes of effect. The negative end of the scale used was skewed by question-specific terms, such as the titles of works being researched, so the flagged items in the review had limited service improvement value.

Topic Analysis

Unsupervised topic analysis can also serve as an important step in exploratory data analysis. While to call it unbiased would be inaccurate, it is safe to say that it sorts information into buckets of similar interactions that are not tainted by imposed categories. Thus, it can serve as a springboard for generating manual analysis code categories or as a final litmus test to ensure that something obvious is not being missed. While the initial results did produce many easily recognizable sets for things like articles, books, citations, databases, etc., they were not cleanly divided into such groups. Rather, there tended to be many overlapping categories, which were placed into separate buckets based on common English constructions like, "I am looking for" or "I am having trouble finding." From a service delivery perspective, the distinction between these two categories is moot and less valuable for analysis. In both cases, the patron is trying to get something they are not able to find or access, while the team's interest lies more in distinguishing between the things they are looking for, or the reasons why. Are they not able to find or access it because something is broken, because the library does not have access, or because the user doesn't have permission accidentally or by design? Considering these minor details, a deeper review held more value for creating self-help material and other service improvements than analyzing the language used.

Accomplishing a deeper analysis would require taking what is learned from first round of topic analysis and using it to improve the data input for a second round of processing. The team decided against another iteration, because manually collapsing the existing groups and moving on to the supervised learning analysis was of greater interest. That said, the unsupervised analysis was time well spent, since the lessons learned were applied to the supervised analysis.

SUPERVISED LEARNING

With a large corpus of manually categorized interactions in hand, the team had the opportunity to explore how effective supervised learning techniques could potentially be at categorizing chat interactions. Since we are not experts in machine learning, this was very much a learning-by-doing endeavor. Thus, conclusions should only be taken as exemplary of what is possible and not the upper or lower limit of what may be obtained by additional attempts. With more sophisticated model tuning and data cleanup, better results may be possible. Based on existing skills and available training materials, the team opted to constrain our exploration to techniques possible using SciKit Learn (Pedregosa et al., 2011). Models we tried include KNeighborsClassifier, MultiNomialNB, LogisticRegression, GradientBooster, RandomForest, DecisionTreeClassifier, and C-Support Vector Classification.

Vectorization

As a first step, the team needed to vectorize the chat data to transform it from words into sets of numbers that could be analyzed by the largest number of potential machine learning algorithms. Initially, a great deal of time was spent trying to curate the perfect stop word list, but in the end, the team settled on a combination of statistical techniques as well as Python code that removed common constructions. While various combinations were run, a grid search testing a range of values for many variables was determined to be the most successful combination, seen in Figure 2.1. It drops any words that appear in 55 percent or more of the chats. No limit was set on how many words would be used, with a minimum threshold of appearing in at least four chats. The team considered both words in isolation as well as two-word combinations using the ngram_range setting.

```
vect = CountVectorizer(max_df=.55, max_features=None, min_df=4,
ngram_range=(1, 2),stop_words=None)
```

FIGURE 2.1. Vectorization

Machine Classification

The team focused on the primary assigned category in the study testing, as most of the models available did not support multi-category classification. The manual classification process produced the labeled input in Figure 2.2. A few items that did not have at least five examples were discarded at this step, and the training/testing split cross-validation methodology requires at least one exemplar in each split.

The team came in with zero assumptions about which method would work best. We did a simple train test split with the following models: KNeighborsClassifier, MultiNomialNB, LogisticRegression, GradientBooster, RandomForest, DecisionTreeClassifier, and C-Support Vector Classification. After this initial test, MultiNomialNB, LogisticRegression, and GradientBooster showed the most promise, so these were included in both exhaustive and randomized grid searches using days of compute time on a 2019 Mac laptop. In testing, logistic regression ended up being the clear winner with a peak performance of 69.3 percent for accuracy despite or perhaps due to its simplicity. It typically exceeded MultiNomialNB by five or more percentage points. Linear regression used significantly more compute time, but with a small dataset, it would still take under a minute to complete. Gradient booster accuracy was close but not quite as good while simultaneously taking about eight times as long to compute. Thus, linear regression was the winner because it had the highest accuracy and tolerable testing efficiency.

At first glance, 69.3 percent accuracy may appear unremarkable; however, it exceeds the null model. In that case, you would

```
General Research 552
Known Article 196
Known Book 125
Circulation 74
Databases 72
Technology 65
Citations 62
CSU+/ILL 53
Video 31
Dissertations/Theses 11
Study Space 9
Known Journal 8
Campus 8
Community Member 7
Subject Librarian Referral 6
Instruction 5
```

FIGURE 2.2. Machine classification

guess the most common answer by 26.4 percent, but it is still wrong about 3 out of 10 tries. Thus, it is not an ideal analysis tool for categorizing items without additional human intervention. However, it may be very useful as a first pass that can be sorted before handing off to humans to correct where the algorithm fell short. This could theoretically increase accuracy and efficiency, lowering the labor cost and tedium of such endeavors.

MANUAL CHAT TRANSCRIPT REVIEW AND CODING

In order to add further clarity to the supervised and unsupervised analysis, a deeper dive into chat transcripts with a detailed manual review was necessary. The team divided all chat data pulled from LibAnswers covering the period of June 1, 2020 through November 10, 2020, which totaled 3,510 recorded chat interactions. Available transcripts during the study period were reviewed and categorized based on specific analysis codes (see Table 2.1). The 19 analysis codes were fashioned from existing statistical fields or tags. Additionally, there were codes added that targeted pandemic-specific information, such as requests for streaming video, study spaces, and questions about community access. Due to the complexity of reference interactions, the team allowed for the option to add a secondary analysis code, if appropriate. For example, in this study, using the Technology analysis code included all technical issues with library-managed resources as well as troubleshooting issues typically handled by the campus's information technology (IT) support. If it was desired to know how often users chat with the library in error and are referred to campus IT, another analysis code could be added to capture this data. Consequently, the more analysis codes included in the coding scheme, the greater the time required to review each transaction. Even though the analysis codes represented a wide range of chat transaction types, this coding scheme mirrored the team's assessment goals.

There were both complications and unforeseen benefits to completing the review process itself. Early on, it was clear that uniformity was essential for coding anomalies such as disconnected chats or repeated questions to allow for a more controlled dataset. The team met regularly to discuss observed trends, suggestions for improved categories, and particularly frustrating transactions. As a next step, the team began to develop a set of revised practices to include in training sessions. Some of these practices, such as explaining steps to guide patrons rather than just sending a link, placed an emphasis on teaching. Some recommendations, such as using natural language and even emojis to humanize chat interactions, aimed to create a more positive user experience.

In other cases, specific behaviors were recommended to chat operators for more practical reasons, such as improving data collection and providing additional user context. It was discovered early on that, when applicable, chat operators should record any subject or course codes volunteered during the interaction, particularly during the more in-depth research consultations.

Table 2.1 Analysis Codes and Totals

Analysis Codes	Summer Primary	Summer Secondary	Summer Total	Fall Primary	Fall Secondary	Fall Total	Overall Totals
Campus	14	5	19	19	2	21	40
Circulation	104	9	113	136	7	143	256
Citation	24	2	26	146	7	153	179
Community Access	7	3	10	11	1	12	22
CSU+/ Interlibrary Loan	39	39	78	98	55	153	231
Databases	17	1	18	86	60	146	164
Dissertation/ Theses	11	0	11	14	0	14	25
General Research	369	3	372	1352	24	1376	1748
Instruction	1	0	1	7	3	10	11
Known Article	107	5	112	251	5	256	368
Known Book	127	6	133	211	7	218	351
Known Journal	20	0	20	9	0	9	29
Printing	1	0	1	4	0	4	5
Study Space	2	0	2	12	4	16	18
Subject Librarian Referral	3	1	4	10	33	43	47
Technology	70	27	97	148	41	189	286
Titan Card	4	0	4	2	0	2	6
University Archives	6	1	7	3	1	4	11
Video	31	0	31	33	2	35	66

Collecting this additional data provides critical insights into patron needs and behaviors, and it helps establish future resources that specifically address these subjects and courses. Sometimes, commonly seen research assignments were identified, allowing for the creation of custom asynchronous resources that target these needs. These resources can be used directly by students, and thus they reduce the workload for the librarian, who can direct patrons to explore them independently.

Another suggested practice was to mention the appropriate subject librarian to the patron, even if no actual referral is provided. The goals of this practice are to introduce more casual reference users to their subject librarians, who can then offer more specialized assistance, and to reduce congestion in the main reference queue. As we revised our training practices, transcripts were reviewed for adherence. A full year of interactions, beginning three months before our revised training began, was analyzed in order to measure both the effectiveness of training and how regularly it should be conducted.

PROACTIVE CHAT IMPACT

The Pollak Library's implementation of proactive chat features in June 2020 impacted virtual reference services in several ways. Comparing total chat reference transactions term over term in 2019, chat transactions experienced a 556 percent increase in the summer semester and a 165 percent increase over the fall semester. This is in line with prior research indicating proactive chat features lead to increased chat traffic (Blizzard, 2018; Epstein, 2018; Gardner et al., 2019; Kemp et al., 2015; Rich & Lux, 2018; Wilairat et al., 2021; Zhang & Mayer, 2014). When examining chat transactions year over year, it is clear that traffic has remained steady since the initial activation gains (see Figure 2.3).

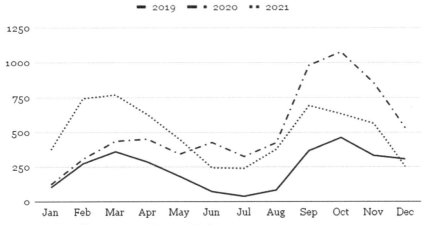

FIGURE 2.3. Chat transaction totals by year

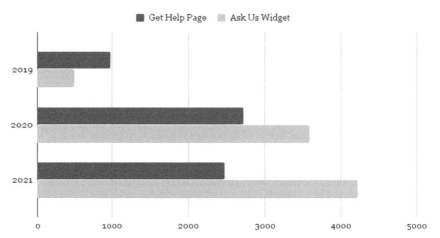

FIGURE 2.4. Chat transactions by referring location

Subsequently, the rise in chat interactions impacted library staffing in unanticipated ways. For example, patrons can request to be contacted directly within the system at the conclusion of a chat exchange. This follow-up feature creates help desk tickets that are routed back to the library to resolve. In contrast to the previous year, the amount of LibAnswers tickets placed after a chat interaction on this page rose more than tenfold during the summer and fall of 2020. Consequently, the growth in overall chat traffic resulted in unforeseen workload for other departments, such as Circulation, Electronic Resources Management, and Discovery.

Interestingly, one significant finding is evident in the location data that indicates where patrons initiate chat interactions (see Figure 2.4). Prior to activating the pop-up chat feature, the static widget on the library catalog results page established in 2019 did not influence users significantly, with more than double the chats originating from the "Get Help" page. The number of chats initiated via the pop-up widget increased significantly in 2020 and has continued to climb in 2021. This trend proves that adding proactive chat to a single library web page encourages users to respond more frequently.

MANUAL REVIEW OF DATA

Examining the results of the manual review of chat transcripts provided enormous insight into the needs of patrons early on in the pandemic. It also provided a timely glimpse into the common behaviors of chat operators and the state of the library's data collection infrastructure more broadly. After aggregating the manual review analysis codes, it became clear that most chat patrons assisted during this period requested help with general research, such as to explore topics or to find sources on a particular subject. This was followed by known item requests (questions concerning how to locate a particular article, book, dissertation, or journal). Circulation queries regarding resource-sharing services such as interlibrary loan and CSU+ (the California State University lending consortium) were the third most popular type of interactions. Naturally, during an unprecedented shift to virtual learning, it was expected that several patrons may request assistance with their technology. Technical issues were the fourth highest concern, followed only slightly by questions on how to create source citations and how to use library databases.

The manual review of chat data also showed the increasing level of interest in library resources available virtually. For instance, the number of questions about access to library video resources indicated the growing demand for streaming video during the lockdown. Particularly during the initial pandemic, the availability of full-text e-resources was one primary underlying reason for patron interactions. In light of these outcomes, the manual review contributed practical, data-driven insights that informed COVID-19 responses and ensured essential patron concerns were heard.

DISCUSSION

The outcomes of this project present both broad and local implications for academic libraries considering activating proactive chat features or exploring chat data. The lessons learned underscore the benefits and drawbacks of each analysis strategy for future use. Specifically, the analysis project led to the implementation of best practices to better capture data, provide support in a more uniform manner, and train staff. In addition, this data-driven approach also informed timely updates and improvements to online content.

REVIEW OF ANALYSIS STRATEGIES

The team uncovered a number of notable benefits to conducting a systematic manual review analysis of chat transactions. In addition to providing greater insight into users' needs, reviewing chat transcripts allowed the team to identify practices both beneficial and detrimental to the service mission of the library. For example, its insight into operator behaviors informed the revision of best practices and internal training material. Furthermore, reviewing chat transcripts while assessing for specific information requires the investigator to consider the data collection process itself. This was ultimately the largest benefit, since the manual review revealed multiple statistical categories and tags that could be updated for clarity and more accurately applied in the future.

There were also drawbacks to undertaking this kind of assessment technique. For instance, precise planning is required to target data points prior to beginning the review process. Without this preliminary step, essential data points identified mid-review may end up requiring duplicative efforts. The process of reviewing transcripts also requires a considerable amount of time and manpower, especially for larger institutions with heavier chat traffic.

The benefits of utilizing Python script analysis can vary widely depending on the success of its execution. Advantages are certainly seen in the time investment and the ability to improve the analysis processes over time. Nevertheless, the team discovered that utilizing more effective categorizations in the script resulted in only about 60–70 percent accuracy. In the end, while the Python script review was a critical part of the project, it was only when it was conducted in tandem with the manual review analysis that the team saw a more holistic view of the trends and practices occurring. Once the team determined that the initial results required a manual review, time was better spent conducting this deeper evaluation. However, the exploration into utilizing supervised and unsupervised techniques for data analysis underscored the importance of assessment as standard practice and revealed the limits of applying these tools.

LOCAL RECOMMENDATIONS

The local implementation of proactive chat features proved an easy and effective way of enhancing visibility and increasing chat traffic; however, a number of considerations made for a smoother transition. Staffing concerns must be seriously addressed, since pop-up feature activation can cause lasting increases in use. For understaffed libraries or those operating at maximum efficiency as is, proactive features should be wielded with caution. Related library departments should be made aware of any activation so they can prepare for the potential additional workload. Also consider local preferences and service needs. Proactive chat features can be customized accordingly, with options to change the proactive box language, data collection fields, timing delay, location, and even schedule.

Important adjustments were made to the library Web site and other online content to reflect the timeliest interests of users. For instance, essential updates were made to the official COVID-19 library home page banner. New FAQ entries in the LibAnswers knowledge base were created to reflect a surge of new questions stemming from the closure. The most immediate changes included guidance on local concerns like how to renew items, return library materials, and use new library lockers. Other helpful additions to online content included guidance for basic technical issues, such as clearing a browser cache and cookies.

It was clear that regularly revisiting and revising training strategies is vital to maintaining ideal practices. Not only is more rigorous training required, but it also needs to be ongoing to match more regular and systematic data analysis. For example, topics such as citations need to be approached in a more standardized way and referring patrons to subject specialists should be a routine part of chat transactions. In terms of data collection, the review revealed gaps and frequent misuse of tags by operators. Controlled vocabulary required updating to help improve tagging accuracy and application, and to better reflect the underlying needs of patrons. Encouraging the use of built-in transcription tools also better captures essential data over manual transaction inputs and minimizes operator subjectivity.

IMPLICATIONS

In light of assertions that virtual reference is experiencing a downward trend (Wells, 2003) or that low use justifies removing librarians from reference work (Bravender et al., 2011), the greatest implication of proactive chat use is the potential for libraries to more effectively assert themselves in virtual spaces. It is clear that libraries experiencing continued COVID-19 closures or other limitations to physical spaces would be wise to consider activating proactive chat features; however, this recommendation extends to any library with the desire to increase patron engagement. Considering both the impact on chat traffic and the increase in legitimate research questions asked, the potential of proactive chat to add convenience and improve service visibility is undeniable.

Looking to the future, this allows for a potential tiered staffing model. Growth in chat use demands strategic investments in human resources in order to prioritize, sustain, and scale up services and the data analysis process itself. An ongoing commitment to this form of data measurement and follow-up training is necessary to identify trends over time and be responsive to the evolving needs of patrons. While there are limitations to the interpretation of the project data, most notably the impact of the library's closure on the rise in overall chat traffic, evaluating the trends from the start of the lockdown reveals that virtual chat usage has mostly remained steady since the initial increase. It is unknown whether or not this extended increase is the result of the long pandemic, but it is telling that this trend persists despite the campus's return to in-person learning in the fall of 2021.

While the need to assess services and improve workflows became more immediate as a result of COVID-19, broader trends in online learning and information access, which surfaced pre-pandemic, only confirmed the importance of this kind of data analysis. Indeed, the move to expand online educational opportunities has been decades in the making. At present, about 5 percent of students at California State University, Fullerton are enrolled fully online as the university moves to offer more degree programs virtually (Metzger, 2021). Colleges and universities that plan to increase online or hybrid programs will require virtual library services that can scale with growth. As a result, both sustainability and scalability of services will continue to demand data-driven decision making at the local level. As this study shows, with proper preparation, proactive chat functionality is a sustainable way to expand and scale virtual reference services. Furthermore, when used along with robust data analysis, updated online content, and ongoing training, it can help ensure that libraries appropriately adapt to serve patrons during unprecedented times.

REFERENCES

Barrett, K., Logan, J., Pagotto, S., & Greenberg, A. (2020). Teaching and user satisfaction in an academic chat reference consortium. *Communications in Information Literacy, 14*(2), 181–204. https://doi.org.10.15760/comminfolit.2020.14.2.2

Blizzard, K. (2018). Proactive chat in a discovery service: What users are asking. *Internet Reference Services Quarterly, 23*(3–4), 59–66. https://doi.org/10.1080/10875301.2019.1643435

Bravender, P., Lyon, C., & Molaro, A. (2011). Should chat reference be staffed by librarians? An assessment of chat reference at an academic library using LibStats. *Internet Reference Services Quarterly, 16*(3), 111–127. https://doi.org/10.1080/10875301.2011.595255

Chen, X., & Wang, H. (2019). Automated chat transcript analysis using topic modeling for library reference services. *Proceedings of the Association for Information Science and Technology, 56*(1), 368–371. https://doi.org/10.1002/pra2.31

Epstein, M. (2018). That thing is so annoying: How proactive chat helps us reach more users. *College & Research Libraries News, 79*(8), 436. https://doi.org/10.5860/crln.79.8.436

Fan, S. C., Fought, R. L., & Gahn, P. C. (2017). Adding a feature: Can a pop-up chat box enhance virtual reference services? *Medical Reference Services Quarterly, 36*(3), 220–228. https://doi.org/10.1080/02763869.2017.1332143

Flierl, M. (2019). Opportunities for reference services after Covid-19. *Internet Reference Services Quarterly, 24*(3/4), 59–63. https://doi-org10.1080/10875301.2021.1910891

Gardner, G., Kimmitt, J., DeMars, J. M., & Baker, S. (2019, April 30–May 3). If you build it, will they come?: Natural experiments with Springshare's proactive chat reference [Presentation]. *ELUNA, Atlanta, Georgia, United States.* http://eprints.rclis.org/34456/

Garvey, M. (2021). Virtual reference amid COVID-19 campus closure: A case study and assessment. *Reference Services Review, 49*(2), 132–150. https://doi.org/10.1108/RSR-01-2021-0005

Gerbig, M., Holmes, K., Mai, L., & Tang, H. (2021). From bricks and mortar to bits and bytes: Examining the changing state of reference services at the University of Toronto Libraries during COVID-19. *Partnership: The Canadian Journal of Library & Information Practice & Research, 16*(1), 1–10. https://doi-org/10.21083/partnership.v16i1.6450

Hockey, J. M. (2016). Transforming library enquiry services: Anywhere, anytime, any device. *Library Management, 37*(3), 125–135. https://doi.org/10.1108/LM-04-2016-0021

HyunSeung, K., & Fienup, M. (2021). Topic modeling as a tool for analyzing library chat transcripts. *Information Technology & Libraries, 40*(3), 1–24. https://doi-org/10.6017/ital.v40i3.13333

Imler, B. B., Garcia, K. R., & Clements, N. (2016). Are reference pop-up widgets welcome or annoying? A usability study. *Reference Services Review, 44*(3), 282–291. https://doi.org/10.1108/RSR-11-2015-0049

Jacoby, J., Ward, D., Avery, S., & Marcyk, E. (2016). The value of chat reference services: A pilot study. *Portal, 16*(1), 109–129. https://doi.org/10.1353/pla .2016.0013

Kathuria, S. (2020). Library support in times of crisis: An analysis of chat transcripts during COVID. *Internet Reference Services Quarterly, 25*(3), 107–119. https:// doi.org/10.1080/10875301.2021.1960669

Kemp, J. H., Ellis, C. L., & Maloney, K. (2015). Standing by to help: Transforming online reference with a proactive chat system. *The Journal of Academic Librarianship, 41*(6), 764–770. https://doi.org/10.1016/j.acalib.2015.08.018

Labrake, M. (2019). Getting your FAQs straight: How to make your knowledgebase. *Computers in Libraries, 39*(8), 14–19.

Logan, J., Barrett, K., & Pagotto, S. (2019). Dissatisfaction in chat reference users: A transcript analysis study. *College & Research Libraries, 80*(7), 925–944.

Maloney, K., & Kemp, J. H. (2015). Changes in reference question complexity following the implementation of a proactive chat system: Implications for practice. *College & Research Libraries, 76*(7), 959–974. https://doi.org/10.5860/crl.76.7.959

Mavodza, J. (2019). Interpreting library chat reference service transactions. *The Reference Librarian, 60*(2), 122–133. https://doi.org/10.1080/02763877.2019 .1572571

Meert, D. L., & Given, L. M. (2009). Measuring quality in chat reference consortia: A comparative analysis of responses to users' queries. *College & Research Libraries, 70*(1), 71. https://doi.org/10.5860/crl.70.1.71

Metzger, C. (2021, January 29). CSUF is no. 1 online college in California. *CSUF News Service.* https://news.fullerton.edu/2021/01/csuf-is-no-1-online-college -in-california/

Mungin, M. (2017). Stats don't tell the whole story: Using qualitative data analysis of chat reference transcripts to assess and improve services. *Journal of Library & Information Services in Distance Learning, 11*(1–2), 25–36. https://doi.org /10.1080/1533290X.2016.1223965

Ozeran, M., & Martin, P. (2019). "Good night, good day, good luck": Applying topic modeling to chat reference transcripts. *Information Technology & Libraries, 38*(2), 49–57. https://doi.org/10.6017/ital.v38i2.10921

Pedregosa, F., Varoquaux, G., Gramfort, A., Michel, V., Thirion, B., Grisel, O., Blondel, M., Prettenhofer, P., Weiss, R., Dubourg, V., Vanderplas, J., Passos, A., Cournapeau, D., Brucher, M., Perrot, M., & Duchesnay, É. (2011). Scikit-learn: Machine learning in Python. *Journal of Machine Learning Research, 12*(85), 2825–2830.

Pomerantz, J., & Luo, L. (2006). Motivations and uses: Evaluating virtual reference service from the users' perspective. *Library & Information Science Research, 28*(3), 350–373. https://doi.org/10.1016/j.lisr.2006.06.001

Radford, M. L., Costello, J., & Montague, K. (2021). Surging virtual reference services: COVID-19 a game changer. *College & Research Libraries News, 82*(3), 106–113. https://doi.org/10.5860/crln.82.3.106

Rich, L., & Lux, V. (2018). Reaching additional users with proactive chat. *The Reference Librarian, 59*(1), 23–34. https://doi.org/10.1080/02763877.2017 .1352556

Strategic Communications and Brand Management. (2021). Fact sheet. *California State University, Fullerton.* http://www.fullerton.edu/about/#facts

Waltman, J., & McGinniss, J. (2020). How can we help? Supporting online students through asynchronous and synchronous library services. *Theological Librarianship, 13*(2), 23–25. https://doi-org.lib-proxy.fullerton.edu/10.31046/tl.v13i2.1940

Warner, A., Hurley, D. A., Wheeler, J., & Quinn, T. (2020). Proactive chat in research databases: Inviting new and different questions. *The Journal of Academic Librarianship, 46*(2), 201–134. https://doi.org/10.1016/j.acalib.2020.102134

Wells, C. A. (2003). Location, location, location: The importance of placement of the chat request button. *Reference & User Services Quarterly, 43*(2), 133–137.

Wilairat, S., Svoboda, E., & Piper, C. (2021). Practical changes in reference services: A case study. *Medical Reference Services Quarterly, 40*(2), 151–167. https://doi.org/10.1080/02763869.2021.1912567

Zhang, J., & Mayer, N. (2014). Proactive chat reference: Getting in the users' space. *College & Research Libraries News, 75*(4), 202–205. https://doi.org/10.5860/crln.75.4.9107

3

Converting In-Person Library Instruction for an Introductory Communication Studies Course into an Online Asynchronous Module: One Team's Experiences

Rachel Olsen and Jenny Dale

INTRODUCTION

Communication Studies 105 (CST 105) is an introductory-level and speaking-intensive course at the University of North Carolina at Greensboro (UNCG). CST 105 is required for many majors and programs on campus and serves as the basic communication course, providing an overview of public speaking and small-group communication concepts. Students complete several research-based assignments in the course, and librarians at UNCG have a long-standing relationship with the course director and campus partners associated with the class. During the COVID-19 pandemic, library instruction for CST 105 needed to shift online while still maintaining its usefulness to students and instructors. In this chapter, we will describe the process of replacing synchronous, face-to-face library instruction sessions for the many sections of this course with an asynchronous module in the Canvas learning management system (LMS).

One of the major assignments in CST 105 is a persuasive speech, which requires students to locate and use several sources, including at least two peer-reviewed journal articles. Since many of those enrolled in CST 105 are first-year students who may not have worked with scholarly sources before, this can be a daunting task. Some of the main goals of library instruction for the course are to help students better understand the peer review process in scholarly publishing and to help them feel comfortable finding and identifying peer-reviewed articles in library databases. The University Libraries at UNCG have had an ongoing relationship with CST 105 for many years; under normal circumstances, most sections of the course participate in an in-person library instruction session each semester. During the 2019–2020 academic year, more than 2,500 students were enrolled in CST 105, and 59 different sections came to the library for sessions.

With the onset of the COVID-19 pandemic during the spring semester of 2020, however, many CST 105 course sections went online, and library instruction had to be completely reimagined. A decision was made at the library level not to allow any in-person instruction for the 2020–2021 academic year, so even sections that were still meeting in person needed a way to get content virtually and asynchronously. This chapter will detail the process of switching to virtual library instruction, including a discussion of various choices that had to be made and workflows that had to be put in place, as well as an honest evaluation of the results and lessons learned.

LITERATURE REVIEW

Literature in both the Communication Studies and Library and Information Science fields has argued for the importance of integrating information literacy into the basic communication course curriculum. This integration is perhaps most commonly achieved through one-shot, course-integrated library instruction sessions, though other, more time- and labor-intensive models have been explored as well. Biddle and Montigaud-Green, for example, describe a "hybrid one-shot/consultation model where the faculty and one or two librarians met with individual students or small groups of students during their class period for 10–20-minute consultations" (Biddle & Montigaud-Green, 2020, p. 1).

Embedded librarianship models have also been effective in the context of the basic communication course. Weaver and Pier (2010) describe a collaborative basic communication course redesign process in which librarians were heavily involved in integrating information literacy into a communication course and embedding it within course sections. Hall (2008) describes a partnership with a professor who taught the basic communication course. The professor was concerned that her students were using poor quality sources (or no sources) and were also failing to attribute sources appropriately (p. 28). Hall became embedded in the course as a librarian, participating regularly in course discussions and providing multiple instructionsessions (p. 29). Anecdotally, the course instructor felt that

Hall's interventions made for better and more effective source use among students (p. 30).

Using a pre-test/post-test experimental design with sections of a basic communication course, Meyer et al. (2008) compared a higher contact experimental group, which "received three contact sessions with librarians, two in-class visits and one in the library, and completed three research logs" (along with some other additional instruction), with a control group, which received a typical one-shot session from a librarian, mostly focused on using databases to find sources (pp. 27–28). Students in the experimental group were "able to improve their information literacy skills significantly over time," while those in the control group were not (p. 31). The authors argue that, "[b]ecause information literacy forms the basis for lifelong learning, not only should it be a part of the basic course in the first year, but also students should be encouraged to continue building upon their information literacy skills throughout all 4 years of college in other curricular areas" (p. 31).

The research discussed above provides compelling evidence for the effectiveness of librarian-faculty partnerships in helping students in the basic communication course develop stronger information literacy skills. The overall theme seems to be that more involvement from librarians leads to better outcomes for students. Unfortunately, the basic communication course at UNCG offers far too many sections and enrolls too many students for an embedded librarian model to be possible.

Well before the COVID-19 pandemic necessitated a quick shift to online learning, many academic libraries were already offering asynchronous online instructional materials in a variety of formats, including research guides, videos, interactive tutorials, learning management system modules, and more. Library professionals working with high-enrollment first-year courses like the basic communication course have long struggled to keep up with the instructional demand of synchronous, face-to-face sessions and have explored more sustainable options. The most common approach to providing a sustainable, scalable alternative to face-to-face sessions for high-enrollment, multi-section first-year courses is to replace those sessions with asynchronous online instruction.

Librarians at James Madison University created a set of asynchronous online tutorials that would provide information literacy instruction to classes in the first-year writing program. They worked to re-create classroom activities in an asynchronous format and took a careful instructional design approach, using the ADDIE model and considering research related to student motivation (Thompson & Carrier, 2016). Though data from the resulting pilot study was limited, the authors concluded that student responses "seem to indicate that the tutorials kept student attention, but that there is room for improvement" (Thompson & Carrier, 2016, p. 89). Pilot data also suggested that students understood the content of the tutorial based on their responses to questions about topic selection, searching for information, and citing sources (Thompson & Carrier, 2016, p. 90); overall, these "tutorials met the primary objective, which was to create scalable, asynchronous instruction materials that students would actually use" (Thompson & Carrier, 2016, p. 91).

Moran and Mulvihill (2017) describe the challenge of providing library instruction that is both sustainable and personal to the large student population at the University of Central Florida (UCF):

> In recent years, UCF librarians have come to realize that some forms of library instruction are not sustainable or scalable. The efforts that are sustainable and large-scale sometimes lack the personal touch of a librarian. It is a struggle to find the balance between these two, and deliver instruction that is sustainable yet personal. While there may be no perfect solution, librarians are making strides in recognizing effective sustainable instruction, and how the personal can be embedded into online instruction opportunities. (p. 13)

Librarians at UCF have responded to this challenge by providing asynchronous information literacy instruction in different formats, including interactive modules, an online course in Canvas (the LMS) for students in the first-year writing program, and a course-specific online library assignment for a nursing course (Moran & Mulvihill, 2017). Collaboration is key in all of these projects, which rely on partnerships between teaching faculty and academic programs (Moran & Mulvihill, 2017, p. 24).

Marineo and Shi (2019) describe another challenge for academic libraries; "[t]he need to provide sustainable and effective library instruction to rapidly growing student populations, particularly of online and distance students" has led to more exploration of sustainable and scalable instruction, while "the imperative for academic libraries to demonstrate their impact on student success has librarians assessing their instruction in new ways" (p. 40). Marineo and Shi conducted a study of LMS-based asynchronous instruction at their institution, Nevada State College, a public institution with a student profile that is similar to UNCG's. Study participants were students in a first-year experience course. The results of the study showed no "significant difference between research assignment grade or semester GPA and instruction delivery type," which the authors argue "suggests that online library instruction can be an effective and scalable alternative to the one-shot, in-person instruction model" (pp. 47–48).

Taken together, these research and case studies speak to the potential of asynchronous online library instruction for high-enrollment first-year courses. Asynchronous models can provide sustainable, scalable, and consistent information literacy instruction to students. A common factor in all of the research summarized here is that library-faculty partnerships and collaborations are clearly crucial to the success of asynchronous learning projects, particularly in situations where the asynchronous content is developed to replicate a face-to-face library session connected to a specific course and assignment.

CST 105 INSTRUCTION BEFORE COVID-19

The University Libraries at UNCG have worked with this course since at least 2005, and the relationship between librarians, the CST 105 course director, and the UNCG Speaking Center faculty and staff has been an important collaboration that greatly benefits students in the course. Prior to 2016, students in the course had some research requirements, but expectations for numbers and types of sources were largely different from the present. Library one-shot sessions have been the primary method of research instruction for quite some time. These sessions attempt to cover a great deal of information literacy content, including topic selection, evaluation of sources, keyword development, specific demonstrations of library resources, and APA citation. The sessions are typically either 50 or 75 minutes in length, depending on the section's schedule. There are several challenges that librarians frequently encounter when teaching these one-shot sessions, including limited time to cover requested content and students being unfamiliar with the assignment. The fact that many of the sections of CST 105 cover research in the same one or two weeks of the semester also means that the First-Year Communication and Social Sciences Librarian is often double- or triple-booked and has to bring in other librarians, interns, or practicum students to manage the teaching load for this course.

The persuasive speech assignment requires that students choose their own topics and make a 5-minute presentation related to that topic. Students must do research to support the claims they make, citing at least two peer-reviewed journal articles and several other credible sources. There is also a roundtable dialogue assignment toward the end of the semester for which students work in groups of three to five to create a structured debate on a topic, which is then presented to the rest of the class. The roundtable dialogue requires research, so students need to draw on the skills they began to develop with the persuasive speech. Librarians work with students late in the semester in workshops designed to help with research and speaking skills in preparation for these dialogues. These workshops involve members of the Speaking Center and UNCG University Libraries, and each group in the class gets 10 minutes to work with specialists from both departments, as well as time to work independently in their groups. An article was published in *Communication Center Journal* detailing the roundtable workshop model (McCall et al., 2017). Shortly after the publication of the 2017 article, the current First-Year Communication and Social Sciences Librarian was tasked with coordinating CST 105 instruction.

ONSET OF COVID-19

In mid-March 2020, upon the outbreak of COVID-19 in the United States, UNCG made the decision to suspend classes for a week in order to facilitate a move to online instruction for most courses. The decision was also made that all library instruction would be virtual for the rest of the 2020 spring semester; this policy was then extended through the 2020–2021 academic year. Because of the timing of the initial shift to online learning, CST 105 students had already completed their persuasive speech assignments, so no instruction needed to be redesigned for the 2020 spring semester. The decision to provide only online library instruction for the 2020–2021 academic year, however, meant that a new approach was necessary for high-enrollment classes like CST 105. The librarian responsible for CST 105 instruction spent a good deal of time during the summer of 2020 brainstorming and experimenting with ways to effectively provide information about library resources to the hundreds of students who would now be taking CST 105 virtually. Luckily, there were nearly five full months between the time COVID disrupted in-person learning and the time when the online content would be needed. During this time, numerous questions about the design and delivery of the module needed answering.

CONTENT DELIVERY DECISIONS

The first major issue was content delivery. How could the information be best delivered to students? During the 2018–2019 school year, the First-Year Communication and Social Sciences Librarian had attempted to offer alternatives to in-person CST 105 library instruction through a Google site. While the site was easy to create and manage from an instructional design perspective, students struggled to follow directions and navigate the site successfully, resulting in the retirement of that particular delivery method. After consulting with the Online Learning Librarian at UNCG, it was determined that students prefer using the systems that they already depend on for resources, such as Canvas, UNCG's LMS. This had been demonstrated by the results of a survey conducted by the Online Learning Librarian previously, in which 76 percent of student respondents expressed a reliance on and preference for Canvas when completing any tasks associated with coursework (Harlow & Hill, 2020). This resulted in the creation of a Canvas module in 2019, which was offered to CST 105 instructors who did not have time to have a "library day" in their course schedule but still wanted students to get library instruction asynchronously. The module was initially popular, with at least a dozen Canvas Commons downloads in its first year. It was decided, therefore, that a Canvas module that could be downloaded from the Commons would be the best way to provide library instruction in response to COVID-19.

DESIGNING STUDENT ASSESSMENTS

The next major concern was student engagement. How would the librarian ensure that students were paying attention to the content in the module? How would students demonstrate their understanding? The easiest way to

Instructor:			Class Average:	
Student Name	**Student Score (100 points possible)**	**Notes**		
			Retakes will be available toward the end of the semester	
			Students can email Rachel with questions but must cc the instructor	

FIGURE 3.1. Score sheet template for reporting to instructors

do this might have been to create a graded quiz in Canvas that students would complete at the end of the module. However, there were several issues with this approach. First, if the quiz were done in Canvas, it would have required the librarian to be enrolled in each individual section of the course in order to be able to grade quizzes and offer feedback, which would have been overwhelming, as there are dozens of sections each semester (to be more specific, 78 in the fall of 2020 and 38 in the spring of 2021). Not being able to see results would have been a major disadvantage from an instructional design perspective for the librarian, as quiz results and other assessments would help determine what changes or improvements were needed in the module. Instructors needed a way to see the results in order to give students credit for completing the module. Ultimately, using Google Forms embedded in the module pages was determined to be simplest method. This would allow the librarian to see and check student progress and responses, which would then be reported to instructors via Box, a secure online cloud storage system. A score sheet template was created for reporting results in Box, and this template could be easily copied and shared with each individual instructor securely. See Figure 3.1 for the template.

Since the module covers a great deal of content, and it may be overwhelming for students to try to remember details from previous pages at the end of the module, the decision was made to integrate formative assessment as "checkpoint" Google Forms on certain pages. A total of six checkpoints were created and placed strategically throughout the module:

1. Choosing a Research Topic
2. Forming Keywords
3. Finding Books Using the Library Catalog

4. Finding Scholarly Articles

5. Evaluating Sources

6. Final Questions and Survey

Because Google Forms has a feature that allows users to create auto-graded questions, most of the checkpoints are graded automatically after users submit their answers. This auto-grading feature has saved the librarian and the graduate assistant working with CST 105 a great deal of time. Only checkpoints #3 and #4 require manual grading. The final checkpoint features survey questions at the end which ask students to give feedback about their experiences with the module. They are informed before this section that their answers will not affect their scores. All six checkpoints combined add up to 100 possible points.

GRADING WORKFLOW AND GRADUATE ASSISTANT

Google Drive is the main tool used to manage the module grading work-flow. All six checkpoints, as well as a survey that students take before completing the module, are housed in a single folder. At the beginning of each semester, a Google Sheet labeled "Scores" is created (see Figure 3.2). This includes columns for the student's name, their instructor's name, and their score on each of the six checkpoints. A simple formula is used to make the Google Sheet calculate the student's total score. From here, the scores go into Box sheets and are shared with instructors as previously explained.

This workflow is the result of a significant amount of trial and error on the part of the CST 105 librarian. During the 2020 fall semester, the first in which this module was used, approximately 588 students attempted the module. During the 2021 spring semester, approximately 465 students attempted the module, totaling more than 1,000 students for the academic year. One important note: the number of students that attempted the module is slightly higher than the number of students that completed the module, though the difference is not significant. Predictably, this was extremely over-whelming to organize and execute, particularly during the first semester in which it was used. The CST 105 librarian spent hours each week inputting data from the Google Forms into the Google Sheet and sharing the results with instructors via Box.

Name	Score 1	Score 2	Score 3	Score 4	Score 5	Total Score	Teacher
Joe Example	5	10	20	10	45	90	Professor X

FIGURE 3.2. Google Sheet with student scores setup

Thankfully, during 2021 spring and fall semesters, two graduate assistants (GAs) began working with the librarian as part of their required MLIS practicum capstones. The GAs were able to significantly lower the workload associated with this process for the librarian, whose job responsibilities include significantly more than just managing CST 105 instruction. Without the graduate assistants, the process would have continued to be difficult and time consuming. Their presence has allowed for increased quality in grading, assessment, and communication with instructors; needless to say, these contributions have been invaluable.

ASSESSMENT OF STUDENT RESULTS: FALL 2020 AND SPRING 2021

Pre-module Assignment

For the 2020–2021 academic year, students completing the module were asked to take a pre-module survey to determine their prior experiences (if any) with library instruction and citation. Of the respondents, 73.4 percent indicated that they had cited a source using APA style before, and 69.2 percent indicated that they had visited one of the two libraries at UNCG. Students were also asked to read a chapter from their course textbook that covers research basics, and they were required to answer a few basic open-ended questions about that reading in the pre-module form.

Checkpoint #1: Choosing a Research Topic

The module begins with a short recap of the assignment and an overview of what students can expect to learn in the module. A video is embedded in the checkpoint that relates to topic selection and the importance of choosing research subjects carefully. The video comes from the North Carolina State University (NCSU) Libraries YouTube channel. A question follows to make sure students viewed the video. More importantly, the next item is a true/false question, which reads as follows: "[True or false] When you pick a research topic, you cannot change it. It is set in stone." The vast majority of students answered correctly (false). This was an important question to include in order to introduce the idea of research as a fluid, nonlinear process.

Checkpoint #2: Forming Keywords

The next part of the module introduces students to the concept of keyword formation and the importance of using short phrases or single terms rather than complete sentences to search for information on a topic. This checkpoint also helps students understand that "the perfect source" does not exist. In addition to a brief written explanation of these concepts, another video from the NCSU Libraries YouTube channel reiterates the content. Another Google Form at the end of the page asks students about segmented searching and poses another true/false question. A great majority of students (98.3 percent) responded to this question correctly, indicating at least an introductory-level understanding of keyword formation and search strategies.

Checkpoint #3: Finding Books Using the Library Catalog

In this checkpoint, students are asked about their specific topics and are required to locate a book from the libraries' collections that may be helpful. This survey is not fully auto-graded; the librarian or GA goes through and manually looks at the title, author, and publication date of the book submitted by each respondent. The average score on this checkpoint was 94.3 percent. Students also respond to a multiple choice question about the difference between the library catalog and library databases. The correct answer to this question states that the library catalog can be used "to find many different things, including books. You can also find scholarly articles, but databases have more filters that allow you to do this easily." About 94.9 percent of the students answered the question correctly, showing that students are generally aware of what the catalog and databases provide.

Checkpoint #4: Finding Scholarly Articles

Similar to checkpoint #3, this part of the module asks students to locate one scholarly article related to their chosen topic. They must submit the title, the author(s), the name of the journal, and a permalink to the article. Again, this question is open-ended and graded manually. Most students submitted their article and its information correctly; however, many missed the important step of applying the "scholarly/peer-reviewed" filter in the database.

Checkpoint #5: Evaluating Sources

The Evaluating Sources checkpoint asks students to compare two Web sites and to choose the one that they would consider most reliable based on their understanding of the ABC framework for source evaluation, which is introduced in this section of the module. ABC is an acronym which stands for Authority and Accuracy, Bias, and Credibility. This concept also appears in the course textbook chapter that students are required to read before completing the module.

Checkpoint #6: Final Questions and Survey

The final checkpoint combines several previously reviewed concepts and recaps key points from earlier module pages. It also includes a brief survey that does not count toward students' overall score. The survey includes a space for students to share open-ended feedback or questions that they may still have about the module content. Of the 45 students that chose to share written feedback, the majority (27) asked questions about the research process, including clarifying questions about using the catalog, comments expressing anxieties about doing research on their own, and questions about topic selection. Other written feedback fell into one of four categories: questions about the assignment, queries about how to contact the CST 105 librarian, inquiries about the library's hours and access policies, and citation questions. When possible, the CST 105 librarian sent follow-up messages to students to try to answer their questions.

GENERAL OBSERVATIONS

The overall average student score on the entire module was 83.9 percent for the academic year. Overall, this is an encouraging indicator that the majority of students understood the content and were able to complete the activities successfully, demonstrating their attention and (hopefully) retention of the concepts covered in the module. The questions that showed lower overall scores tended to be multipart questions, and the main issue was missing information that was likely a result of students not fully reading the question and instructions. In terms of instructional design, more detail could have been given about parts of a scholarly article and perhaps another short question could have been included to test students' ability to apply filters correctly in databases.

FEEDBACK FROM INSTRUCTORS

A brief, anonymous survey was sent to CST 105 instructors to ask for their feedback related to the course module. The survey was sent to more than 30 instructors, with just seven responses received. Of these respondents, six indicated that their satisfaction with the module was at either a four or a five on a five-point Likert scale. When asked what they would choose in terms of CST 105 library content delivery given multiple options, respondents seemed split.

If you were to teach CST 105 again, would you prefer going back to in-person instruction for library sessions or would you rather keep using the Canvas module? (7 Respondents)

1) I would prefer going back to in-person instruction.	42.9%
2) I would prefer to continue using the Canvas module.	42.9%
3) I have no preference.	14.3%

One instructor requested that a video be created at the beginning of the module to show students how to complete it successfully; a video like this is already in place, indicating that the instructor may not have thoroughly reviewed the module before assigning it to their students. To remedy this issue, instructors are now being asked to complete the module for themselves as a "test run" before assigning it to their students.

FUTURE DIRECTIONS AND CONCLUSION

As of the writing of this chapter, the pandemic continues to be a major issue for the university. CST 105 instruction will, for the foreseeable future, continue to be virtual and asynchronous. Several important points of feedback have been collected, and changes have been made to the module. First, students from the 2020–2021 academic year found the module to be too long compared to their other course assignments. The instructors and course director agreed with this assessment, and so the module has been shortened. There are now three checkpoints instead of six, and much of the content is presented as optional and recommended for students who would like to investigate concepts further. There have also been issues related to the use of Google Forms in the module; some feel that it would be more beneficial to instructors and students to have the checkpoints changed to Canvas Quizzes. This comes with a variety of logistical issues, so this change is still under consideration. It remains to be seen how the pandemic will affect CST 105 library instruction in the long term, but for now, librarians are using feedback as discussed above to make the module as effective and beneficial for students as possible.

For librarians who find themselves in similar situations, the authors of this chapter offer a few suggestions for moving library instruction online:

- Make sure that expectations from campus partners and instructors are clear before instructional design begins.
- Consider what content is truly necessary for students to learn and what content can be made optional; this can take the form of links to suggested resources or a page on a LibGuide.
- Conduct frequent assessment of student results; do not change materials like quizzes, videos, etc., during the semester, but consider making adjustments between semesters.
- Ask for feedback from library colleagues; even those with little experience facilitating online instruction can provide helpful suggestions for improving online learning objects.

REFERENCES

Biddle, C. L., & Montigaud-Green, V. (2020). A measure of success? Utilizing citation analysis to evaluate consultation strategies in oral communication courses. *Virginia Libraries*, 64(1), 1–11. https://doi.org/10.21061/valib.v64i1.597

Hall, R. A. (2008). The "embedded" librarian in a freshman speech class: Information literacy instruction in action. *College & Research Libraries News*, *69*(1). https://doi.org/10.5860/crln.69.1.7922

Harlow, S., & Hill, K. (2020). Assessing library online patrons use of resources to improve outreach and marketing. *The Serials Librarian*, *79*(1–2), 200–227. https://doi.org/10.1080/0361526X.2019.1703873

Marineo, F., & Shi, Q. (2019). Supporting student success in the first-year experience: Library instruction in the learning management system. *Journal of Library & Information Services in Distance Learning*, *13*(1–2), 40–55. https://doi.org/10.1080/1533290X.2018.1499235

McCall, J. D., Ellis, E., & Murphy, M. (2017). It takes three to enhance: A pilot study of collaboration in the basic course. *Communication Center Journal*, *3*(1), 34–52.

Meyer, K. R., Hunt, S. K., Hopper, K. M., Thakkar, K. V., Tsoubakopoulos, V., & Van Hoose, K. J. (2008). Assessing information literacy instruction in the basic communication course. *Communication Teacher*, *22*(1), 22–34. https://doi.org/10.1080/17404620801926925

Moran, C., & Mulvihill, R. (2017). Finding the balance in online library instruction: Sustainable and personal. *Journal of Library & Information Services in Distance Learning*, *11*(1–2), 13–24. https://doi.org/10.1080/1533290X.2016.1223964

Thompson, L., & Carrier, H. S. (2016). Scalable equals asynchronous and asynchronous equals boring. Or does it? *Internet Reference Services Quarterly*, *21*(3/4), 81–92. https://doi.org/10.1080/10875301.2016.1241202

Weaver, K. D., & Pier, P. M. (2010). Embedded information literacy in the basic oral communication course: From conception through assessment. *Public Services Quarterly*, *6*(2–3), 259–270. https://doi.org/10.1080/15228959.2010.497455

4

Data: How Do You Drink from a Waterfall?

Laura Passos Santana and Sueli Mara Ferreira

INTRODUCTION

Through the eyes of the COVID-19 pandemic, where social disparities were broadly revealed, access to education significantly shifted, and the information overload—or *Infodemic*, the overabundance of information that occurs during an epidemic (World Health Organization, 2021)—surpassed all of its previous landmarks. How can learners approach the magnitude of the metaphoric waterfall of digital resources while holding such small cups? Not only is this limitless source too vast to qualitatively fill individual cups without filters to fight misinformation (leaning toward both critical analysis and research literacy), but the size of the cup is not large enough to leverage the ever-growing—and, *hopefully,* high-quality—volume of water.

Not only has the COVID-19 pandemic shed light on the issue of access to information, a human and universal right, but it has also revealed the previously misunderstood importance of public policies that guarantee the *openness* of access to the educational resources required to advance health care workers' educational development during health emergencies. Given the importance of formulating and applying public and institutional policies aimed at information and communications technology (ICT) and open educational resources (OER) in Latin America and the Caribbean (LAC), the objective of the research presented in this chapter is to evaluate the characteristics of public policies relevant to the use of technologies in education based on the selection of a specific thematic area: health.

We chose to approach this issue through the lens of Open Access (OA) initiatives. We aim to observe the public policies related to the Network of Open Educational Resources (OER Network) from the Pan American Health Organization (PAHO). The regional digital repository seeks the promotion of free, collaborative learning environments, with the capacity to make the processes of knowledge transfer and democratization exponential by favoring the production of content with a regional reach. However, understanding that the network, as a group of national repositories, is also buoyed by local policies to ensure the openness of information access, infrastructure, and skills development, we will zoom in and analyze the group of repositories from the Southern Common Market (Mercosur) countries—Argentina, Brazil, Paraguay, and Uruguay.

Realizing the region lacks policies to attend to emergency outbreaks, we seek to understand if and how these repositories meet the objectives of public policies within the scope of ICT in each country. For this, we will begin this chapter with a theoretical review of the themes relevant to OER and ICT public policies. We will then follow this with a discussion of the study's methodological design, and a quantitative analysis of the resources available in each repository. Then, we will present a list of recommendations that can serve as input to provide solutions for LAC's regional demands.

PUBLIC POLICIES IN THE CONTEXT OF ICT

Given the recent and disruptive transformations affecting access to scientific information around the world due to Open Access, we are moving toward a scenario of greater scientific collaboration and promotion of knowledge about science. Suber (2012) emphasizes that, although digital technologies have facilitated countless revolutions in our society, the current one, caused by Open Access, is the "Access Revolution." In addition to enabling communication within the scientific community, Open Access facilitates the appreciation of science by society, which could potentially use the results of various research democratically.

This process expands the flow of information within and outside the scientific community and qualifies the movement itself as a social research environment based on *sharing*. During the pandemic, the growth of preprints within the biomedical field has caused consumers of scientific content globally to pay attention to this model of information sharing. Else (2020) reported in *Nature* that nearly one tenth of all preprints published across the globe were about COVID-19.

In order to secure the change of pace and movement accelerated by the pandemic and facilitated by the Digital and Open agendas, public policies are essential to foster digital technologies in the educational context. Although the focus of the policies explored for this analysis target the access and use of ICT, it is imperative to consider the legislation (both local and regional) around copyright. The lack of robust copyright laws in a region that legally favors access to information foments the dependency of public and institutional policies to provide digital repositories with a guardrail in order to fulfill their purpose of guaranteeing this human right.

The official report from the Inter-American Development Bank (2019) estimates that by the year 2040, the Latin American region, which today has 11 million health professionals, will demand a total of 13 million professionals to manage the growing number of patients due to a global trend of population aging and an increase in comorbidities. Mainly, to meet the latent demands of the region and its health care workforce, we see an opportunity to treat digital and open educational tools as a means for learners to navigate through the overwhelming amount of data, information, and evidence shared among the community on a daily basis.

In the field of education, the incorporation of ICT studies in the digital sphere in the LAC region began in the late 1980s and early 1990s as a priority to promote the reduction of the digital divide, the modernization of learning processes, and the acquisition of cognitive skills or abilities by learners. The impact of globalization on education increases the value of information, which, together with the production of knowledge, contributes to the reproduction of values in society.

Thus, we consider technology as a means to ensure more inclusive social, human, and economic development, which makes its different aspects core elements in the transition toward an information (as well as a knowledge) society. On the other hand, in order to guarantee the sustainability of digital development strategies on the way to an information society (IS), the introduction of technologies in social processes must be supported by public policies focused on ICT that advocate both access to high-quality infrastructural resources and the legal support that guarantees access to information.

Present in all aspects of our lives (social, economic, and political), the Internet plays a significant role in our relations in the public sphere and requires us to understand some elements that enable its real insertion into our ethos. Since the Internet is nothing more than a network of computers that communicate with one another, a "network of networks," in its current social structure, the Internet is an intrinsic element of survival, or, in Castells's words, the very "fabric of our lives" (Castells, 2000).

This definition goes beyond the meaning of technology. The Internet is a means of communication, interaction, and social organization. It reflects Lévy's (1993) view of a network of human relations but is translated to a cognitive environment susceptible to time and the technical aspects of computing and ICT. In this scenario, public policies in the LAC region should go beyond securing access to infrastructure to guarantee the cognitive skills that allow the the transformative use of ICT in education to thrive.

Access to sources of knowledge has the potential to promote changes in the social fabric of the region and, taking the consequences of the

COVID-19 pandemic into consideration, to enable improvements in health care through professional qualification. The development of ICT in this context may reduce access barriers and the appropriation of technology, contributing to a scenario of equal access in order to achieve quality health care and improve professionals' digital skills.

A region that lacks infrastructure and training in health care, education, and technology has in *collaboration* a tool to evolve its weaknesses. However, the public policies coming from LAC's vast territory reveals a plethora of different challenges regarding access to ICT, health information, and skills for the transformative use of *digital* technology. Although the heterogeneity makes each country's context and needs unique, the embodiment of initiatives that strengthen knowledge sharing in the region may represent a sustainable dissemination of experiences. We do, nonetheless, find answers in ICT, which offers a range of possibilities to face inequalities in access to (health) information in the countries of this region.

The massive incorporation of ICT in formal education represents the fastest, most economical, and most extensive way to bridge the digital divide between communities, countries, and institutions. The extinction or reduction of the digital gap does not only depend on digital devices, but also on processes and exchanges of information as well as the incorporation of new technological supports for learning that enable democratization and access to knowledge. This requires putting into place public policies and legislation that favors access to information. Thus, it is undeniable that a condition for the integration of digital technologies in learning environments and educational systems is the existence of policies aimed at ICT.

However, since the implementation of public policies at the national level must be guided by the needs of each country, for the elaboration of national digital agendas required for an information society, it is recommended to carry out diagnoses of local ICT development. It is imperative to establish the terms of infrastructure growth, particularly the terms for the incorporation of technologies into production and social processes. Given the heterogeneity of digital advancement among countries, the common element of the objectives of the national agendas of the Latin American region is the vision of ICT as a tool for development and social inclusion.

The evolution of ICT has created new scientific communication networks, informational flows, and possibilities of access to information. These new forms of knowledge exchange under new space-time parameters were made possible by technologies that are the basis for an information society. In this perspective, open educational resources are one source of free and democratic access to higher education. Through technologies such as virtual learning environments, it is possible to make educational resources available online, along with all the resources necessary for its pedagogical use.

Because open digital repositories are dedicated to the gathering, storage, organization, preservation, recovery, and dissemination of information and educational resources, Volder (2008) believes that policies that favor digital repositories must be promoted. However, the lack of success or continuity in the LAC region may also be linked to the lack of knowledge and commitment of the authorities, the lack of economic and technological support, the lack of knowledge as well as the distrust of academics and researchers, and the lack of communication and cooperation between institutions. Torino (2017) corroborates Volder's reasoning by stating that policy making is one of the most important steps in the planning of a repository since it guides its implementation, form, and speed of development. Consequently, when analyzing a regional network, the institutional policy from each individual repository must be aligned with its local legislation, including authors' rights.

However, more than guiding the implementation of digital repositories, policies need to guarantee their permanence through the establishment of strengthened objectives and forms of action that make them reliable sources of information for the scientific community and society.

OPEN EDUCATIONAL RESOURCES DIGITAL REPOSITORIES

These challenges must be leveraged into opportunities in line with information science in order to develop a strong relationship with Open Access initiatives. As such, open educational resources (OER) repositories seek to democratize access to scientific information by providing open access content and transforming educational processes, and they are considered part of a potential strategy to develop an information and knowledge society in Latin America and the Caribbean.

In discussions on the use of technologies in education, Open Access policies emerge as a solution for sharing knowledge, and OER provide a means to enhance the dissemination of educational content that help learners navigate through an escalating number of informational resources. Related to OA policies, authors' rights also play a significant role in the pole of *access*, as they protect scientific expressions through intellectual property (Couto et al., 2022). Namely, OA policies are also useful for defining *open* authorizations regarding authors' productions. However, since the LAC region also lacks robust OER policies, digital repositories may need to comply with restrictive copyright laws.

In terms of typology, UNESCO (2015) characterizes OER as materials of a pedagogical nature, provided that they are made available under open access or public domain licenses. Open licenses give platform users the freedom to make use of their content, including the ability to retain materials, reuse them, review and adapt them, combine them, and redistribute them. These safeguards are fundamental for both producers and consumers of the resources to demonstrate the requirements of the conceptualization of OER.

First, by removing payment barriers (making materials free of charge), we promote greater accessibility to materials, since readers are not limited by their own budgets or those of their institutions. Second, by removing permission barriers (*free, open*), we allow researchers, students, and scholars to use and reuse them freely for the research and reading process; redistribution; translation; migration to other media; and long-term archiving. Thus, it is imperative to consider one of the main attributions of the term "OER," whose determination is the differentiating element between the highlighted concepts: the obligation of open licenses for use.

Wiley (2002), who coined the term "open content" in 1998 to promote the use of open educational content, characterizes OER as small instructional components that instructional or educational designers can create with a high potential for reuse, adaptation, and scaling. For Wiley, this context attributes a great benefit to the learner: that of collaboration. Another benefit of OER is that it is granular, which facilitates reuse by educators and accelerates the educational development process, making it more efficient. The possibility of regrouping and coupling these small resources to compose larger blocks turns them into key elements for the development and availability of pedagogical content in online learning.

Repositories are also seen as protagonist tools in the democratization of access to knowledge, scientific information, and/or educational objects. The democratization of access to education can be raw material for scientific advancement, and this movement has been accelerated by the COVID-19 pandemic.

In its turn, technological advances cause radical changes in access to information and knowledge. Consequently, these factors are fundamental to the democratization processes of contemporary society. Inevitably, the implementation of OER digital repository initiatives in Latin America impacts political, social, and democratic movements and favors the democratization of access to information and educational resources. This is because these platforms behave as alternative ways of scientific communication aligned with institutional, national, and regional Open Access policies.

Thus, OER can bring solid advantages for education in the public sphere by increasing learning opportunities, granting greater access to knowledge, strengthening educational communities, promoting a robust educational system, reinforcing and diversifying educational curricula, and reducing educational costs. These characteristics ultimately result in a more accessible education (Toledo, 2014).

OBJECT OF ANALYSIS: PAN AMERICAN HEALTH ORGANIZATION'S OER NETWORK

Due to the impact of the COVID-19 pandemic on access to educational resources for health care workers, the OER repositories that are the focus of this chapter are part of the Pan American Health Organization's (PAHO)

OER Network. The OER Network's objective is the dissemination of health knowledge and the encouragement of health research by bringing together different types of educational resources in an open format, the conceptual foundation of which is based on content availability through licenses that allow free and perpetual use. The scope of our analysis considers the Mercosur countries of Argentina, Brazil, Paraguay, and Uruguay. These countries are responsible for more than 60 percent of the users of PAHO's OER Network.

By diving deeper into the number of resources that Mercosur countries make available in PAHO's OER Network repositories, different levels of OER engagement can be perceived within the region. The low number of resources available in the platforms of Argentina, Paraguay, and Uruguay (171, 33, and 5 OER available, respectively, while Brazil made 12.589 resources available) may represent a lower-than-expected engagement among the Latin American countries that make up PAHO's OER Network. Although this factor might even directly influence the infeasibility of inferences about the Mercosur bloc in general, all countries share the same main audiences and educational objectives: resources aimed at the demands of professional training for health care.

Out of various sets of metadata collected to conduct a quantitative and qualitative analysis of the OER Network, three common variables were identified: language, thematic axes, and open access guarantee. Individually, Mercosur countries predominantly produce, use, and reuse materials written in their native language, and since the Network's OER are mostly in Spanish, users from Argentina, Paraguay, and Uruguay can consume and reproduce open educational resources from other countries, unlike Brazil, due to language barriers. Regarding the predominant thematic axes in the repositories, "Public Health," "Health Education," and "Primary Health Care" stood out. As for the dissemination of knowledge in the region, all countries that acquire open licenses for the use of each resource in their repositories confirm their open access recommendations by allowing the use, adaptation, and reuse of materials in a flexible and accessible way.

The infeasibility of a bloc-level analysis under all the quantitative variables studied is essentially due to the discrepancy between the number of open educational resources available in each country's platforms and the unique characteristics of the Brazilian repository. In this sense, we can mention the quantitative difference from Brazil's repository, which individually represents 70 times the total number of OER available in the repositories of Argentina, Paraguay, and Uruguay together. We attribute Brazil's highest degree of adherence to the Network to the country's strategy of making resources available independently via integrated research to existing governmental repositories. The existence of a national network in Brazil was the primary reason for the high number of OER in the country.

Furthermore, the question that guided the modeling of the analysis was the evaluation of PAHO's OER Network repositories based on the objectives of its guiding policies at the national and regional levels. To provide context, it was necessary to map out the policies of each Mercosur country regarding their approach to ICT and OER. First, it was necessary to map out the conceptual notions of digital repositories and branches of open science and the Open Education Movement to support the final conclusions. The focus on studying a network aimed at training health care professionals is linked to the importance of the health care workforce in these societies, highlighted by the COVID-19 pandemic.

Repositories as Mediators

While the repositories should represent the educational demands of learners and educators in such countries, they are also consequences of public and/or institutional policies developed from gaps between those who produce and appropriate knowledge and those who work with the resources and infrastructure necessary for its deployment. Thus, repositories are mediators between policies and end users. In addition to using repositories to create a channel for communicating needs and commitments, it is essential to establish direct paths between the policies (and their facilitators) and learners and educators to ensure the adherence and sustainability of these initiatives.

In response, we explore indications of the approximation or distancing between public policies that promote OER repositories and the educational needs of their end users in terms of the sets of metadata that describe the resources present in the platforms. Since the description of these materials have the power to guarantee and expand the dissemination of the content, we wonder if, in fact, they reproduce the research patterns commonly shared by users. On the other hand, since the assessment of the mapping of such policies, we report that the General Policy of PAHO's OER Network is more aligned with the different levels of granulation of the demands and capacities (infrastructure and competence) of these users. In its turn, national policies, even if reflecting international concepts of Open Access, point to the need for greater dialogue about the specificities that health education requires.

Since learners' relationships with technological resources vary according to the different levels of access to technological infrastructure that countries have, it is assumed that the effort to level the digital skills of users is a priority to ensure sustainability of repositories, both in relation to the production of resources and access to them. The platforms in question did not contain specific instructions in their interface for any of these audiences, nor guidelines regarding the different types of licenses for open resources and interoperability. These guidelines were located on external PAHO platforms, as well as local events with the aim of fostering this instrumentalization.

Learner and Educator Engagement

Also reflecting on the different potential audiences of these repositories, we identified an opportunity to engage with policy and decision makers at institutional, national, and regional levels. Considering that PAHO's OER Network has open educational resources focused on these decision makers, the greater the involvement of this audience with the repositories, the greater the potential for reorienting existing public policies and for valuing them. By promoting quality resources for managers and by demonstrating the impact that OER can have on the educational process, the chances of expanding these initiatives are more likely to happen, especially in professional and higher education, since, due to the contextualization of OER in the region, there is still evidence on the focus of these initiatives toward basic education.

Mainly, by attributing value to OER and open (digital) education, an opportunity is identified for the development and implementation of policies aimed at technological training, especially for educators. High ratings on the design of interfaces and features increase the usability rates of these educational tools and express greater assurance of continued encouragement. When a user has their educational experience positively impacted by these platforms, both by the quality of the materials and by the availability of mechanisms that expand their study framework, it is expected that the user will make recurrent use of the materials and will contribute to the sustainability of the repositories.

Finally, we identified factors that can contribute to the lack of participation within these repositories. Even after being created, supported, and encouraged by international and relevant institutions related to health, both learners and educators demonstrate the need for tools that fit their natural learning and work needs. Without embedding this new model of education locally and institutionally so that the platforms are integrated into the users' routine processes, it will hardly be possible to reach high levels of user engagement.

Sustainability Recommendations

A list of five recommendations with notions that can favor the creation of local or regional programs with the goal of dealing with the challenges and opportunities raised is proposed in Table 4.1. The goal is to leverage the average parameters within the Latin American region and training initiatives that aim to meet the educational demands of students and teachers, to ensure not only the development of new materials, but also their reuse. Secondly, outreach initiatives are identified as facilitators of collaboration in the region and as an opportunity to reach more individual and institutional users. Institutional partnerships, in addition to favoring integration and

Table 4.1 Recommendations for Developing a Sustainability Program Template

Recommendation	Objective	Expected Results	Expected Resistances
Capacity building	Unification of training and workshops on building interactive content, digital competence, handling open licenses, metadata, and language skills	Improve resource quality, ensure appropriate open license assignment, interoperability, and language mastery	Adherence of personnel to activities, absence of professionals from work posts
Promotion initiatives	Local and regional campaigns and contests	User growth and increased engagement	Investments in campaign production and dissemination on social networks
Institutional partnerships	Development and integration of resources and platforms, dissemination actions and exchange programs	Strengthening local and regional collaboration, optimizing resources	Absence of technical terms of cooperation, language
Institutional recognition policies	Scholarships for the purchase of technical equipment, courses, and career development plans	Encouragement and promotion of researchers and resource producers, differentiated student assessment	Absence of budget forecast for recognition standards
Continued education	Implementation of educational actions in the workflow of health care professionals	Continuous use of resources promoting the production of new materials and the sustainability of the repository	Adherence to changes in the scope of work for education

collaboration, optimize resources and act on the Open Access recommendations. Additionally, institutional policies and continuing education actions are also recommended to ensure the sustainability of their areas of activity.

The five recommendations do not intend to exhaustively solve all the challenges faced in the repositories, but they aim to propose measures that help guarantee the sustainability of the platforms through two pillars: the growth in the number of engaged users and the growth in the quality of open educational resources available. The OER Repository Sustainability Program Template was developed to illustrate the efforts to increase the quality, retrieval, and visibility of materials available in OER repositories and to increase the number of materials available through the digital training of those who produce and consume educational resources.

Naturally, the potential consequence of this movement is the increase in the number of active users in the repositories who, in addition to consuming—using, adapting, and reusing—the materials, also become potential contributors to the growth of the platforms. This model does not seek to advocate an order of actions, but rather to demonstrate the cyclical and systemic movement that these exert over the repositories.

The cooperation potential that Open Access environments and tools make possible for scientific collaboration can be transported to a scenario of regional and professional collaboration between Mercosur countries, despite the potential challenges related to the predominance of different languages (Portuguese and Spanish) in the repositories. We realize the value of this repository network for the institutional caliber it carries, but mainly for the opportunities it represents for the culture transformation regarding Open Access and the development of relevant skills to help advance learners' practices through technology.

KEY TAKEAWAYS

In this investigation, only one of the excerpts of the insertion of information and knowledge technologies in health education was studied, opening space to expand the views achieved here to the myriad transformations that ICT can generate in the development and implementation of new resources in the post-pandemic world.

More specifically, it was observed that OER digital repositories can contribute as a mechanism to guarantee access to high-quality educational resources, particularly as a tool for responding to health emergencies when public policies are prioritized. These perspectives have prompted new questions and challenges, especially around the importance of fomenting fair copyright laws that help guarantee access to information as a truly universal right.

By demonstrating the possible efficiency of public policies in Mercosur countries through inferences from the analysis presented, we contribute to understanding the impact of the COVID-19 pandemic within the growing educational and technological demands faced by health care professionals in the region. From this perspective, the results of this research can be treated as a thermometer of the progress of Open Access initiatives and policies in the region, as well as the commitment that the states in Mercosur countries have established with this community.

PAHO's network of digital repositories are a consequence of public and/or institutional policies developed from gaps between those who produce and appropriate knowledge and those who provide the resources and infrastructure necessary for its deployment. Repositories, then, play a mediation role between policies and end users and require efforts to improve users' digital skills to secure the sustainability of these instruments.

The Latin American and Caribbean region presents a plethora of differences regarding access to ICT, health information, acquisition of skills for the transformative use of OER, and the necessary skills to live in a globalized and increasingly complex world. On the other hand, the region also shares a new layer of possibilities for advancement in the resolution of shared problems, with the main tool to approach the common issues being *collaboration*.

To approach this challenge, the following recommendations are proposed: digital skills training; community outreach and institutional partnerships to promote collaboration; and continuing education programs. Putting the Open Movement's collaborative approach into practice can facilitate the process of sharing and disseminating, which, in the region, also holds the power to advocate for new institutional policies that value OER. Thus, the transformation proposed by the Open Movement reveals that the biggest challenges faced in LAC are not technical, legal, or economic, but *cultural*.

The inclusion of Open Access practices requires a cultural transition in the scenarios of development and implementation of technologies in health education among its community. This community motion not only represents a larger cup to approach the voluminous information waterfall currently magnified by the pandemic, but mainly counts on the power of collective intelligence to gather, analyze, criticize, and make informed decisions based on the *quality* of the water. This notion does not intend to exhaustively solve all the challenges faced in the repositories, but they aim to at least propose measures that contribute to guaranteeing the sustainability of the platforms through two pillars: the growth in the number of engaged users and the growth in the number of high-quality open educational resources available.

REFERENCES

Castells, M. (2000). Toward a sociology of the network society. *Contemporary Sociology, 29*(5), 693–699.

Couto, W. E., Ferreira, S. M., Souza, A., & Valente, M. (2022). Guia para bibliotecas: Direitos autorais e acesso ao conhecimento, informação e cultura [Guide to

libraries: Authors' rights and access to knowledge, information and culture].
FEBAB. Retrieved from http://repositorio.febab.org.br/items/show/6214

Else, H. (2020). How a torrent of COVID science changed research publishing—in seven charts. *Nature, 588*(7839). https://doi.org/10.1038/d41586-020-03564-y

Inter-American Development Bank. (2019). The future of work in Latin America and the Caribbean: Education and health, the sectors of the future? *Inter-American Development Bank*. http://dx.doi.org/10.18235/0001524

Lévy, P. (1993). As tecnologias da inteligência: O futuro do pensamento na era da informática [Intelligence technologies: The future of thought in the era of informatics]. *Editora 34*.

Nosek, B. (2019). Strategy for culture change [Blog]. *Center for Open Science*. Retrieved from https://www.cos.io/blog/strategy-for-culture-change

Suber, P. (2012). *Open Access*. MIT Press.

Toledo, A. (2014). Gasto público en la educación de América Latina: ¿Puede servir a los propósitos de la Declaración de París sobre los Recursos Educativos Abiertos? [Public spenditure in Latin America's education: Can it serve the Paris Declaration's purpose on Open Educational Resources?]. *UNESCO. Cuadernos de Discusión de Comunicación e Información [Communication and Information Discussion]* 1. Retrieved from https://digital.fundacionceibal.edu.uy/jspui/handle/123456789/194

Torino, E. (2017). Políticas em repositórios digitais: Das diretrizes à implementação [Policies in digital repositories: From guidelines to implementation]. In F. Vechiato (ed.), *Repositórios Digitais: Teoria e prática* [Digital Repositories: Theory and practice] (pp. 9–114). EDUTFPR. Retrieved form http://repositorio.utfpr.edu.br/jspui/handle/1/2755

UNESCO. (2015). Guidelines for open educational resources (OER) in higher education. *UNESCO*. Retrieved from https://unesdoc.unesco.org/ark:/48223/pf0000213605

Volder, C. (2008). Los repositorios de acceso abierto en Argentina: Situación actual [Open access repositories in Argentina: Current situation]. *Información, Cultura Y Sociedad [Information, Culture and Society]* (19), 79–98.

Wiley, D. A. (2002). Connecting learning objects to instructional design theory: A definition, a metaphor, and a taxonomy. *The Instructional Use of Learning Objects: Online Version*. Retrieved from http://reusability.org/read/chapters/wiley.doc

World Health Organization. (2021). WHO public health research agenda for managing infodemics. *WHO*. Retrieved from https://apps.who.int/iris/rest/bitstreams/1330207/retrieve

5

Exploring the Feasibility of a Hybrid Approach to a Post-pandemic Information Literacy Lesson

Brianna B. Buljung, Lisa S. Nickum,
Patricia E. Andersen, and Gyasi Evans

INTRODUCTION

As the 2020 fall semester approached, librarians at the Colorado School of Mines (Mines) faced the task of transitioning the information literacy lesson for the university's Design I (EDNS 151) course to a fully virtual lesson. Design I is an introductory course taken by nearly 600 students each semester, and it includes a required information literacy lesson tied to the "Authority Is Constructed and Contextual" frame of the Association of College and Research Libraries (ACRL) Framework for Information Literacy in Higher Education (Association of College & Research Libraries, 2016). Between 2017 and 2020, the lesson was successfully taught using a flipped model that paired an online lesson with an in-person librarian meeting. Prior to the COVID-19 pandemic, teams of five students met in person with a librarian to discuss the course's semester-long project.

Due to COVID-19, the library's instruction team conducted all team meetings online using the virtual meeting tool Zoom in both the 2020 fall semester and the 2021 spring semester, with approximately 120 sessions each semester. When Mines relaxed some pandemic-related restrictions for the 2021 fall semester, librarians began offering an in-person option for the

Design I lesson. Student teams were allowed to select either a fully in-person or fully virtual meeting for their team, allowing students to choose a format to suit their specific team needs.

This chapter explores what an effective post-pandemic Design I information literacy lesson could look like. Surveys were administered to students over the course of three semesters in the fall of 2020, the spring of 2021, and the fall of 2021. The surveys were used to gain perspective on student perceptions of the meeting format and to evaluate the feasibility of utilizing the hybrid approach in future semesters. A similar survey distributed in the fall of 2020 and informal focus group discussions were used to better understand the perspectives of teaching librarians and any pain points experienced. This chapter discusses lessons learned as the library's Design I meetings shifted in format throughout the pandemic. Lessons included mitigating Zoom overload for teaching librarians, addressing the impersonal nature of online learning, and successfully navigating the use of new online instructional support tools. A creative use of Zoom virtual meetings, Springshare's LibCal appointment booking product, honest conversations, and a lot of patience ensured this foundational teaching collaboration was maintained and that students had reasonable access to learning opportunities regardless of their location.

INFORMATION LITERACY AND DESIGN I AT MINES

The Colorado School of Mines is a medium-sized university located in Golden, Colorado, with approximately 6,500 students (5,500 undergraduates). The university is focused on science, technology, engineering, and mathematics (STEM), and all undergraduate students graduate with a bachelor of science degree. The Arthur Lakes Library supports research across the university with twelve academic library faculty and utilizes a functional model for organizing library faculty. At Mines, each faculty member leads library efforts in a particular area, such as instruction. Faculty participation in projects outside their lead area is voluntary; there is no traditional reference or liaison department. The information literacy program is coordinated by the Teaching and Learning Librarian, but program success depends on the goodwill of and participation from the rest of the faculty to teach lessons across the curriculum, especially large-scale instruction like Design I.

The Design I course at Mines introduces students to the principles of engineering design through project-based learning (Engineering Design & Society Department, 2020). Each semester is focused on an overarching problem, and students work in teams of four to six to design a solution, including a final report and works-like prototype. In the fall of 2020, the students addressed the problem of the COVID-19 pandemic. In the spring of 2021, the students explored outdoor activities and adaptive outdoor equipment, and in the fall of 2021, they addressed rapid response to disasters.

Throughout the semester, students complete milestone assignments individually and in teams that build up to a final research project, which is presented in a trade-fair setting. To complete the final project, students combine scholarly research, testing of their design, and stakeholder input. Their research for the project can include journal articles, standards, government reports and regulations, materials for their prototype, and more.

Most students take Design I in their first year, and the course is often their first encounter with the Mines Library. The library and course faculty have a long history of collaboration, including for the information literacy lesson in this course. Prior to 2017, that lesson took the form of a one-shot session early in the semester that helped students practice evaluating different types of sources. In the spring of 2017, the lesson was changed considerably to better meet the needs of students and course instructors (Buljung & Light, 2018). It was flipped to combine a brief module in the Canvas learning management system (LMS) and a required team meeting with a librarian. The Canvas portion of the lesson introduced students to scholarly and authoritative sources and included a short quiz. Student teams were then required to meet with a Mines librarian for 30 minutes to discuss how their team planned to narrow the semester's problem to a manageable topic for researching. For example, in the fall of 2020, students narrowed the problem of COVID-19 to topics like grocery store robots, classroom technology, and masks for athletes. The librarian also helps students explore library resources available to them. The lesson and final research project help students explore the contextual nature of authority and practice evaluating sources for their work. While the meeting is led by a librarian, the discussion can differ from team to team and is driven by their specific questions. In a typical 30-minute appointment, the librarian will review concepts of scholarly and authoritative sources from the Canvas module, then help the team brainstorm keywords and stakeholders for their narrowed topic and end by discussing a few databases or Web sites of special interest to that team. Approximately 600 students complete the course each semester across 24–26 course sections, resulting in more than 120 team meetings each semester. Depending on their schedules and other commitments, 8–10 librarians participate in the lesson in any given semester.

THE DESIGN I LESSON DURING THE PANDEMIC

Design I's information literacy lesson is early enough in the semester that it was not impacted by the sudden shift to remote learning in March 2020. However, as the 2020 fall semester approached, it became evident that the university would not return to the pre-pandemic norm of fully in-person undergraduate classes. Prior to the COVID-19 pandemic, Mines offered very few fully online undergraduate courses. That semester, the university, including the library, officially remained open, but many courses were moved online. To reduce capacity on campus, first-year and senior-level courses were prioritized for in-person learning, and most of the Design I content was taught in person. However, course faculty and librarians determined that it would be both safer and less complicated to offer the library's lesson in a fully virtual format only. The shift to a fully virtual lesson enabled maximum participation for both students and librarians. While most students were taking the course in person, a few were attending class online. Also, there could be students quarantined due to close contact with a COVID-19 case. A fully virtual meeting provided remote students the opportunity to participate alongside their teammates. This shift also ensured that more librarians felt comfortable teaching the information literacy lesson. Most teaching librarians meet with a minimum of 5–10 teams, and this was too much close contact for most librarians to feel comfortable participating in person.

In a typical semester, students complete the Canvas module portion of the lesson during the second week of the semester. The last section of the lesson contains instructions for scheduling their team's librarian meeting. Prior to the pandemic, sign-up consisted of selecting an open slot on a shared, editable Google Sheet. Although this spreadsheet was not ideal, it was a feasible tool for fully in-person meetings. However, it would not work for the 2020 fall semester, as more than 120 Zoom sessions would need to be created manually. Library staff had previously considered utilizing Springshare's LibCal to book the sessions but had never fully explored that option. LibCal provides functionality for creating events and booking appointments with individual librarians. Mines intended to use the appointments portion of the tool to replace the Design I Google Sheet. In the summer of 2020, in collaboration with the Digital Projects Librarian and campus technology services, Zoom integration was added to LibCal, enabling auto-generation of Zoom links for every appointment booked. One student from each design team would select an available appointment slot on the Design I calendar and complete the booking form on behalf of their team. Then, that student received an automated confirmation e-mail containing the details of the appointment and the Zoom link to share with their teammates. The new integration made LibCal a much more attractive option for students booking meetings, and it incentivized teaching librarians to explore this workflow further.

Overall, the fully virtual lessons in the fall of 2020 and the spring of 2021 were very successful. There was a bit of a learning curve for librarians during the first semester. Beyond attending staff meetings, Zoom was a new tool for most of the teaching librarians. Few had the opportunity to use it in a class setting prior to the fall of 2020. They also had to learn to navigate webcam issues and slower Internet speeds if working from home while other family members were also online. The appointment features of LibCal were new to most of the teaching librarians. They had to learn to add and remove availability to the Design I group calendar and update content in the auto-generated confirmation e-mail to ensure that students understood the meeting portion of the Design I lesson was held via Zoom.

The information literacy lesson was also largely successful for students. The Design 1 course project can be daunting to students, especially those in their first semester of college. They are navigating campus, completing college-level coursework, working in groups, and conducting substantial research. The meeting, even when held virtually, connected them to real people in the library they could contact with additional questions or concerns throughout the semester. The fully virtual nature of the lesson ensured that all teammates could contribute and participate. Students taking classes virtually or in quarantine would not be the only teammates calling into an in-person class. During the first fully virtual semester, there were some basic netiquette issues that librarians had not anticipated before the meetings began. Some students called in from less-than-ideal environments; for example, while driving, during sports practice, or while their roommates were also attending class virtually. Extra noise and other people wandering through the frame could be disruptive to the meetings. To mitigate this issue, in the spring of 2021, sign-up instructions were more explicit about asking students to find a quiet place from which to participate.

PILOTING A HYBRID MODEL

By the summer of 2021, course faculty, students, and librarians were hoping that Mines would return to the pre-pandemic norm of fully in-person classes. Most courses across the university were offered in person, and many restrictions on capacity and activities were reduced. Several of the teaching librarians were comfortable returning to meeting in person with Design I teams in the library. They missed the in-person interaction with students. However, the library could not return to a fully in-person lesson because students could be quarantined at any time, and some librarians were still unable to safely participate in person.

The most important consideration for librarians when piloting the hybrid model was ensuring there was no confusion for students when scheduling and then attending their meetings. Librarians were concerned that teams would arrive in the library, unaware they had signed up for an online slot. Teaching librarians created two separate "locations" in Springshare LibCal to differentiate between in-person and virtual meetings. This approach ensured that fully online meetings could continue to take advantage of the integration that auto-generated the Zoom link. In the Canvas lesson, students were given links to the calendars for both locations so they could select the format best suited to their team's needs (see box). This attempt to avoid confusion was highly successful. All of the scheduled teams met in the format they had selected at sign-up, and most importantly, no teams arrived at the library for online meetings. Although highly successful, the solution is imperfect, as teams may have to check both calendars to find a time that works for them.

Once you have been assigned to a project team, set up a 30-minute team meeting with a Mines librarian. Only **1 member per team** should sign the entire team up and share out the confirmation e-mail.

Your team has the option to meet with a librarian in person in the library or online. There are no hybrid options, **the whole team** must be either in person or online.

Sign-up

Friday, September 3 through Monday, September 13

To schedule an **IN-PERSON** meeting use this link: https://libcal.mines .edu/appointments/bookalibrarianf2f?g=14625Links to an external site.

To schedule an **ONLINE** meeting use this link: https://libcal.mines .edu/appointments/bookalibrarian?g=7135Links to an external site.

Contact Brianna (bbuljung@mines.edu) if you have questions or are unable to find a time that works for the majority of your team members.

Another important consideration in the return to in-person meetings was library space. Prior to the pandemic, physical constraints led to a restriction of two teams maximum per time slot. This restriction was managed via the Google Sheets sign-up form, which only allowed two teams per time slot. However, a bit more coordination was required in the LibCal environment when individual librarians could control their own availability. Librarians began populating their initial availability approximately one week prior to when students would begin sign up. Then, as the course's library coordinator, the Teaching and Learning Librarian used administration rights in LibCal to view individual librarians' calendars and created a master list of meeting availability. Fourteen of the 111 available in-person appointment slots had more than two librarians available. Librarians then negotiated among themselves to drop availability as needed to ensure a maximum of two meetings per time slot.

Although managing the in-person schedule is a bit more complicated, having too many librarians available to help is a good problem to have. The information literacy lesson for Design I can be exhausting and time-consuming, especially as most Mines librarians are also balancing other duties and responsibilities. Research conducted in 2018 demonstrates that the flipped lesson helps students more than the previous, less intensive one-shot lesson

(Buljung & Light, 2018). Librarians participate in the meetings because they enjoy the engagement with students and value the impact the lesson has on student learning at Mines. In the spring of 2021, librarians made themselves available for a total of 213 appointment slots (111 in person and 102 online), comparable to the two online semesters (250 and 221, respectively). This continued support from Mines librarians is essential to ensuring the long-term sustainability of the Design I information literacy lesson.

COMPARISONS OF HYBRID AND FULLY VIRTUAL SEMESTERS

Students were given a brief survey at the end of their librarian meeting in all three semesters. The survey sought to gain their perspective on their use of LibCal to book the appointment, their perceived usefulness of the information literacy lesson, and ideal timing of the meetings moving forward. In the fall of 2020, 260 students completed the survey; in the spring of 2021, 208 students responded; and in the fall of 2021, 351 students filled out the survey. During fully virtual meetings, the link to the survey was put into the Zoom chat at the end of the session. During in-person meetings, a sheet with a QR code that linked to the survey was used. Sharing the survey with students was optional for librarians, as was completing the survey for students. The most likely reasons the survey was not completed were if a meeting ran long, the librarian forgot to share the link, or students were rushing to their next obligation.

In the fall of 2020, librarians also completed a survey that asked similar questions. In the spring and fall of 2021, the survey was replaced with an informal after-action discussion to gain a more nuanced understanding of librarians' perspectives. Given the small population size of 8–10 librarians per semester, the librarian survey was not as informative as this group discussion. Ensuring that students had a useful and high-quality educational experience comparable to previous years was an essential thread woven through all the work done with the course during the pandemic. The informal discussions provided the authors with a better understanding of the successes and pain points experienced each semester. Teaching librarians were also able to learn and adapt before the next semester.

Using LibCal to Schedule Library Appointments

All three semesters, students were asked to rate the ease of completing different tasks related to the meeting process using a five-point Likert scale from very easy to very difficult. The most difficult task for students in all three semesters was finding a time to meet with the librarian that worked for their team, with n = 38, 22, and 79 students, respectively, finding it moderately or very difficult to find an appointment slot that worked for their entire team. Students found other aspects of the meeting process to be much easier. They overwhelmingly found using Zoom to be very easy (n= 188, 150, and 210 students, respectively). Importantly, it was relatively easy for students to get to the Design I LibCal calendar from the Canvas lesson (Figure 5.1) and schedule their meeting using the booking form (Figure 5.2). In Figures 5.1 and 5.2, each point of the Likert scale is represented as a percentage of the total student responses for that semester. In both figures, responses of "Very Difficult" comprised 0 percent of the total

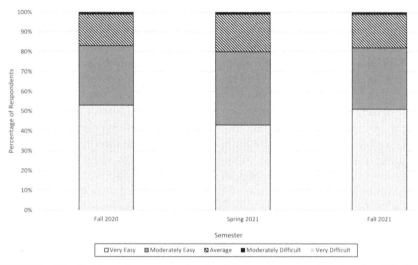

FIGURE 5.1. Rating the ease of scheduling the meeting in the LibCal calendar

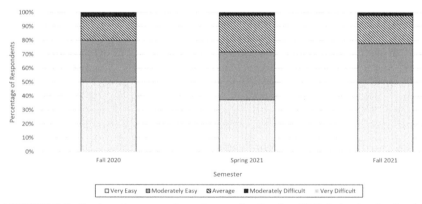

FIGURE 5.2. Rating the ease of getting to the Design I LibCal calendar in the Canvas lesson

for each semester. The students' perceived ease when using the LibCal booking system is promising for continued use in the course. Design I can be overwhelming, and students are often using systems and processes that are unfamiliar. It is important for Mines librarians to make completion of the Design I lesson as straightforward and easy to navigate as possible for students.

Despite the initial learning curve, teaching librarians also found it easy to use LibCal to manage the meeting schedule, especially with the Zoom integration auto-generating the Zoom link. Transitioning from an editable Google Sheet to LibCal appointments had several benefits for the teaching librarians. Going virtual gave librarians more control over their own schedules. After publishing their initial availability, more than 250 slots were added to the calendar, greatly increasing flexibility for the student teams to select a time. One hour on the second afternoon of meetings even had five librarians available in the same slot. Also, librarians could add or remove availability as needed, instead of having to coordinate schedule changes through the Teaching and Learning Librarian. They could adjust their calendar independently and communicate directly with their scheduled teams. This also facilitated easier follow-up with additional resources after the meetings. In a typical semester, it was inevitable that extra teams would occasionally arrive at the library, claiming to have signed up. Google Sheets was so easy to edit that teams ended up editing over each other. The shift to LibCal mitigated this issue, making it easy for students to see only the available appointment slots.

Usefulness of the Meetings

To rate the students' perceptions of the helpfulness of the library's information literacy lesson, students were asked to select the most helpful aspect of the curriculum. They could choose one of the following answers: the Canvas module as a whole, videos included in the module, the Design I research guide, the librarian meeting, or other. Students in all three semesters overwhelmingly chose the librarian meeting as the most helpful aspect (n= 180, 131, and 226 students, respectively). The next most helpful aspect selected was the Design I research guide (n= 52, 61, and 98 students, respectively). Their selections also could be based partially on proximity to the survey, as the research guide is often discussed by their librarian, and the surveys were administered at the end of the meeting. Students appreciate that the session is tailored to their team's approach to the semester problem and addresses their specific questions.

To gain a more nuanced understanding of students' perceptions of the meetings, they were also asked to describe their appointment in three words. In the fall of 2020, students entered 646 total words and phrases (139 unique). In the spring of 2021, students entered 502 total words

(116 unique). In the fall of 2021, students entered 854 total words (173 unique). "Helpful" and "informative" were overwhelmingly the most commonly used terms across all three semesters. "Helpful" was used 132, 97, and 202 times, respectively, while "informative" was used 129, 103, and 187 times across the three surveys. The next most used term each semester was "useful," with 19, 22, and 31 uses. These three words were often used in combination with each other and other terms, such as insightful, productive, quick, educational, easy, and interesting. Some terms found across the three survey response pools describe students' perceptions of the librarians, including friendly, nice, supportive, fun, cheerful, cool, entertaining, and genuine. A few other terms used by students included inspiring, empowering, inspirational, motivational, peaceful, and approachable. Teaching librarians were encouraged to see that students found the meetings helpful and that they also had a pleasant experience. Five students in the spring of 2021 found the lesson to be repetitive, redundant, or boring. Students who take Design I in the spring are likely to have engaged with a Mines librarian during information literacy lessons in other core courses already. While librarians try to differentiate lessons in different courses as much as possible, they can occasionally be perceived as redundant.

Learning new tools for this course while navigating their other job duties from home was stressful for the teaching librarians. All the librarians who led meetings in 2020 and 2021 had participated prior to the pandemic. They hold themselves to a high standard in all aspects of their work, especially when working with students. Librarian responses to the 2020 fall semester survey showed their stress and perceptions that they were not working at their normally high standards. In comparison to the student responses, the librarians were more likely to use a critical term when asked to describe their experience in three words. Six of the seven responses included at least one critical term or phrase, including disconnected, frustrating, Zoom overload, unconnected, and impersonal. Positive terms in the librarians' responses included efficient, new, exciting, flexibility, better than expected, and fast. Disparities in responses between the students and librarians could be related to relative experience using Zoom or librarian expectations for the meetings based on past experience. Late in the 2020 fall semester, the authors held the first informal discussion with participating librarians to learn more about their perspective. The teaching librarians provided additional details about their experience teaching, and largely they did not feel that it was a negative experience. Instead, they used critical terms because they hold themselves to a high standard based on their past experience teaching the Design I lesson. As one librarian described, they felt they could have done a better job managing technology and teaching the lesson.

The feelings of frustration decreased somewhat in the second full semester of online teaching in the spring of 2021. Librarians had become more comfortable with Zoom meetings, LibCal appointment booking, and online teaching. They had also largely navigated the bandwidth issues arising from multiple family members working at home at the same time. In the fall of 2021, participating librarians also felt the transition to the hybrid model was successful. Those who prefer to teach in person were able to, while those who preferred teaching online could still contribute to the library's work with the course.

Suggestions for Scheduling and Format

The switch to a virtual lesson and responses to the survey gave librarians the opportunity to gauge student perspectives on meeting times and formats. In past semesters, appointment availability was primarily dictated by individual librarians' schedules and the typical 9 to 5 workday. To learn more about when students preferred to meet, they were asked what day of the week and what times of the day were ideal for this type of class activity. In the second and third semesters (the spring and fall of 2021), they were also asked to select their ideal day of the week. Results were fairly mixed, but students tended to prefer later in the week (Figure 5.3). This data helped librarians add more availability later in the week to accommodate the teams interested in those days.

Students in all three semesters were asked about their preferred time of day for the librarian meeting. They were asked to select one of the following options: morning (8:00–11:00 a.m.), lunch (11:00 a.m.–1:00 p.m.), afternoon (1:00–5:00 p.m.) or evening (5:00–7:00 p.m.). Afternoon was the

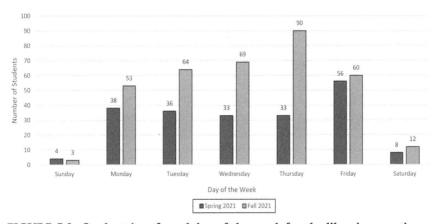

FIGURE 5.3. Students' preferred day of the week for the librarian meeting

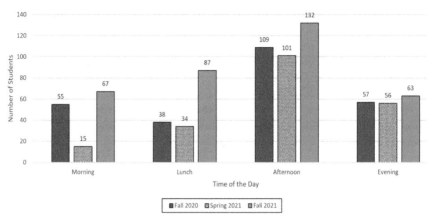

FIGURE 5.4. Students' preferred time of day for the librarian meeting

most popular time period for students in all three semesters (Figure 5.4). During the all-virtual semesters, students had evening as their second favorite time, but this time period fell to last when students returned to largely in-person learning in the fall of 2021. Many sports teams and clubs meet in the evening, so students prefer to keep course commitments separate as much as possible. Across all three semesters, morning was consistently either the third or fourth most popular choice.

In their 2020 fall semester survey, librarians were asked to rank their preferred times of day to meet with students. Ranking was used because librarians will have meetings in multiple time periods over the course of a semester's lesson. To analyze the results, each ranking was weighted as points (for example, one point for rank #1 and four points for rank #4). Then, the total for each time slot were added and averaged. The lowest number of points indicated the time slot the librarians most preferred. Librarians prefer to have student appointments earlier in the day, with morning being the most desirable (Table 5.1). Most librarians have families and/or other obligations in the evening.

Table 5.1 Librarians' Ranking of Meeting Time Slots

Time of day	Total points	Average
Morning	11	1.57
Lunch	17	2.43
Afternoon	19	2.71
Evening	23	3.28

In response to the data from the three student surveys, librarians have been able to adjust their availability. While morning slots are still available for booking, there is typically only one librarian available prior to 10:00 a.m. During the hybrid semester, a couple librarians increased their late afternoon and early evening availability by offering online appointment slots from home. They would participate in person during the late morning and afternoon, then be available online for a couple meetings in the evening. Based on anecdotal feedback, this appears to be a feasible approach moving forward. It allows librarians to be available when the students are and offers more flexibility for student teams navigating work, sports, and other obligations in the evenings.

LESSONS LEARNED

The start of the pandemic forced a lot of new tools on students and librarians alike, including Zoom. Others, like LibCal appointment booking, had been available to Mines librarians, but there had been no urgency to learn to use some of its functionality. The use of LibCal has already made significant improvements for librarians in terms of scheduling Design I meetings with students. Shifting the power to add and remove availability to individual librarians removes the responsibility from the Teaching and Learning Librarian. It also helps librarians to better structure their commitment to the course around their other duties and responsibilities.

When adapting a program or lesson, especially at the scale of the Design I lesson, to an online or hybrid model, librarians need to practice patience and listen to collaborators' needs and frustrations. They are highly likely to experience a learning curve, especially if new tools or processes are implemented. There will be a period of adjustment for both librarians and students. Netiquette and distractions during meetings were a problem in the 2020 fall semester but much less of an issue in following semesters as students adjusted to the norms of online learning. Librarians also face unexpected complications, even if they are meticulous planners. For example, in the fall of 2020, one design team's meeting was cut short by a fire drill in their dorm building. The librarians had avoided the library's annual drill that often conflicts with Design I, but they had not anticipated the drills in the dorms. Adequate time for instructor self-care is also a necessity. Librarians cannot expect the same level of colleague participation in a fully online setting, especially during a pandemic. Instructors should be given the ability to spread out appointment availability and the time to decompress in between if need be. Meetings may need to be spaced over more days to accommodate Zoom fatigue and competing priorities for participating librarians.

Moving forward into the spring of 2022 and beyond, the hybrid approach offers the most flexibility for offering appointment slots when students are most likely to need them. Offering virtual sessions from home in the later afternoon and early evening can help meet the needs of both students and participating librarians. Across the three semesters, students expressed their preference for afternoon and evening time slots. The librarians also largely prefer to meet with student teams in person. Scheduling more in-person meetings earlier in the day and offering a few late afternoon and evening virtual slots from home helps address both preferences. Due to other commitments, some librarians will not be able to participate later in the day. But, for those who can, this method of scheduling provides a hybrid path forward for the library's collaboration with the course. Over time, the authors will be able to track available slots offered by librarians against the slots chosen by student teams. This longitudinal data will help librarians continue to refine the meeting scheduling process and best meet the needs of students.

Students in the hybrid 2021 fall semester were asked to select their preferred meeting format. They were asked to make their selection regardless of how their team participated during the semester. They overwhelmingly preferred to meet in person (n= 269 students). Only 36 students preferred to meet virtually, and 44 students had no preference. The significant preference for the in-person format could be due to fatigue with online classes. It could also be due to the highly collaborative and hands-on nature of the Mines curriculum, and specifically the Design I course. The highly interactive, project-based learning that occurs throughout the course is more difficult to translate to a fully online environment than other types of courses. The librarian meeting is yet another interactive aspect of the course. Participating librarians also expressed more comfort and interest in working with students in person when possible. They were frustrated with the impersonal nature of Zoom, especially if some or all team members chose not to have their cameras on. From the librarians' perspective, although the online meetings were successful, the in-person format is more interactive and engaging. The authors will be able to continue tracking the number of appointments offered in each format as well as the slots ultimately selected by students to gauge long-term desirability of offering meetings in both formats.

FUTURE OF THE LESSON

Is the hybrid approach to the Design I information literacy meetings the way forward for the Mines library? Yes, it is the most feasible model, at least for now. The hybrid approach offers the flexibility necessary to address the needs and interests of both students in the course as well as participating librarians. As the pandemic moves into 2022, the Mines librarians are still monitoring the health situation and adapting the lesson as needed. While writing this chapter, the authors are preparing for the 2022 spring semester; the topic of the lesson will be aging populations. It is anticipated that some students and librarians will need an online option to fully participate. Experiences throughout the pandemic have taught the authors that the future is unpredictable and maximum flexibility is needed to provide stability and support for the students in the Design I course. Due to the prevalence of the COVID-19 Omicron variant on campus in January 2022, the automated appointment confirmation e-mail for all in-person meetings will contain the following note: "If you have booked an in-person meeting but your entire team is unable to meet in person due to quarantine/isolation, let me know no later than the morning of your meeting so that I can convert your meeting to online. Just reply to this confirmation e-mail, and I'll send a Zoom link to share with your team." This extra note will help students navigate the changing health situation on campus, ensure maximum team participation, and remove the stress of having to reschedule meetings due to quarantined team members.

The student surveys conducted throughout the three semesters also provided insights into their preferences for day of the week and time of day for meetings. Librarians are able to offer availability that better matches student preferences, making better use of the librarians' time during the workday. Instead of having time slots go largely unfilled earlier in the day, librarians can adapt their schedules as much as possible to meet students' desired time frames. Prior to the fall of 2020, librarians were curious about student preferences but had yet to make any formal attempt to investigate. Ongoing tracking of the data from availability and scheduled meetings will provide a more nuanced understanding of students' needs with regard to the meeting portion of the course's information literacy lesson.

The hybrid approach is currently the most feasible, but the authors will need to determine under what circumstances the meetings would revert to the traditional fully in-person schedule. As this chapter has demonstrated, a shift to a fully online information lesson will largely be dictated by the situation, but it can be accomplished successfully. At what point will the hybrid approach no longer be needed? What criteria should be used to make that decision? For the next few semesters, the authors will continue to monitor the situation on campus, gain further perspective from teaching librarians, and gather data from the Design I LibCal calendar slots selected by students. The Mines library will use this qualitative and quantitative data to make informed decisions about the format and organization of the Design I librarian meetings. Further development of the Design I information literacy lesson will be an iterative process that accounts for the needs of students and teaching librarians while ensuring maximum participation, savvy use of available technologies, and open dialogue about successes and areas for improvement.

REFERENCES

Association of College & Research Libraries. (2016). Framework for information literacy for higher education. Retrieved from http://www.ala.org/acrl/standards /ilframework

Buljung, B. B., & Light, L. (2018). Using a flipped lesson to improve information literacy outcomes in a first-year design class. *ASEE Annual Conference and Exposition, Conference Proceedings, 2018-June.* Retrieved from https://peer .asee.org/31193

Engineering Design & Society Department. (2020). Cornerstone design @ mines. *Colorado School of Mines.* Retrieved from https://cornerstone.mines.edu/

6

Finding New Ways to Support Social Connections for Older Adults: Rural Public Libraries Innovate during the Pandemic

Noah Lenstra, Joseph Winberry, and Fatih Oguz

INTRODUCTION

When the COVID-19 pandemic spread across the United States of America in March 2020, public librarians grappled with the challenge of how to continue supporting social connections and social infrastructure (Klinenberg, 2018). For many older adults living in rural communities, the public library had become a "de facto senior center" (Cline & Jarvis, 2019), a space to gather, to socialize, and to learn. Librarians in these rural communities seeking to continue to support these social connections faced the double challenge of 1) limited Internet and technology availability, and 2) limited digital literacy among older adults, as they worked to continue supporting the social needs of their older populations (Osei, 2021).

To understand this reality, and any innovations rural librarians may have developed in this context, the authors sent an online questionnaire to 1,123 randomly selected small and rural public libraries in the spring of 2021. The e-mail addresses of these libraries came from directories maintained by state library organizations. The authors received 353 usable responses, a response rate of 32.4 percent. More information on this larger study can be found in Lenstra et al. (2021). This chapter focuses primarily on the open-ended responses provided by rural public librarians. Findings show that in some communities, rural librarians used a wide variety of modalities to continue supporting social connections among older adults—not only technology, but also the telephone, the postal system, and socially distant in-person communication. Findings also highlight how some rural library workers understand that their roles in the lives of older adults transcend the informational to include a kind of caring, social role. Finally, struggles with technology and attempts to stay abreast with what other librarians are doing animate responses.

This chapter serves to inform both public librarians and those responsible for providing them master's degrees in library and information science and continuing education about the innovations rural librarians experimented with as they sought to continue supporting social connections among older adults during the COVID-19 pandemic and the implications of these experiments for public library services going forward.

LITERATURE REVIEW

Rapidly evolving technology and growing patron expectations in the 1970s indicated that there were numerous social and economic advantages for academic libraries that innovated (Drake, 1979; Musmann, 1982). Beyond recognizing its value, early studies yielded lessons in how to build support for such transformation as library staff were found to be more supportive of this change when they were able to participate in its development (Howard, 1977; Luquire, 1976). Research on innovation in academic libraries has grown in the past few decades (Brundy, 2015), but related research in public libraries has been more limited (Damanpour & Childers, 1985; Pungitore, 1995; Widdersheim et al., 2019). More recent studies in public libraries have focused on the perspective of library administrators on innovations (Potnis et al., 2020a; Potnis et al., 2020b) as well as how innovations can support communities and marginalized populations (Gorham & Bertot, 2018; Suchá et al., 2021; Winberry & Potnis, 2021). Few studies, however, have focused on innovations in small or rural public libraries or on the existence of public library innovations meant to serve older adults specifically (Chase, 2021; Jia, 2015; Lenstra et al., 2020; Lenstra et al., 2021).

The budgetary limitations which have, at times, spurred innovation in the past have continued into and progressed throughout the COVID-19 pandemic (Todorinova, 2021). In recent years, rural communities have come to rely on the strategic positioning of the public library in delivering vital services to local residents—a role the library has continued to play during the crisis (Chase, 2021). Much of the research that has focused specifically on the role rural libraries have served during the COVID-19 pandemic has emphasized the role of technology. For instance, Rubenstein et al. (2021a, b) examined the kinds of information rural libraries shared over Facebook;

while in some cases discussion of the pandemic itself was minimal, there was information about modifications made to library hours or processes as well as discussion of virtual programming options for patrons. Another set of studies found that rural public libraries may have the Internet access necessary for rural individuals who need to engage with telemedicine resources, making libraries more vital in a time when so much of life transferred online (DeGuzman et al., 2022; DeGuzman et al., 2020). Other research has examined how technology can help public libraries remain relevant in both rural and urban settings given the pandemic-related facility shutdowns that some communities have required (Nageswari & Thanuskodi, 2021; Wakeling et al., 2021). A common thread throughout these various studies is the lack of accessible broadband Internet for many people in rural communities. This requires additional consideration, as do non-technological issues facing the staff and patrons of rural public libraries during the COVID-19 pandemic (Lenstra et al., 2021).

Despite years of previous research confirming it, the pandemic has reinforced the importance of digital literacy in the lives of older adults; digital literacy refers to high "levels of skilled, competent use of technology" in daily life (Van Jaarsveld, 2020, p. 3). A comparative study of the United States and India found that Internet use by older participants increased during the pandemic (Lund & Maurya, 2021). Generally, however, older adults have been among the most negatively affected by the health risks of COVID-19 as well as those most likely to lack the technological access and literacy skills necessary for circumventing the isolating elements of social distancing (Davies et al., 2021; Seifert et al., 2021; Shah et al., 2021). Without the proper digital literacy skills, older people may have to choose between protecting their physical health by keeping their social distance and their mental health if they lack the digital literacy necessary to maintain social connections virtually (Cosco et al., 2021).

There is other evidence connecting digital literacy and social connection together. For instance, while lacking digital literacy makes a person more isolated, research has shown that the strength of an older person's social network is a greater indicator of them having the support necessary to learn new technology than their age (Lopez et al., 2021). Other scholarship examining the role of social connections of older adults during the COVID-19 pandemic found that the resilience of older people in times of crisis is not just an issue of individual resilience but of community and resources resilience as well (Chen, 2020). This suggests that there is a need to understand social connection and digital literacy as closely related constructs that should be studied together in research and built together in practice (Hansmann et al., 2020).

This is not to say that the digital divide is only a community-level issue. A lack of personal interest in technology is cited as a reason for the digital divide and requires more work to see how technology can be provided and framed in such a way that makes it more valuable to hesitant older users (Song et al., 2021). For instance, online group meeting tools can be sold as resources for building and maintaining relationships with people who would not be able to stay connected without the technology, such as those living in other parts of the country or world (O'Connell et al., 2022). Nevertheless, community-level technological infrastructure can help older people become more comfortable with technology before ending up in a situation, such as another pandemic, in which digital literacy is an essential skill (Seifert et al., 2020). This is especially true for those living in rural communities (Golomski et al., 2022). Given the connections that digital literacy has with personal health, economic well-being, and relationships with others, the research suggests there is a need for better implementation of digital literacy training and resources for older adults and the institutions that serve them (Morrow-Howell et al., 2020).

METHODS

Qualitative data used in this chapter is drawn from a larger study that explores the roles of libraries in supporting healthy aging of older adults in small and rural communities (Lenstra et al., 2021). The chapter focuses on innovations related to how public librarians contribute to social connectedness in these communities, based on the open-ended responses included in the dataset. The data were collected between March and April 2021. The sample of small and rural public libraries for the study was drawn from the Fiscal Year 2018 Public Libraries Survey (PLS) dataset (US IMLS, 2020) using a cluster sampling method. A total of 353 usable responses were received from 17 states out of four U.S. regions. For the purposes of this chapter, those (n=173) who responded to three open-ended questions are included in the data analysis. These included:

1. During the pandemic (March 2020-present), did your library offer any other types of programs or services for older adults? If so, please specify in the field below.

2. Does your library have any other priority areas that relate to services for older adults? If so, please specify in the field below.

3. Thinking about the topic of public libraries supporting social connectedness among older adults during the COVID-19 pandemic, do you have anything else you'd like to share or add that has not been addressed by this survey? If so, please provide your response below.

These responses ranged from 2 words to 184 words, with an average of about 33 words between them.

Although frequently brief in length, these open-ended responses reveal volumes about the context and content of innovation in rural librarianship during the pandemic. To understand the significance of that content, the authors employed standard coding procedures, using the "classification of innovations in public libraries" developed by Potnis, Winberry, Finn, and Hunt (2020b) as a rudimentary code book to classify content. Two authors independently coded the dataset and then discussed any differences in coding.

RESULTS AND DISCUSSIONS

Quantitative results suggest that during the COVID-19 pandemic rural librarians utilized a wide variety of communication channels to stay connected with older adults. Within the full dataset, of those that reported offering services for older persons during the pandemic (n=245), nearly 55 percent reported offering "Check-in /conversation services (e.g., library workers call library regulars to check in with them)"; 35.5 percent reported "Social distanced in-person programming outside the library space"; and 31.8 percent reported "Correspondence programming, facilitated in whole or in part by the library (e.g., pen pal programs, or the distribution of Valentine's Day cards to older adults)" (Table 6.1). Furthermore, 39 percent reported offering check-in services on a regular basis during the pandemic, 22 percent offered in-person programming, and 15 percent offered correspondence programming.

Less evidence was found of the development of new processes, partnerships, or technologies by rural librarians during the pandemic. Turning to the qualitative data, within the 105 responses to the prompt "During the pandemic, did your library offer any other types of programs or services for older adults?" a majority focused on new programs (53 percent), with less on new processes (21 percent), new partnerships (13 percent), or technologies (5 percent) (Potnis et al., 2020b).

Table 6.1 Offered at Any Point during the Pandemic (n=245)

		. . . and check-in services	. . . and in-person programming
% Offered check-in services	54.7%		
% Offered in-person programming	35.5%	21.2%	
% Offered correspondence programming	31.8%	20.8%	14.3%

Table 6.2 Offered on a Regular Basis, Defined as Respondents Who Specified This Activity Was Offered "More Than Once a Week," "Once a Week," or "Once a Month" (n=245)

		. . . and check-in services	. . . and in-person programming
% Offered check-in services	38.8%		
% Offered in-person programming	21.6%	10.6%	
% Offered correspondence programming	15.1%	11%	6.12%

Programming as Innovation

The following quote illustrates some of the innovations in programming discussed by respondents:

> We set up a live chat through our website to help our patrons through questions or issues they had with their card. We also provided telephone services for older patrons to have someone to talk to during the pandemic, capped off at 10 minutes, so they felt connected with the library and community.

This quote also illustrates some of the tensions rural librarians navigated: the caveat "capped off at 10 minutes" suggests a concern with feeling overwhelmed by the challenge of keeping older adults connected.

Partnerships and Processes as Innovation

Given this potentially overwhelming challenge, some librarians did develop innovative partnerships and processes. These librarians supported social connections by working collaboratively with others, rather than developing new programs in-house. One wrote:

> In response to the Pandemic, the Library took on the job of creating and hosting the webpage for the newly formed "[Name of Community] Helpers" Community group. This group formed in the wake of the health crisis to help organize volunteers, and to connect those in need with those who could provide help. . . . It has included publicizing a newly created 'Everyone Eats' Community Action social service program which provides free meals to those in need, many of whom are elderly and live in senior housing. The program has been very successful, providing food and a feeling of stability for those in need. The Library is one of many organizations working together to coordinate and publicize community services.

In other cases, innovative partnerships allowed librarians to meet older adults where they were during the pandemic:

> The Library entered into a partnership with our County Senior Center. Library staff members created materials to advertise outreach & home delivery to Seniors receiving pick-up on-site or home-delivered meals. The Librarian spoke with each person who participates in the meal program in person and described library services available to them, rode with a meals delivery volunteer to distribute information, registered patrons for library cards, and delivered requested materials to the Senior Center for pick-up.

Others discussed partnerships as a core part of how they saw themselves building back after the pandemic subsides. One wrote, "Once all is safe [our priority is to] develop a facility for aging populations that is co-located with a library." Another wrote that their priorities included "[utilizing] the library for services such as early voting, food distribution, rental assistance, COVID[-19] vaccine access. Nontraditional library services but essential for our senior patrons with limited access."

In still other cases, librarians discussed coordinating behind the scenes with partners, even in cases when those conversations did not translate into actions:

> We worked with the health department to come up with ideas for keeping seniors connected—one example was the idea of a drive-in movie using our blow-up movie screen—but [we] eventually decided that it would be too hard to avoid close contact in the bathroom.

Whereas most responses spoke to the librarians themselves coming up with ideas, these quotes imply that in at least some rural communities the "innovation space" expanded beyond the library to encompass the wider community.

Crisis Intervention as a Form of Innovation

The responses also suggest the need for a new innovation category in public libraries focused on crisis intervention. Crisis intervention is a form of innovation in that it requires libraries to speedily find new ways to serve their patrons in a safe and effective manner (Temiz & Salelkar, 2020). Crisis interventions in past research has referred to libraries taking on roles outside of their day-to-day services to help their community through unforeseen challenges, such as the opioid epidemic or natural disasters (Allen et al., 2020; Hagar, 2014). Many of the public libraries in our sample took on a crisis intervention role in checking in on their older patrons by calling them during the pandemic.

For instance, consider the following quote: "An online Book Club was set up and facilitated by our staff. Our adult services librarian did outreach calls to those persons who were in her adult programs, and called once a month to do a check in." In this example, we see traditional library functions (outreach and programming) complemented by nontraditional, innovative services—"a check in." The growth of these types of "check in" services during the pandemic suggests innovation related to crisis intervention for potentially isolated older adults in at least some rural libraries.

Another example of the crisis intervention check in can be seen in rural Appalachian Ohio, where "The Chillicothe & Ross County Public Library partnered with Ross County 211 and area service organizations" to develop the "Checking In: In This Together" service during the pandemic wherein library staff made "friendly phone calls to check on qualifying folks who may be isolated and lonely" and to help coordinate assistance to those in need.

The closeness of library staff to patrons (and vice versa) can be a factor in the creation and success of these check-in innovations. The study adapted Burt's (1997) emotional closeness measure (Distant, Less Close, Close, and Especially Close) to assess the closeness between the library staff and patrons. Although a minority of quotations were coded as "especially close," those that were coded as such suggest that at least in some communities these caring innovations may have grown out of librarians' perceptions of the library's role as a caring space prior to the pandemic.

This especially close relationship can be seen in this quote:

> As a small town in Northern Maine I have made it our mission to reach out to our senior members of our community. A 91-year-old patron came in when we reopened June 1st and cried when she saw us. Hugs and masks were necessary, but I am so happy she wanted to see us. We care for our elders in many ways.

One librarian wrote in response to the prompt "Does your library have any other priority areas that relate to services for older adults?" that "Just the fact that our population is 800 on a good day, and most folks know they can come to the library just to visit if they want. I have several who will drop in for a visit 1–3 times a month," suggesting that this library's main priority is simply to keep functioning as that caring third place in the lives of older adults.

Another wrote that their priority going forward was "[being] a place for seniors to go without judgment and having an ear that listens." A third wrote that "pre-COVID we functioned as a kind of a community center." This caring role of the rural library overlaps with the idea of the library as multigenerational social infrastructure, as seen in this quote:

> In our small community, the Library was the center of social activity prior to the pandemic. We quickly moved our programs online and have been a lifeline for our older residents. Families were less interested in online programs so we started setting up storywalks. We were pleasantly surprised when we started hearing from older adults who visited our storywalks too.

This quote also speaks to how, in rural areas of the United States, library services for older adults are not always explicitly labeled as such. In the context of small staff, library services are sometimes for all ages, including older adults, who demographically are becoming a larger segment of the population year after year in rural parts of the United States. The folding of older adults into the catch-all service population also appears in these quotes: "Since most of our patrons fall under the category of older adults virtually all our programs are for older adults" and "many of our virtual programs were attended—and continue to be attended—by older adults."

Digital and Analog Media in the Context of Innovation

Nevertheless, some libraries did report that engaging older adults via digital services during the pandemic was a challenge. Although in some communities older adults did participate fully in virtual programs and services, in other communities librarians said technology posed a barrier.

As one respondent wrote: "Technology is a vital piece in working with our aging population, but we were aware it will not be a sufficient bridge. We needed to find a way to physically open and be even safer than the grocery store during the pandemic," given how older adults were especially vulnerable during the pandemic. Another wrote:

> Internet access has been a limitation for many older adults in our community during the pandemic. Virtual programming with older adults has not been successful for this reason. WiFi hotspots are available for checkout, but the area around the library has many hills and valleys and signal is drastically reduced outside of city limits.

In addition to challenges accessing technology, librarians reported challenges related to digital literacy: "Most of our outreach was dependent upon whether patrons had access to computers and broadband. Too many in our area either do not have access, or the skills, to participate in virtual programs."

The combination of older adults with low digital literacy compounded by spotty access to digital devices and Internet connectivity can also be seen in this quote:

> Much of the attempt at solutions to pandemic closures involved technology, while many seniors do not have the technology skills to utilize them. Additionally, since there isn't free community internet service available, seniors have difficulty affording home internet service.

In some places, public librarians framed themselves working with others to address digital inequalities. One wrote, "We worked with our [partner] to provide a curriculum and taught classes to seniors who received a free iPad after completing a technology course to assist them in staying connected. This was funded through a grant [our partner] received."

In many other cases, though, librarians developed multimodal approaches to engagement that included "old" media like telephone and mail, as well as perhaps the oldest media of all—face-to-face communication, inside and outside of the library building itself. This multimodal strategy can be seen in this quote:

> [Our library offered] curbside and phone service, deliveries to homes, we miss you cards & mailings, friendly newsletters to older adults, now outside picnic table service to those not wanting to enter the building, Facebook times, finally have a new website for older adults, esp. keeping in touch w/them because our phone conversations were sometimes some older adults' only visiting times for them during the pandemic. We have reopened w/safety precautions, and many are coming back after being vaccinated and esp. the ones we stayed in touch with.

Others utilized what they had to keep older adults connected, including local newspapers and parking lots. One wrote, "We did Parking Lot Bingo (bingo from inside of cars and we used a megaphone—so fun). We also did a drive-thru meal, and something we called Senior Surprise—seniors drove up to the library and got a goodie bag of surprises." Another wrote, "We paid for ad space in the local newspaper and offered some library themed word searches and word challenges for adults to participate—thought it was a fun way to reach those who don't use a computer but still wanted to feel engaged in some way."

In U.S. rural librarianship, technology is seen as important, but it was not in and of itself the vital component that enabled rural librarians to continue supporting social connections among older adults during the pandemic.

Other Constraints to Innovation

Finally, it is worth noting that in addition to the innovations discussed above, some librarians did articulate some of the reasons why innovation seemed impossible during the pandemic, with one writing as follows:

> We have had the goal of providing more technology instruction to all adults, but specifically older adults, for the past couple of years. We were beginning to add programs before the pandemic hit. Unfortunately, our adult service staff had severe health issues and ended up retiring in 2020. We have had other staff shortages as well. We are slowly getting back to a point where we can add more programming and services.

Another challenge centered around not knowing where to go to engage in peer-to-peer learning with other rural librarians grappling with these challenges. One wrote:

> I saw on a library Facebook group where a library in Canada had started doing what amounted to welfare calls to their seniors and another poster called them

out on it saying that librarians are not trained social workers and questioning how they would handle it if the senior was actually in need. We are in a rural area with few resources to connect to, but I wondered about this myself. We've worried about seniors we know through library visits who haven't come in or connected with us at all during the pandemic, but have hesitated to call because it would be weird or intrusive. Would welcome suggestions.

Here we see a librarian thinking about the issues and innovations discussed in this chapter, but who is not sure where to go to really learn about these topics in ways that would prepare them to try something new in their own local context.

CONCLUSION AND IMPLICATIONS

A major finding of this study centers around the heterogeneity of responses. Rather than a univocal response to the pandemic, results instead suggest that rural librarians explored and experimented in a wide variety of ways, which supports the diverse representations of innovation found in previous research on innovations in public libraries (Potnis et al., 2020b; Winberry & Potnis, 2021). Rural librarians in many communities explored different options to continue supporting older adults, including digital technology, analog media, outdoor spaces, and community partnerships. The findings of this study add to a small but growing pool of studies that examine the role of innovation in serving older patrons in public libraries, and rural public libraries specifically.

A second major finding is that innovation in public librarianship could be productively expanded to encompass more intangible aspects of social belonging, community care, and social connectedness that add to and move beyond just the digital literacy focus of recent related research (Van Jaarsveld, 2020; Hansmann et al., 2020. Innovation can include new systems and strategies to foster and sustain social connections, social inclusion, and caring communities for older adults and other populations.

Limitations and Future Work

It is also possible that those librarians who chose to complete this survey were in some ways outliers—librarians already thinking about this topic— and thus inclined to complete the questionnaire. For instance, one librarian wrote, "We were the first library in our area to help seniors or anyone register for vaccines."

It is also possible that these respondents represent early adopters of, and developers of, innovations. Regardless of how representative these respondents may be, there is still value in attending to the innovations of librarians, representative or not, as we seek to expound on the lessons learned from practicing librarianship during the COVID-19 pandemic. The goal of this chapter has been to open a window into the world of innovation taking place in rural public libraries during the COVID-19 pandemic.

Learning from the pandemic, per the theme of this book, will require a much deeper engagement with rural librarians by researchers, including potentially academic librarians, who could learn alongside rural public librarians, utilizing some of the emerging frameworks of the Service Learning Librarian as a guide (University of Northern Iowa, 2022).

Implications

One implication of this project is the need for better platforms for sharing of innovations among rural librarians. Although there are many spaces in which rural librarians *could* share their experiences—including the Association for Rural and Small Libraries, the Public Library Association, and state library associations—there is also some evidence that some rural librarians do not know where to go to find out what others are doing, and to engage their peers in productive dialogue.

A second implication of this study is to think about how to better support multi-sector partnerships involving public librarians. On April 19, 2021, the National Association of Area Agencies on Aging (2021) hosted a webinar entitled "More Than Books: Libraries as Hubs for Social Connection," suggesting that at the national level there is increased interest in library-aging agency partnerships. The library profession needs to continue communicating to potential partners, at the local, state, and national levels, how public librarians support, and have supported, social connections among older adults, including during the COVID-19 pandemic, with an eye toward informing, supporting, and funding innovative cross-sector partnerships at these three levels.

REFERENCES

Allen, S. G., Clark, L., Coleman, M., Connaway, L. S., Cyr, C., Morgan, K., & Procaccini, M. (2020). *Call to action: Public libraries and the opioid crisis.* Dublin, OH: OCLC.

Brundy, C. (2015). Academic libraries and innovation: A literature review. *Journal of Library Innovation, 6*(1), 22–39.

Burt, R. S. (1997). A note on social capital and network content. *Social Networks, 19*(4), 355–373. https://doi.org/10.1016/S0378-8733(97)00003-8

Chase, S. (2021). Innovative lessons from our small and rural public libraries. *Journal of Library Administration, 61*(2), 237–243.

Chen, L. K. (2020). Older adults and COVID-19 pandemic: Resilience matters. *Archives of Gerontology and Geriatrics, 89*, 104124. https://doi.org/10.1016/j.archger.2020.104124

Cline, D., & Jarvis, M. (2019, January 23). From movies to meals: Senior services and spaces at your local library [Webinar]. *Network of the National Library of Medicine, Bethesda, MD.* https://www.youtube.com/watch?v=AxRh9UmHxz8

Cosco, T. D., Fortuna, K., Wister, A., Riadi, I., Wagner, K., & Sixsmith, A. (2021). COVID-19, social isolation, and mental health among older adults: A digital Catch-22. *Journal of Medical Internet Research, 23*(5), e21864.

Damanpour, F., & Childers, T. (1985). The adoption of innovation in public libraries. *Library & Information Science Research, 7*(3), 231–246.

Davies, A. R., Honeyman, M., & Gann, B. (2021). Addressing the digital inverse care law in the time of COVID-19: Potential for digital technology to exacerbate or mitigate health inequalities. *Journal of Medical Internet Research, 23*(4), e21726.

DeGuzman, P. B., Abooali, S., Jain, N., Scicchitano, A., & Siegfried, Z. C. (2022). Improving equitable access to care via telemedicine in rural public libraries. *Public Health Nursing, 39*(2), 431–437. Online ahead of print. https://doi.org/10.1111/phn.12981

DeGuzman, P. B., Siegfried, Z., & Leimkuhler, M. E. (2020). Evaluation of rural public libraries to address telemedicine inequities. *Public Health Nursing, 37*(5), 806–811.

Drake, M. A. (1979). Managing innovation in academic libraries. *College & Research Libraries, 40*(6), 503–510.

Golomski, C., Corvini, M., Kim, B., Wilcox, J., & Valcourt, S. (2022). Aspects of ICT connectivity among older adults living in rural subsidized housing: Reassessing the digital divide. *Journal of Enabling Technologies, 16*(1), 17–27.

Gorham, U., & Bertot, J. C. (2018). Social innovation in public libraries: Solving community challenges. *The Library Quarterly, 88*(3), 203–207.

Hagar, C. (2014). The US public library response to natural disasters: A whole community approach. *World Libraries, 21*(1).

Hansmann, K. J., Cotton, Q. D., & Kind, A. J. (2020). Mind the gaps: Supporting key social safety nets across the digital divide in rural Wisconsin. *WMJ: Official Publication of the State Medical Society of Wisconsin, 119*(4), 227.

Howard, H. (1977). The relationship between certain organizational variables and the rate of innovation in academic libraries. *Unpublished doctoral dissertation, Rutgers, the State University of New Jersey.*

Jia, G. U. O. (2015). Study on the innovation of public library's digital service for aged group. *Sci-Tech Information Development & Economy, 2015,* 18.

Klinenberg, E. (2018). *Palaces for the people: How social infrastructure can help fight inequality, polarization, and the decline of civic life.* New York: Broadway Books.

Lenstra, N., Oguz, F., & Duvall, C. S. (2020). Library services to an aging population: A nation-wide study in the United States. *Journal of Librarianship & Information Science, 52*(3), 738–748.

Lenstra, N., Oguz, F., Winberry, J., & Wilson, L. S. (2021). Supporting social connectedness of older adults during the COVID-19 pandemic: The role of small and rural public libraries. *Public Library Quarterly,* 1–21. https://doi.org/10.1080/01616846.2021.1970446

Lopez, K. J., Tong, C., Whate, A., & Boger, J. (2021). "It's a whole new way of doing things": The digital divide and leisure as resistance in a time of physical distance. *World Leisure Journal, 63*(3), 281–300.

Lund, B. D., & Maurya, S. K. (2021). How older adults in the USA and India seek information during the COVID-19 pandemic: A comparative study of information behavior. *IFLA Journal*, *48*(1), 205–215, https://doi.org/10.1177/03400352211024675

Luquire, W. C. (1976). *Selected factors affecting library staff perceptions of an innovative system: A study of ARL libraries in OCLC.* Indiana University.

Morrow-Howell, N., Galucia, N., & Swinford, E. (2020). Recovering from the COVID-19 pandemic: A focus on older adults. *Journal of Aging & Social Policy*, *32*(4–5), 526–535.

Musmann, K. (1982). The diffusion of innovations in libraries. A review of the literature on organization theory and diffusion research. *Libri*, *32*(4), 257–277.

Nageswari, N., & Thanuskodi, S. (2021). Usage of public library services in long beach city, California-USA during COVID-19 pandemic: An analysis. *International Journal of Information Science & Management (IJISM)*, *19*(2), 49–64.

National Association of Area Agencies on Aging. (2021). More than books: Libraries as hubs for social connection [Webinar]. https://www.viddler.com/v/1dda2331

O'Connell, M. E., Haase, K. R., Grewal, K. S., Panyavin, I., Kortzman, A., Flath, M. E., . . . & Peacock, S. (2021). Overcoming barriers for older adults to maintain virtual community and social connections during the COVID-19 pandemic. *Clinical Gerontologist*, *45*(1), 159–171. doi:10.1080/07317115.2021.1943589

Osei, D. (2021). For older Americans, COVID makes closing the digital divide a vital matter. *Nonprofit Quarterly*. https://nonprofitquarterly.org/for-older-americans-covid-makes-closing-the-digital-divide-a-vital-matter/

Potnis, D. D., Winberry, J., & Finn, B. (2020a). Best practices for managing innovations in public libraries in the USA. *Journal of Librarianship & Information Science*, *53*(3), 431–443. doi:10.1177/0961000620948567

Potnis, D. D., Winberry, J., Finn, B., & Hunt, C. (2020b). What is innovative to public libraries in the United States? A perspective of library administrators for classifying innovations. *Journal of Librarianship & Information Science*, *52*(3), 792–805.

Pungitore, V. L. (1995). *Innovation and the library: The adoption of new ideas in public libraries* (No. 86). Westport, CT: Greenwood Publishing Group.

Rubenstein, E. L., Burke, S. K., D'Arpa, C., & Lenstra, N. (2021a). Health equity and small and rural public libraries during COVID-19. *Proceedings of the Association for Information Science & Technology*, *58*(1), 827–829.

Rubenstein, E. L., D'Arpa, C., Burke, S. K., Lenstra, N., Rose, A., Schneider, G., & Floyd, R. (2021b). Staying afloat, staying connected: Comparing small and rural public libraries' Facebook use during Covid-19. *Association for Library & Information Science Education*.

Seifert, A., Batsis, J. A., & Smith, A. C. (2020). Telemedicine in long-term care facilities during and beyond COVID-19: challenges caused by the digital divide. *Frontiers in Public Health*, *8*, 690.

Seifert, A., Cotten, S. R., & Xie, B. (2021). A double burden of exclusion? Digital and social exclusion of older adults in times of COVID-19. *The Journals of Gerontology: Series B*, *76*(3), e99–e103.

Shah, M. K., Gibbs, A. C., Ali, M. K., Narayan, K. V., & Islam, N. (2021). Overcoming the digital divide in the post–COVID-19 "Reset": Enhancing group virtual visits with community health workers. *Journal of Medical Internet Research*, *23*(7), e27682.

Song, Y., Qian, C., & Pickard, S. (2021). Age-related digital divide during the COVID-19 pandemic in China. *International Journal of Environmental Research & Public Health*, *18*(21), 11285.

Suchá, L. Z., Bartošová, E., Novotný, R., Svitáková, J. B., Štefek, T., & Víchová, E. (2021). Stimulators and barriers towards social innovations in public libraries: Qualitative research study. *Library & Information Science Research*, *43*(1). https://doi.org/10.1016/j.lisr.2020.101068.

Temiz, S., & Salelkar, L. P. (2020). Innovation during crisis: Exploring reaction of Swedish university libraries to COVID-19. *Digital Library Perspectives*, *36*(4), 365–375.

Todorinova, L. (2021). One year in: A Survey of public services librarians on the effects of the COVID-19 pandemic. *Journal of Library Administration*, *61*(7), 776–792.

University of Northern Iowa (UNI). (2022). *Service Learning Librarian*. https://sllibrarian.uni.edu/

US IMLS (United States Institute of Museum and Library Services). (2020). Public Library Survey Fiscal Year 2018. Institute of Museum and Library Services. https://www.imls.gov/research-evaluation/data-collection/public-libraries -survey

Van Jaarsveld, G. M. (2020). The effects of COVID-19 among the elderly population: A case for closing the digital divide. *Frontiers in Psychiatry*, *11*. https://doi .org/10.3389/fpsyt.2020.577427

Wakeling, S., Garner, J., Hider, P., Jamali, H., Lymn, J., Mansourian, Y., & Randell-Moon, H. (2021). "The challenge now is for us to remain relevant": Australian public libraries and the COVID-19 crisis. *IFLA Journal*, *48*(1), 138–154. https:// doi.org/10.1177/03400352211054115

Widdersheim, M. M., Lund, B. D., & Kemboi, B. J. (2019). Change management in public libraries: Research-based political strategies. *Journal of Library Administration*, *59*(7), 693–742.

Winberry, J., & Potnis, D. (2021). Social innovations in public libraries: Types and challenges. *The Library Quarterly*, *91*(3), 337–365.

7

Keeping Instruction Sustainable Post-COVID-19 with a Learning Objects Repository

Tracy Coyne

INTRODUCTION

No one saw the pandemic coming in early 2020, at least no one on the Instruction and Curriculum Support (ICS) team at Northwestern University Libraries where I am a librarian. Our nine-person unit was humming along with the usual activities of providing instruction support and workshops to colleague librarians interested in building or honing their teaching skills. Northwestern is a research university located near Chicago, with 21,000 total students (8,000 undergraduate, 13,000 graduate) among 12 schools. The University Library, or NUL, where I am based, supports nine of those schools, while separate library administrations serve the law and medical schools, as well as Northwestern's campus in Qatar.

Suddenly, COVID-19 hit in March, and our ICS team leader gathered us together via Zoom—our new normal for department meetings—and asked us to construct a teaching resource in the university's learning management system, Canvas. The pandemic had shut down our library building a few weeks earlier, and no one could foresee how long we would be working remotely. It was a perplexing time for all, but the need was clear: create a digital repository that would give academic librarians tools that they could share with faculty members in their Canvas courses that would last beyond the pandemic. Content could include instructional videos, handouts, and other relevant tools for undergraduates who were learning how to use the library and conduct research.

Our team leader asked for volunteers, and four of us formed a cohesive unit and got right to work. We met frequently over the next few months and divided the workload into areas in which each of us had experience. By September 2020, we had a robust repository. We shared the tool with our fellow librarians and encouraged them to spread the word to faculty. While the bulk of the content was completed a few months after the pandemic began, we continue to deposit new items to the present day. This chapter explains how we created the learning objects repository, our criteria for selecting content, and how we presented this new resource to our colleagues and faculty. While this repository was a response to the challenge of working remotely, it was designed to be sustainable and used long after the pandemic ended.

CREATING THE REPOSITORY

The ICS unit at Northwestern University Library comprises nine librarians who are responsible for assisting colleagues with teaching techniques and procedures. Of those nine members, four of us volunteered to create a learning repository in May 2020; the repository's eventual name was Library Resources and Research Strategies (LRRS). While we had planned on creating a repository at some point in time, the onset of the COVID-19 pandemic in March 2020 accelerated our plans.

Northwestern uses the Canvas learning management system (LMS) campus wide and NUL uses Microsoft SharePoint, a collaboration software tool, to store and share files among staff in all units. We also used the NUL Box account (cloud storage site) to share our individual work in files that our four-person team could easily access.

Precursors

We did not start from scratch, in that the LRRS had precursor tools from which we could draw: a LibGuide titled "Start Your Research" and our ICS SharePoint site that we populated with teaching resources for librarians. The "Start Your Research" guide contained advice on how to build background on a topic, form a question, and then choose and search databases with keywords. It provided criteria for students to use when evaluating resources, explained the difference between academic and popular publications as well as primary versus secondary resources, and gave advice on how to read a scholarly article.

The other precursor tool that we drew from was the ICS team's resources on the NUL SharePoint site. ICS created our unit's pages in 2018 after a library restructuring created our department. We spent the next two years populating our SharePoint pages with guidance for instruction librarians. Topics covered in the SharePoint content include before-class logistics, planning student-centered teaching, accessible teaching, distance learning, assessment, and professional development.

While the LibGuide and SharePoint site were useful, we found that often our colleagues would forget that these resources existed, and they would get infrequent use after an initial rush of attention after being created. We also wanted a resource that we could share with faculty members so that they could easily use the tools in their own courses.

Creation

The goal was to have a working repository ready by the start of the next academic year (the fall of 2020). Our four-person team convened our first meeting in April 2020, about one month after the pandemic began, with the aim of reviewing existing content for inclusion in the new repository. We wanted to create a branded account that would house relevant resources from the LibGuide and the SharePoint site, as well as other resources, such as handouts and videos that we had used for instruction that were not yet stored in a central location. The obvious choice because of its cost (none), access (campus-wide), and familiarity among faculty was Canvas. Up to this time, the library had not had its own instance in Canvas unlike other schools at NU, such as the business and arts and science schools. It turned out that the library did not need to create its own instance in Canvas but just needed to create a regular Canvas course to which we could add content at will. Although we knew this would present a learning curve for librarians, we felt that Canvas was still the most logical choice for the repository.

Audience

While we knew our audience would include librarians and faculty, we also needed to determine the level of students who would be using the content (i.e., first-year students, undergraduates, graduate students). The consensus was that these learning objects should be aimed at undergraduates, particularly in getting to know the library and learning effective research processes.

Owner

Next, we had to decide who would own and maintain the repository. We agreed that it was important to retain the library "brand" on the Canvas site in order to promote and encourage use of library services. It also made sense that our ICS team should be responsible for its maintenance and therefore act as a gatekeeper for any new deposits.

CRITERIA FOR CONTENT

At our first meeting in April 2020, we confirmed that the repository would be required to serve needs beyond the pandemic, and that we needed to look past the next few months as far as imagining what type of content to include. At our second meeting, we agreed that we wanted to identify best practices for creating videos for the repository, such as intentionally pausing at relevant places within a video so that dated content could be edited and replaced, thus allowing us to preserve the bulk of the video. At this point, we were probably getting ahead of ourselves, and discussion of our hopes for what the repository would become was fairly wide-ranging. In hindsight, this was our way of processing our thoughts, and each one of us had our own ideas and concerns that we wanted to voice, lest we forget by the time of the next meeting. If we had to do this again, we probably would have appointed a notetaker at each meeting, but as it was, we each relied on our own notes to remember the discussion.

Work in Progress

As each of the four of us worked on content to add to the repository, we needed a temporary place to store our files while waiting for NU's information technology (IT) department to create our Canvas course shell. During this time, we used the NUL Box account.

Our content ideas were becoming more concrete by our third meeting, and we each volunteered to start working on specific items, such as creating an outline to shape the blank Canvas course shell; starting a section on library reference resources; and creating a video. We agreed that we would upload our work to the library's Box account. As we started imagining what we wanted to include, we thought of how our fellow librarians would use this resource. We also reviewed the existing "Start Your Research" LibGuide for suggestions on dividing up and labeling content. One of the realizations that we had early on was that the Canvas site would be a combination of a ready-made course site and a repository, meaning that we would have the flexibility to export content to an instructor's Canvas course as a unit or as individual items. Thus, content could be used as needed in a Canvas site, in a LibGuide, or simply for distribution to students individually (e.g., handouts).

Up to this time, many NUL librarians had no experience using Canvas unless they had been invited to a faculty member's course site by the instructor; very few librarians were embedded in courses, and those who had been had done so on a mostly informal basis. However, one of us had experience with using a Canvas course site as part of a collaborative project with one of NU's schools and, with permission of the content owners, shared the course site with the repository team. This gave us a model from which to work and helped us to visualize what a complete Canvas course could look like. It also gave us experience interacting with the digital architecture of the site. Having this as a template helped jump-start our discussion on what we wanted the site to look like from a cosmetic standpoint (i.e., Did we want a highly structured look, or did we want it to be more free flowing?). We eventually added the NUL logo to the Canvas card, a square, digital image that appears on the user's Canvas dashboard, which provides a quick visual summary of all the Canvas course sites to which the user belongs. Later, we added more visual interest to the home page by adding a background photo from the university gardens. We also added content identification logos to the home page; this added color, defined content, and helped in navigating the site.

At the end of our third meeting, we started thinking about naming the site. We each agreed to put forward suggestions on which we'd take a vote. During our fourth meeting, we agreed to do a needs analysis and to identify what learning objectives and outcomes we had for the repository—our homework to be completed by the next meeting. Also, at this point, we were firming up some of our best practices for creating videos. For example, one of us found helpful content on the university's LinkedIn Learning account (formerly Lynda.com) that showed how to storyboard ideas for planning an instructional video. It also suggested including opening and closing statements in the video. We added viewing the LinkedIn Learning video to our homework list.

Filling in the Canvas Shell

By the start of the second month of work, we had obtained the Canvas course shell from the university's IT department (NUIT), the unit that administers Canvas for all the schools and departments at NU. We had originally thought that we would begin by using a Canvas "sandbox," a temporary space in which to work that is assigned to an individual, but NUIT advised us to forgo this and begin working on what would become the actual Canvas course site. Each of us was invited to join the course as a "teacher," one of several roles that Canvas provides. Other role options that have various permission levels are student, TA, participant, support, advisee, grader, designer, and observer.

Now that we had the actual shell, we needed to start thinking about how to visually present our content. Canvas offers different ways to do this, with options ranging from modules (a very structured and "nested" visual appearance where one must click through to reveal a sub-page) to pages (a design with more white space where much of the content appears on the same page [unnested], with links leading to further content). We decided to use Canvas's module option, which provides a visual frame that organizes individual page links within each frame that one chooses to create. One can have several frames on the same page, each with its own category or subject. Frames make the most sense when they are titled logically to reflect the content, such as "Develop a Research Question." Modules are then populated with line-item hyperlinked content that leads to a sub-page when clicked. A nice feature of modules is that one is able to leave content as "unpublished" until such time as it is ready to be accessed by users.

In thinking through the flow of the site contents, the team agreed that we wanted to make the content as user-friendly as possible, especially for faculty who might be exporting sections of content into their own Canvas sites. We were aware that this could affect how we structured and presented the frames and nested content. For example, we wanted the titles to be immediately understandable and the content to be appropriate for export to a faculty member's site. We also did not want to nest the content too deeply; in other words, the content ideally should be only one click away from the frame.

As the frames and modules started taking shape, several of us worked on filling in content on the home page and volunteered to write sections titled "What Is This Canvas Site About?" (a brief paragraph inviting users to export the repository content—either a la carte by page or by entire modules—to faculty course sites); "How Is This Site Organized?" (a display of five distinct content icons with a legend); and "How to Get Started" (a section encouraging users to work with a liaison librarian to determine what content is best suited to the course, followed by a link to instructions on how to export items to another Canvas site). Our team considered creating a style sheet to keep the various submissions consistent, but ultimately, we found we did not need one; with such a small group, a fairly uniform design, and limited outside contributions, we were able to communicate informally with one another. Work on the repository continued, and we set a date of September 7, 2020, to publish the Canvas site, marking 20 weeks since we started the project.

Quizzes

We continued to look for helpful content for the repository, including assessment tools. One issue with Canvas that we experienced was the limitation on quizzes. We observed that exported Canvas-created quizzes often have difficulty integrating into a faculty member's Canvas gradebook, thus affecting the weighting of grade points for existing course assignments. Eventually, we found a solution to this problem: we created quizzes in Google Forms; this allows faculty to copy quizzes into their own Google account, where they can make edits and not worry about affecting point values they have already constructed in their Canvas course. We also realized that to prevent losing or having to replace quizzes (e.g., if someone overwrites the file) within the repository, it is important to remind users not to make changes while in the site, and instead instruct them to copy quizzes into a Google account, where they can make changes as they wish.

Modules Overview

By the time our deadline arrived in September 2020, we had produced a good start to our repository. Since that time, we have continued to add content and, as of the time of this writing, our repository now consists of the following contents: five different content types (Developing a Research Question, Deciding on Sources, Locating Sources, Reading and Note-Taking Tips, and First-Year Student) arranged in eight modules or frames (Start Your Research, Develop a Research Question, Deciding on Sources, Citations, Locating Sources, Reading and Note-Taking Tips, Library Research Module for Fall Quarter College Seminars, and Make Your Mark: Preserve Your Story for Future Wildcats). The content in each frame is labeled with a colorful icon next to the frame's title to help users distinguish among the content choices more quickly. The icons are as follows: Developing a Research Question (blue circle), Deciding on Sources (black square), Locating Sources (orange diamond), Reading and Note-Taking Tips (red triangle), and First-Year Student (stack of books).

Developing a Research Question Module

The first item that appears in the module view is the Developing a Research Question content. We use this module to explain how students can use sources to help them jump-start their research by filling in background knowledge and identifying subtopics, key concepts, methods used, key people, organizations, and events. On the Background Information page we feature two videos that we recorded in-house using Panopto, an application for creating videos that integrates with Canvas. The first video is a three-minute overview of the *Oxford Bibliographies Online* database, while the second video explains how to use the *CQ Researcher* database. The next page (State a Research Question) explains how to form a research question by using the topic + question + significance method suggested in Kate Turabian's *Student's Guide to Writing College Papers*. This page is followed by a worksheet page (Use Your Research Question) to help students generate keywords to use in their search; this is a downloadable handout. This content is reinforced with two videos created in-house on how to choose keywords and how to use the library search engine. The last page in this module is a conclusion that summarizes what was covered in the module.

Deciding on Sources Module

The next module, titled "Deciding on Sources," covers how to select sources appropriate for an assignment. We start by stating the learning outcomes and what students will be able to do after completing this module (i.e., describe different types of articles and what they can contribute to the student's research; select appropriate databases; limit search results to peer-reviewed items; and apply criteria to evaluate resources [a downloadable handout]). The module also includes a section called "Types of Articles." Here, we cover the differences between articles in scholarly publications, trade journals, popular magazines, and newspapers. In the section on academic publishing, we link to a three-minute video by North Carolina State, titled *Peer Review in Three Minutes*, that effectively explains what constitutes peer review. Types of scholarly articles are explained in a brief video by Virginia Commonwealth University Libraries. Next, we point students to an NUL LibGuide page with screenshots that show a step-by-step process for finding peer-reviewed journal articles using the library's search engine, NUsearch. In the popular, trade, and news publishing section, we present a three-minute video from the Ethical Journalism Network that states the common code of conduct of five basic values to which journalists adhere. We also link to the Code of Ethics page at the Society of Professional Journalists' Web site to further acquaint students with the values that journalists respect. We include a section with search tips, including an eight-minute NUL video that we produced in Panopto on tips for finding news articles. We follow up with a brief video on news sources at the university library. We finish this content with a link to *The Information Cycle*, a short video from the University of Nevada at Las Vegas that explains the value of including different types of sources in a research assignment. We end the content on this page with a brief slideshow on how to evaluate resources.

Citations Module

The Citations module is presented next and is filled with links to academic integrity resources, both at NU and beyond. We include an eight-minute video that covers the major points of American Psychological Association (APA) citation style. We created this video in-house using Panopto and Camtasia (a video-editing tool) and plan to create a similar one for the Modern Language Association (MLA) citation style. We round out this module with links to the NUL book collection on proper bibliographic citations and academic writing aids.

Locating Sources Module

We filled this section with several helpful aids, such as screenshots and videos for accessing library resources using the NUL search engine or academic databases, and making the most of the research tools they offer. For example, we include screenshots labeled with instructions on how to e-mail an article from a database and how to export a bibliographic citation. We feature a two-minute video that we made using Camtasia animations that explains how to adjust Google Scholar settings to display results that provide a FindIt@NU hyperlink, which links directly to the full text results in our collection. We offer the same information in a text-based handout. Next, we include a short video on how to request an item through the NUL interlibrary loan service. Finally, we explain the benefits of using a search log and provide a link to an example on the University of Southern California Libraries' site.

Reading and Note-Taking Tips Module

We provide content in this module on three topics: reading strategies; active note-taking; and literature reviews. A short video from the University of Minnesota provides guidance on how to read a scientific article, which we pair with their worksheet that shows how to comprehend a complex article by looking at its parts. Next, we include an NU web page that explains how to take notes digitally using Microsoft OneNote. We follow this by providing links to a number of Web sites with advice on how to take notes in college, including an interactive tutorial from Penn State. Finally, we provide numerous links that explain what a literature review is and how to write one, including resources in the academic database *Sage Research Methods*, which provides a project planner tool that explains what makes a successful literature review. Finally, we link to books on how to write literature reviews.

Library Research Module for Fall Quarter College Seminars

This module was created by our liaison librarian for first-year seminars for the purpose of introducing first-year students to the university library. It includes links to relevant LibGuides on the First-Year Seminar and to our "Start Your Research" LibGuide. Next, we feature a six-minute video that provides an overview of how to use the library and its services. A quiz in Canvas and one in Google Forms test students on how to find e-books in the library. We then include a Beginning Your Research worksheet that we created in Google Forms that asks students to answer a brief set of questions about their assignment. We then offer some group activity learning objects (information time line using Jamboard; source analysis using Google Docs; and evaluating articles with Google Forms. Quizzes review how to read a scholarly article and how to contact a subject librarian (in Canvas and in Google Forms). Next, the section on academic integrity presents an in-house video on what a citation is and why it is important, a document with screenshots that shows how to generate citations in library databases, and interactive quizzes on how to write citations in APA, MLA, and Chicago style. We then link to NUL workshops on EndNote and Zotero bibliographic citation management tools. Wrapping up, we finish with two assessments in Google Forms: a 3-2-1 assessment (three things you learned; two resources to help with your project, one question you have), and Check Your Knowledge (check-the-box answers to seven questions on research practices).

Make Your Mark: Preserve Your Story for Future Wildcats Module

This module was created by NUL's special collections unit as a self-paced training course for students who would like to deposit student organization artifacts in the university archives. While this content departs from the other types of items deposited thus far in the repository, it is an effective way to house and present the material, and it lends itself very well to this Canvas site. The content is presented in three sections and includes an 8-minute video that explains the benefits of donating artifacts, a 30-minute video explaining how to prepare records for transfer to the archive, what types of records are appropriate, and how to transfer them, and a 7-minute video in the final section that describes what happens after the records are transferred and how the university cares for them. All three sections are followed by a comprehension quiz created with the Canvas quiz template.

PROMOTING THE REPOSITORY

From the beginning, our four-person team wanted to start sharing our progress on the learning objects repository with other team members; to do so, we added our ICS unit members to the Canvas site at about week six. At week twelve, each of the four of us planned to add one deliverable (e.g., a video) to the Canvas site. At this point, some of us were further along than others. One of us exported videos created in Panopto to Box, as a holding area, until we could add animations to the videos in Camtasia; the Camtasia animations would help us highlight details or important points. While this step added extra time to our production schedule, we felt the added features were worth it.

Four months into the project, we were ready to think about presenting the draft Canvas site to our NUL colleague librarians beyond our ICS unit. We planned to add (enroll) anyone to the Canvas site who expressed interest, rather than adding everyone automatically. We began spreading the word about the repository by meeting with our instruction librarian colleagues in small groups. We outlined the purpose of the repository and offered to add them to the Canvas site. We explained that this would give them a chance to look around and consider if this was a tool they would use while working with faculty.

Our deadline was to have the repository and learning objects ready for the new academic year in September 2020. We planned to present the site at a library liaisons meeting in early October. We started preparing sample questions and answers in anticipation. We finished on time and presented the site to our colleagues. Several asked us to enroll them immediately, while others preferred to wait and take some time to consider how they would use the site. Eventually, more library colleagues enrolled, and while our enrollment isn't too huge, we are encouraged by colleagues such as those in the special collections unit who saw this as a good fit for their work.

CONCLUSION

Although building the repository was a serious amount of work by our four-person team over a four-month period during the pandemic, this project did yield unexpected benefits. For example, it accelerated the production of instructional videos that we had in the planning stages but had not yet produced by the time the pandemic hit. It also helped us demonstrate the value of our ICS team to the library and faculty. Importantly, it introduced a lot of our colleagues to Canvas, something that might not have happened unless they were already embedded in a faculty member's course. Finally, the repository gave us another tool with which to engage faculty and offer our services, showing how the library can be a great partner in providing research instruction to NU's students.

Takeaway Tips

Build your repository with the end users in mind (e.g., librarians, faculty, students); agree on a target completion date and any other milestone dates as you progress; use concise wording for titles; start with a small team; have frequent progress meetings and decide whether to appoint a notetaker; when accepting content from others, be sure to limit to resources that will be useful for a wide audience; consider using a style sheet to ensure consistency in adding new content, especially if you don't have an appointed content editor or gatekeeper to oversee new additions; be on the lookout for any impending software changes or migrations; and build time into your schedule to accommodate any delays.

8

Keeping the Focus on Patrons at the Salisbury University Libraries

Beatriz Betancourt Hardy, Amy M. Jones, and Mou Chakraborty

INTRODUCTION TO SALISBURY UNIVERSITY AND THE LIBRARIES

Salisbury University (SU), where the authors of this chapter work, is a member of the University System of Maryland and is a public regional comprehensive institution on Maryland's Eastern Shore. It offers 46 undergraduate majors, 15 master's programs, and 2 doctoral programs to nearly 7,000 FTE students. It consistently earns inclusion in lists of best colleges and best college values.

The SU Libraries, ranked in the top 20 college libraries nationwide in 2021 by *the Princeton Review*, comprise the main campus library and the Edward H. Nabb Research Center for Delmarva History and Culture, both located in the Guerrieri Academic Commons, and the Dr. Ernie Bond Curriculum Resource Center (CRC), located in the Seidel School of Education's building. Our staff includes 26 full-time and 7 part-time employees, plus around 30 student workers. We are part of the University System of Maryland and Affiliated Institutions (USMAI) library consortium, which shares a catalog, some databases, and other services. The SU Libraries also belong to the Maryland Digital Library, OCLC, Lyrasis, RapidILL, GetItNow, and Reprints Desk.

HOW THE PANDEMIC PLAYED OUT

Early in 2020, we lived in blissful ignorance of what lay ahead. On January 25, the provost e-mailed the deans about a coronavirus in China, noting there were only two confirmed cases in the United States. On March 2, the provost announced that a COVID-19 working group had been established, despite there being no cases in Maryland. On March 5, Governor Larry Hogan declared a state of emergency. On March 6, the SU chief of staff e-mailed senior leadership to be prepared to move classes online and develop guidance for employees who did not feel safe coming to work.

At this point, the library dean asked unit heads to begin planning to provide services if the campus closed and what staff could do while teleworking. She worked with the technology librarian to create a survey of staff teleworking capacity and sent it out to all library staff. The survey included questions asking whether staff members had a Windows-based computer, Microsoft Office, and reliable broadband Internet access at home. The survey also asked if they knew how to access the campus Virtual Private Network (VPN), access e-mail from off-campus, connect a laptop to their home network, and so on. This survey proved extremely helpful.

PHASE ONE: PAUSE

On March 10, a Tuesday, the president's office announced that classes were canceled that Thursday and Friday, two days before spring break, to allow faculty to prepare to hold classes online for the two weeks after spring break. In-person classes would then resume. On March 12, all buildings on campus were immediately closed to the public, per the governor's order, and all events were canceled.

Starting on March 12, the main library remained open with limited hours. This was to allow faculty to visit the teaching center, which is in the library, and provide computer access for local students who lacked computers/Internet at home. Only medically vulnerable staff were teleworking at this point, but we did begin, based on the teleworking survey, to prepare for everyone teleworking by providing training and seeking out the hardware needed by each person.

PHASE TWO: ONLINE AND CLOSED

On March 23, the university shifted classes online for the rest of the semester, closed dormitories, suspended athletics, and closed buildings to most people. The library then closed on March 24 for the rest of the semester. Staff, now all teleworking nearly 100 percent of the time, scrambled to provide virtually as many services and collections as possible.

PHASE THREE: REOPENING

Initially, we believed campus would reopen for summer sessions with most classes online and fully open in the fall with largely in-person classes. Just in case, however, the library began planning in April for different scenarios ranging from campus being fully open for in-person classes to classes starting on campus and moving to online to being entirely online. This scenario planning by each unit proved beneficial, allowing us to fully explore staff concerns and prepare actively for different possibilities. For example, we bought plexiglass shields for our service desks in late April rather than waiting for campus administration to make decisions about what to do.

The university ended up keeping classes online throughout the summer and reopening for in-person and hybrid classes in the fall. In preparation for reopening, we worked with facilities staff to de-densify library spaces and posted signs all over reminding patrons to do their mandatory daily screenings and keep wearing their masks. The main library building reopened on August 12 to faculty and staff and on August 24 to students. While we opened for our normal hours, very little else was normal about the 2020–2021 academic year, and you will read elsewhere in this chapter how we modified our services and policies.

ACCESS SERVICES

The Access Services Department encompasses circulation, course reserves, interlibrary loan, billing, and stacks management, supported by 3 full-time and 5 part-time staff and 12–15 student employees. Access Services provides customer service at the Library Service Desk in the Guerrieri Academic Commons (GAC), where the main library and the Nabb Center are located. The GAC serves as an academic and social hub on campus, and in addition to library spaces, it houses two food establishments, a large public event space, classrooms, computer labs, academic support services, faculty and graduate student spaces, and more. The pandemic challenged us to reconsider how to fulfill this traditionally public-facing role in new ways and exposed various inequities and risks unique to staff in these roles.

CONSORTIUM AND LOCAL EFFORTS

With circumstances changing hourly during the early days of closure, we initially took a reactionary approach. As it became clear the pandemic would redefine our lives for the foreseeable future, we transitioned to a more proactive stance from which we devised more comprehensive communication strategies and contingency plans for various scenarios. During all phases, we attempted to exercise what limited agency we had amid a global pandemic, with the goal of protecting health and safety while preserving as much access as possible to collections, services, resources, technology, and equipment. As part of the USMAI library consortium with a shared integrated library system (ILS), decisions about loan periods, over-due fines, and other circulation policies had to be coordinated among the member institutions. Some of our first collective steps were to suspend all overdue fines and recalls, advance the due dates for all items on loan at the time of closure, and suspend resource-sharing (patron-placed holds) within the consortium. Access Services staff from USMAI member libraries met regularly to share information, coordinate policies, commiserate over our challenging situations, and strategize in order to advocate on behalf of public-facing staff who were most at risk. As libraries gradually reopened at varying levels of access, we collaborated extensively to resume consortia resource sharing and to enable various contactless services. These joint efforts fostered improved communication within the consortium that con-tinues to the present, and USMAI has permanently ended overdue book fines for undergraduates.

On the local level, we tailored services to meet our patron and staff needs and to reduce students' financial and emotional burdens. While the libraries remained closed, Access Services staff worked exhaustively with faculty to make print course materials accessible online, either with limited scans or open access sources. In phase two, we worked with the technology librarian to implement a Controlled Digital Lending program that offered a limited structure within which students could borrow materials online. This proved extremely successful, generating goodwill among our faculty and student patrons, promoting accessibility, and easing student burdens. We are con-tinuing Controlled Digital Lending on a limited basis.

PLANNING

The preparation for transition from phase two to phase three involved careful, thoughtful discussions and planning for various reopening scenarios, strengthened by cross-departmental collaboration among all staff with public-facing roles. Not knowing the precise circumstances under which we would reopen, the User Services and Outreach Team (comprising staff from library administration, Access Services, Research and Instructional Services, the Nabb Center, and the Curriculum Resource Center) met regularly on Zoom to develop plans for varying levels of building access, desk operations, staffing, materials access, services, and outreach. We also discussed ways to move among various scenarios in response to changing circumstances and guidance. Next, the Access Services staff held extensive planning meetings on Zoom to discuss more specific desk and department operations, down to the minutest detail of office supplies and telephone use. Once the decision was made to reopen the building to the campus community, the libraries had vari-ous plans in place that could be communicated easily to our patrons.

Our goal in reopening the Library Service Desk was to balance our commitment to student-centered service with the protection of health and safety for patrons and staff. The desk hours were shortened minimally compared to pre-pandemic times, and we maintained pre-pandemic staffing levels, with two people on duty at all times (usually one student employee and one staff member). To lessen exposure, we rearranged furniture to provide adequate space between staff and rearranged work schedules, dividing staff and student employees into two alternating groups (one group working Monday-Wednesday-Friday-Saturday, and another working Tuesday-Thursday-Sunday).

Virtually all spaces within the GAC remained open and accessible, with changes only to ensure social distancing. Group study room capacity limits were lowered, and policies were changed to permit individual use of these spaces. The stacks remained open since they shared space with the only quiet study areas in the building. The housekeeping staff played an important role in cleaning these shared spaces, and Access Services staff communicated frequently with them to coordinate and offer gratitude for their efforts.

CONTACTLESS SERVICES

We focused much attention on modifying our operations and services to offer contactless options. One computer at the Library Service Desk was set aside as a supervised self-checkout station, with a dual monitor where staff could observe patrons as they checked out their own books and DVDs, with plexiglass barriers offering a layer of protection. Later, we added three Meescan stations where patrons could participate in a true self-checkout experience using their mobile devices. To eliminate the risk of handling cash payments, we worked with the university's Accounts Receivable Office to offer online payments for color printing and other library services. The cornerstone of our contactless operations was our curbside pickup service, which began in a limited capacity with our Leisure Reading Collection and later was expanded to include most books and DVDs in our collections. We were proud to be the first institution in the consortium to execute the service. We also implemented a paging service, pulling books from our shelves for patrons to pick up at the Library Service Desk. We will continue offering these services.

TECHNOLOGY

As part of our efforts to ease stressors for students, we modified our technology lending policies to offer extended loan periods for equipment and devices students needed to succeed academically. We added Chromebooks to our circulating devices and permitted students to borrow these along with our laptops, iPads, calculators, and other equipment for two weeks at a time. Our equipment lending services complemented a university-led initiative to provide laptops and other technology needed by students participating in courses remotely. Even without the threat of overdue fines, we experienced minimal damage and losses to our equipment, and our efforts helped build positive relationships with the students who benefited from this trust and flexibility.

In the early stages, before research pointed to airborne particles as the main source of transmission, we followed REALM guidelines to implement strict controls over the handling and quarantining of physical materials, and we limited the number of staff processing them (REALM 2022). We continued these controls in phase three to ease concerns for patrons and staff. Access Services staff created a Quarantine Room from unused office space and devised a detailed workflow for safely processing incoming and outgoing items. In the stacks and other areas holding print collections, we added signage directing patrons to place any unwanted items they had touched on return carts. To minimize exposure, we had one staff person each day responsible for processing returned and used items. We are no longer quarantining items.

RESOURCE SHARING

The closure of many libraries around the world posed a resource-sharing challenge and severely limited our ability to find scholarly materials for student and faculty patrons. Our interlibrary loan staff persevered, working remotely several days a week while continuing to borrow and lend electronic materials. Our ILL borrowing staff also expanded our document delivery services, scanning and sending electronic copies of items from our collection to student and faculty patrons, a practice we are continuing permanently. Once libraries across the country began reopening, our borrowing staff worked tirelessly to find libraries willing to ship print materials to our patrons. Our lending staff participated in a special RapidILL COVID-19 pod, sharing our electronic materials at no cost with non-RapidILL member libraries from around the world (RapidILL, 2021).

STAFF

In addition to preserving our student-centered services, the Access Services Department also prioritized staff health and morale. As a public-facing department, most of our staff were designated essential employees and continued working in the building at least several days a week throughout the pandemic. Initially, this work was staggered to minimize exposure, meaning staff rarely saw one another in person and began to feel increasingly isolated. Weekly Access Services staff meetings on Zoom provided opportunities to share updated information and helped colleagues feel more connected. Each meeting began with a game or icebreaker to ease tension and strengthen relationships. The department also used Slack channels for a staff "Get Outside" challenge and other activities to promote physical and mental health.

Once the building reopened to the campus community, our staff faced a higher level of physical and mental stress. While many library employees continued teleworking nearly full-time, Access Services staff and student employees played a vital role in keeping the Library Service Desk operational. This public-facing role increased their risk of exposure, and the ongoing burden of enforcing mask wearing and social distancing policies with a reluctant student population weakened morale. In addition to regular departmental Zoom meetings, Access Services leadership strived throughout the pandemic to check in regularly with staff about their physical and mental health. Full-time staff had the option to telework through the 2021 spring semester, granting a level of flexibility and autonomy that boosted their morale and helped renew their motivation. Regrettably, this option did not continue for public-facing staff once operations returned to a more normal level, and telework was never an option for part-time staff, who carried a heavy burden in keeping the Library Service Desk operational. These disparities exposed inequities among various categories of university staff that persist today.

The Access Services Department benefited from cross-training (both across library departments and within our own unit), which helped distribute the risk and workload, and increased adaptability at the Library Service Desk. Within the department, staff created and shared detailed scanning, quarantine, interlibrary loan, and course reserve operations manuals so colleagues could easily move among various roles and help wherever they were needed the most. Access Services staff also conducted a training session on Zoom for library staff willing to offer customer service at the Library Service Desk. We eventually incorporated 10 staff members from Research and Instructional Services and Collection Management into a regular morning rotation of desk shifts. While this contribution from colleagues in other departments represented only a small portion of the weekly desk coverage, it promoted empathy, fostered goodwill, and raised awareness about issues of equity. We continue to make a more conscious effort to share information across departments and have incorporated more cross-training into our permanent processes.

With the pandemic far from over, the Access Services Department remains far better positioned for the inevitability of change. We have developed the skills to respond to evolving patron needs and expectations, and our collaborations within the library, across campus, and within the USMAI consortium have fostered relationships that will strengthen and inform future decisions. In reconsidering how to fulfill our public-facing role in new ways, Access Services staff have demonstrated our value in a student-centered academic environment.

RESEARCH AND INSTRUCTIONAL SERVICES

The Research and Instructional Services (RIS) Department also experienced great changes due to the pandemic but was able to pivot online relatively easily. The six RIS librarians and four student workers typically provide staffing for the Research Help Desk, answering in-person, e-mail, and chat queries. With the library closed during the spring of 2020, nearly all reference inquiries moved to our already-established chat services. Even when we reopened in the fall of 2020, in-person interactions remained low relative to the past. Our chat interactions, meanwhile, reached a historic high, and were more substantive than in the past, with reference queries accounting for 73.9 percent of the chats. While we have long provided virtual research consultations for distance students, the pace increased greatly, with 144 consultations from May 2020 to April 2021.

INSTRUCTION

Most instructional librarians primarily teleworked from the beginning of phase one until the start of phase three. In addition to staffing the Research Help Desk and chat, they continued to collaborate with faculty on course assignments and instruction, support faculty research, and engage in collection development. Since most library instruction classes were normally taught in-person, the librarians had to quickly pivot to online teaching during phases one and two. While several librarians regularly provided instruction for distance classes, most did not have much experience with online instruction. Overall, this meant learning new technological tools, preparing for both synchronous and asynchronous classes incorporating active learning, and ensuring ADA compliance in the online instruction and resources created. These developments will continue to influence our teaching after the pandemic.

The director of External Library Services (DELS), an experienced distance librarian, was our primary point person for virtual instruction. Having used Zoom and many other platforms over the year and having taught hybrid classes, she was able to provide training and advice to other librarians. Early in the pandemic, she did a presentation for the instructional librarians that covered online teaching and learning and explained how to use Zoom's different features. All of the librarians incorporated some kind of educational technologies into their teaching, including tutorials, worksheets, Spring-Share LibGuides, and modules.

Unsurprisingly, the pandemic caused a big decline in face-to-face instruction and led to much more participation by librarians in our learning management system, Canvas. While in 2019–2020 we taught 381 face-to-face sessions, in 2020–2021, there were only four face-to-face sessions and another 195 online. The librarians taught online both synchronously and asynchronously. Previously, instructional librarians only occasionally were embedded in Canvas courses, but the pandemic made it imperative that they have a significant presence. Fortunately, faculty became more open to including librarians, and the DELS provided advice on different ways of participating. Most embedded librarians in Canvas engaged with students through discussion posts and helped with citations and assignments. And even if faculty did not include a librarian in the course, our university added the library chat service to the menu on all Canvas courses, allowing students to contact the library even if a librarian was not embedded in a specific course. We anticipate that the higher level of engagement in the learning management system will continue.

Librarians accustomed to employing active learning techniques in their face-to-face classes had to come up with some creative ways to replicate them online. One librarian, for example, became embedded in a course in Canvas and created a research discussion form. Ahead of his synchronous session, he shared a "Topics to Keywords" worksheet in which students wrote out their research question/thesis and distilled several key concepts and synonyms. At the outset of the library workshop on Zoom, the students used their completed worksheets to search for a library-derived book source and article source with an eye toward relevance, currency, and quality, all of which were covered in the workshop. The students then posted their citations in the forum, and the librarian replied after the workshop, providing additional guidance.

Librarians also took advantage of technology to create different ways of encouraging active learning. Some chose to use the interactive features of Zoom, such as polling, breakout rooms, whiteboards, and chat. Some created online modules within Canvas, such as for our freshmen English classes, while others used Guide on the Side to create tutorials (Brazer, 2020; Plottel, 2020). Several librarians used cloud-based document sharing platforms, such as GoogleDocs, Padlet, and Jamboard, to integrate active learning. The DELS experimented with a variety of tools, such as Flipgrid and Nearpod, and collaborated with a few faculty members to use Glogster for students' presentations.

Some librarians created videos using different tools (for example, Panopto, Camtasia, Zoom, Loom, and PowerPoint). In a series of videos, the DELS added Bitmojis and memes, making them more personal and fun. She also ensured closed captioning for the videos and for the synchronous Zoom sessions. The education librarian created an elaborate database tutorial using PowerPoint voiceover, and it was embedded in several education courses (Ford, 2020). The librarians' newly acquired technological expertise will continue to benefit our instruction program for years to come.

OUTREACH

The library staff, primarily librarians, also provided outreach in a variety of ways. We moved citation management workshops and other programs online. The now-virtual Graduate Student Boot Camp saw an increase in student participation. Finals Fairy (typically done as a physical scavenger hunt during finals week with clues on social media) was only moderately successful in its online iteration, as students were burned out and struggled to continue engaging. We developed pandemic-related LibGuides, one about COVID-19 research resources and another with online activities for kids. We created a cooking guide using recipes from our collections to provide another way of de-stressing. We will continue to offer workshops and the Bootcamp virtually, but other outreach activities have now returned to in-person.

SPECIAL COLLECTIONS

The Nabb Center, our special collections unit, responded aggressively to our initial closure in phase two. It normally supports instruction in face-to-face classes using its collections as well as serving local history and genealogy researchers. It responded to the immediate COVID-19 closure by shifting instruction online, digitizing collections, creating a transcription project, engaging users virtually, and initiating a COVID-19 archive.

The Nabb Center's instruction typically is very hands-on. The staff quickly transitioned to online instruction, developing several different approaches. Two librarians helped a history proseminar conduct unique primary research in a synchronous session, using digitized materials. A History of Art Design class worked with digitized graphic materials made available in Dropbox. The archivist filmed a presentation, and the students then filled out worksheets, developed their research, and wrote essays. For a class on Race and Place in the Environment, the archivist and the exhibits curator created an assignment that had students review race-related digitized archival items and then write new exhibit labels for furniture in the Nabb's permanent exhibit, looking at it from a race-conscious perspective (McPeek et al., 2020). Finally, for a class on Writing in Digital Environments, students reviewed two digitized scrapbooks from the University Archives and then wrote concise descriptions following archival standards. While most special collections instruction in the future will be hands-on, virtual is now an option.

Most of the digitizing of collections was the work of two part-time staff members who normally act as receptionists. The digitization served the dual function of keeping them employed and providing off-site access to the collections. Given the requirement to telework rather than be on-site, we broke with usual archival standards to allow the digitizers to take scanners and collections home. Both digitizers were trusted employees who had already been digitizing collections on-site as part of their jobs and knew how to handle archival materials. They came in once a week to return items and collect more materials to digitize. The archivists chose what materials to digitize, based on need for classes, requests from users, and knowledge of what items were most commonly used in person. The digitized items were then uploaded to the Internet Archive (Nabb, 2022c) or Flickr (Nabb, 2022a), depending on the type of material.

With the closing of campus, many of our student workers and part-time staff members could have been left without work, since their jobs often entail working at our public service desks. Happily, we found a way to keep many of them employed. A couple worked on social media projects, but the majority transcribed handwritten documents and oral histories from the Nabb Center. We already had a workflow for this, as we had been using a dozen volunteers to transcribe documents on-site, but we adapted the workflow for working from home, using digitized materials. We also put out a call for volunteers and quickly got more than a dozen additional volunteers. We put the transcriptions in the Internet Archive (Salisbury Nabb, 2022).

In addition to keeping people employed, the benefits of the transcription project were many. Some people have trouble reading cursive, leading students to sometimes avoid using handwritten manuscripts. Transcriptions make manuscripts accessible for people with disabilities and allow search engines such as Google to mine the text so that they appear in search results. What we had not anticipated was how much digitizing and transcribing collections would increase the visibility and use of the Nabb Center's collections. Most of the items we have put in the Internet Archive have 800 or more views, far more than would be possible in person, and we will continue to make collections available through the Internet Archive.

In March 2020, when the University shut down all buildings, the Libraries had an exhibit, "Friends and Rivals: Baseball on Delmarva," that was part of an NEH grant to create a digital archive of baseball in our area. It was supposed to be on display from January to June 2020. We had already started working on creating online exhibits, including the baseball exhibit, but the COVID-19 pandemic greatly accelerated that trend. The curator and our technology librarian quickly finished the online version of the baseball exhibit as well as several other exhibits using Omeka, an open-source web publishing program (Nabb, 2022b). This has now become a permanent part of our exhibit creation process. As with the digitized collections, having online versions raised the visibility of our exhibits.

The Nabb Center also provided some opportunities for users to engage with our collections in different ways. By far the greatest engagement came through social media, on Facebook and Instagram. The local history archivist created several series of themed posts, such as mystery photos, a photo tour of historic buildings in our home county, cooking challenges using handwritten recipes from our collections, and explorations of our area's rich but often troubled African American history. The archivist also created a Nabb Center page on Jigsaw Planet, an online puzzle site, using images from our collections (Post, 2021). The university archivist created a virtual walking tour of the main campus for SU's virtual homecoming in the fall of 2020; this tour has gotten over 2,000 views (Piegols, 2020). This engagement through social media will continue.

Finally, the Nabb Center established a COVID-19 archiving program. We encouraged people to keep journals documenting their experiences and including anything relevant, such as tweets, photographs, drawings, short videos, and more. To supplement these individual stories, our university archivist also web-captured press releases, executive orders, and official statements from the governor and mayor, COVID-19 dashboards, university Web sites, our university president's video statements, and campus social media and e-mails related to COVID-19.

The Nabb Center, like the rest of the SU Libraries, reopened to our campus community in August 2020. We required social distancing in the reading room and established a reservation system, since only eight people were allowed in at one time. Because the building was not open to the public, we developed an escort system to get members of the public into the building and to the Nabb Center. Instruction continued to be primarily online for the academic year, but we resumed creating physical exhibits. Staff who were able continued to telework at least some of the time, per university instructions for the 2020–2021 academic year. In August 2021, we reopened to the public and staff came back to work on-site full-time.

DR. ERNIE BOND CURRICULUM RESOURCE CENTER

The CRC, with two full-time staff members and four student workers, supports the Seidel School of Education primarily by maintaining a quality collection of children's literature and other relevant, program-based materials. Although it is in a different building, it follows most guidelines and practices of the main library. Its experience was in some ways a microcosm of that of the main library. It closed in March 2020 and reopened in the fall of 2020. The CRC coordinator did his best to maintain morale, checking in regularly with staff members and student workers. His plan for reopening prioritized safety measures, such as shifting seating to force social distancing, providing ample supplies of sanitizing materials, placing plexiglass shields at the service desk, quarantining books, and posting signs to remind students to wear masks and follow the university's daily check-in procedures. He also engaged with users by creating a video tour of the CRC, making social media posts, and even hosting virtual events from the physical library. The pandemic made it evident that even with a couple of staff members, the CRC is now poised to function effectively under different scenarios.

MAKERLAB

The SU Libraries MakerLab, located on the first floor of the Guerrieri Academic Commons, offers 3D printing and scanning, laser cutting and engraving, and virtual reality technology. Since it opened in 2016, the MakerLab has played a growing role in supporting student and faculty academic goals. When three other 3D printing labs on campus closed completely during the pandemic, the technology librarian worked with the 3D printing course instructor to ensure the MakerLab would remain a viable, affordable, and accessible option, even while facing continuing demand for its technologies and equipment.

When the MakerLab closed in phase two, the technology librarian swiftly adapted its services and resources for an online environment. The challenge was to find ways to connect patrons with the technologies they needed. While the technology librarian was permitted to continue working in the physical space of the MakerLab, the student employees who normally work in the space had been sent home, leaving it understaffed at a time of continuing demand. In response, the technology librarian implemented a remote appointment system in which patrons consulted him over Zoom while sharing a computer screen connected to equipment in the MakerLab. The system succeeded in bringing the technology to the patrons, and it proved helpful when the building reopened in phase three, minimizing exposure and enabling students and faculty who could not come to campus to continue using the technologies. The technology librarian also created a way for patrons to upload their design files electronically in advance of the appointment, rather than bringing them in person on a flash drive. Working with Access Services staff, the technology librarian created a contactless pickup and payment system in which students paid directly through their online university account and retrieved printed items placed in lockers in the Guerrieri Academic Commons. Patrons also benefited from an existing service that enabled them to see online photos of printed items to confirm they printed properly in advance of pickup.

It would have been easy to simply suspend MakerLab services when the GAC closed in March 2020, just as other communal spaces and 3D printing labs across the country had done. With modifications, the MakerLab continued as an important link to the SU community. Even when student workers returned in the fall of 2021, some of these modifications were retained, including the option of virtual appointments and the ability to upload design files in advance of appointments. Over 250 MakerLab prints were picked up in 2020, and nearly 390 prints in 2021. While these numbers reflect a decline from pre-pandemic times, they illustrate the value of maintaining services to support students' academic needs and well-being. The MakerLab now has an infrastructure in place to adapt smoothly to various circumstances and ensure continuity of service for the campus community.

COLLECTION MANAGEMENT

The Collection Management Department, typically with a full-time staff of six, handles acquisitions, cataloging, serials, electronic resources, and government documents. While it does not directly interact with our users much, it played a key role in supporting them during the pandemic. The unit quickly made available the many electronic resources that publishers provided at no cost during the pandemic. All book purchasing switched to electronic rather than print to accommodate the reality of so many users being off-site. Very early in the pandemic, we subscribed to EBSCO's Faculty Select program to help faculty find open educational resources and greatly expanded our streaming video offerings. Meanwhile, teleworking staff worked hard at data cleanup in our catalog, making materials easier to find.

The department also worked hard to ensure we would not have the backlogs of materials to process that so many libraries have reported during the pandemic. During phase one, the staff did a great deal of cross-training and documenting of the work of different areas. During phase two, four staff members came in one day per week, each on a separate day, and kept materials moving through the appropriate workflows. Later, that expanded to have Acquisitions and Cataloging staff coming in on Mondays and Tuesdays, while the rest of the staff came in on Thursdays and Fridays, with Wednesday a swing day to be used on a per-request basis.

COMMUNICATION

Clear communications are important in a situation filled with uncertainty. Internally, the Libraries relied on e-mails and meetings, primarily in Zoom. The library dean tried, in her communications with staff, to address not just what was certain but also what was being discussed as likely or possible at higher levels of campus administration, and issues that were causing anxiety among library staff.

A key part of our external communications was to create an online guide to our services. The technology librarian is the only Libraries staff member allowed by the web services office to update the Libraries' pages. However, given the extensive and changeable nature of what we wanted to communicate, we did not want to rely on just one person. Instead, we put a short summary on the Libraries' Web site and linked to a LibGuide with the fullest, most up-to-date information (Salisbury University Libraries, 2021). Using a LibGuide worked well, since many staff could update it and changes appear instantaneously. Even so, in the first month, this only got 1,012 views—not even one-eighth of our faculty and students—and never more than 255 views in any succeeding month.

A second method of external communication was to have the library dean send out e-mails to all faculty, staff, and students. Rather than sending a lot of shorter e-mails, she sent detailed e-mails every few weeks, with information about services, updates to due dates, and a LibGuide link. The e-mails included bulleted lists with the topic of each bullet in bold, making them easy to scan quickly. While long e-mails usually are to be avoided, in this case, having a long, comprehensive e-mail meant people did not have to search through their inboxes for various bits of information about the Libraries. We at least knew everyone received the e-mails, whether or not they read them.

We also used social media as appropriate. This works well for short pieces, such as changes in hours or promoting individual services, but it is not well-suited to longer, more detailed information. However, this is much more hit-or-miss than our other methods of communication and reaches fewer people.

CONCLUSION

While the pandemic presented many challenges, it also provided opportunities to reevaluate existing service models, put into practice activities we had already been considering, and explore new possibilities. Here are some of our takeaways:

- Communication, collaboration, and cross-training are critical, within and across all levels.
- The student-centered approach keeps patrons and staff happy. Remove punitive measures (overdue fines) and offer services patrons want, such as self-checkout, paging, online payments, remote appointments, locker pickups, and curbside pickup. Many of these actually save staff time.
- Provide flexibility and grace for staff, and in the process, you might help address lingering equity issues:
  - Help employees stay motivated by promoting autonomy, competence, and relatedness. (Center for Self-Determination Theory, 2022)
  - Have a conversation about whether full-time public-facing staff must work in the building all the time. Can they telework part-time as long as the service desk is covered?
  - Trust your staff, unless they give you a reason not to. Address violations individually rather than removing an option for everyone.
- Creativity, flexibility, and adaptability are absolutely critical while planning services, whether instruction, special collections, or any other area of the library.
- Significant progress and improved workflows are possible even during adversity when the library is equipped with a plan and staff is able and willing to pull together as a team.
- Virtual reference and instruction, online exhibits, and digitized collections all extend the library's reach greatly.

And, of course, our final takeaway is that as much as we have learned during this pandemic, we would just as soon not have another one.

REFERENCES

Brazer, S. (2020). USDA plant search. Retrieved form https://libapps.salisbury.edu/gots/guide_on_the_side/tutorial/usda-plant-search

Center for Self-Determination Theory. (2022). Theory. Retrieved from https://selfdeterminationtheory.org/theory/

Ford, S. (2020). ERIC database: Content and use. Retrieved from https://youtu.be/LohLyPEDivw

McPeek, M., Piegols, J., & Post, I. (2020). Reconceptualizing the classroom: An immersive digital primary source exercise during COVID-19. *Museum & Society, 18*(3), 337–340.

Nabb Research Center. (2022a). Nabb research center. Retrieved from https://www.flickr.com/photos/nabbresearchcenter/

Nabb Research Center. (2022b). Events and exhibits. Retrieved from https://www.salisbury.edu/libraries/nabb/events-exhibits/

Nabb Research Center. (2022c). Salisbury university libraries, Nabb research center. Retrieved from https://archive.org/details/salisburyuniversitylibrariesnabbresearchcenter?sort=-publicdate

Piegols, J. (2020). Salisbury University walking tour. Retrieved from https://theclio.com/tour/1588

Plottel, T. (2020). HIST 102: Finding and obtaining books. Retrieved from https://libapps.salisbury.edu/gots/guide_on_the_side/tutorial/hist-102-finding-and-obtaining-books

Post, I. (2020). Nabbcenterianpost. https://www.jigsawplanet.com/nabbcenterianpost

RapidILL. (2021). A big thank you to the RapidILL community. Retrieved from https://page.exlibrisgroup.com/hubfs/EMEA/RapidILL/RapidILL%20Thank%20You%20COVID19%20Pod.pdf

REALM Project. (2022). REALM project—REopening archives, libraries, and museums. Retrieved from https://www.oclc.org/realm/home.html

Salisbury University Libraries. (2021). COVID-19 SU libraries updates and resources. Retrieved from https://libraryguides.salisbury.edu/COVID-19

9

Library Workers' Well-Being during a Pandemic

Jahala Simuel and Sophia Sotilleo

INTRODUCTION AND CRISIS LEADERSHIP

The COVID-19 pandemic has changed in many ways how we work in libraries and with our library teams. How we serve our patrons has evolved during the pandemic. Libraries can now virtually serve and work with patrons. This shift to working with patrons remotely and working with the new protocols from the pandemic has created the need to develop and be aware of specific health protocols. Library policies have changed to ensure that we have a plan in place that will serve as a blueprint and documentation on how to serve patrons virtually during a crisis. The pandemic also exposed how we work with our colleagues as well. We are now paying close attention to the well-being of library staff working remotely.

The transition to working remotely revealed how important it is to meet library workers where they are in various areas of their lives. Some of the issues and problems that library leaders observed were related to physical and mental health, family support, work/life balance, technology training, and communication. To confidently work with library workers to ensure their well-being during the pandemic, library leaders had to pause and review how they would work with their team and likewise take time to ensure they were also taking care of their own well-being. The one thing that stayed the same during the shift to working completely virtually and adhering to the health issues from the pandemic was the general mission of all libraries to provide free and open access to a broad range of materials and services to people of all ages and backgrounds. Library leaders continue to develop and share how they can work with their teams to meet the library mission at their specific libraries. This chapter contains a case study describing how two library leaders worked with their staff at two different historically Black colleges and universities (HBCU). One is a small public, state-related university, and the other is a large private university. The leadership roles represented in this case study are director and supervisor at academic libraries. During the pandemic, both leaders at their respective institutions focused on what practices would ensure the well-being of library employees.

ASSESSMENT: GATHERING INFORMATION

Information for this case study utilized professional conversations and surveys from other academic library leaders. Library leaders initially assumed that the only step they needed to take was to work with the Information Technology office to approve access and authentication so the library staff could work from home. After communicating with their staff, leaders quickly realized that the transition process would be more complex. A detailed assessment was used to find out what each team member needed to successfully transition to a virtual workspace. Leaders soon learned that the digital divide that was being experienced in various communities was also evident among staff members. Information from the assessment indicated that staff members needed access to the Internet, laptops, and technology training. Leaders also realized that the tasks that were accomplished in person at their physical library were going to be different virtually, especially for staff who did not have sufficient Internet bandwidth, updated laptops with Microsoft Office software, or certain technological skills. This discovery caused a level of stress and frustration for the team and their leaders, which resulted in a delay of library services because of the additional time it took to completely transition each team member to their remote workspace.

Once clearance was approved, library leaders allowed staff to return to their work location to get whatever equipment and documents they needed to begin working remotely. When all library staff members had what they needed to work remotely, library leaders worked with their team to make sure they could authenticate remotely from home and were able to access the necessary resources to do their jobs effectively. The assessment revealed that not every staff member had access to some of the basic things needed to work remotely. There were also essential technological skills that some staff members did not have, such as basic Microsoft Office experience and the confidence to use technology to chat with patrons or navigate the integrated library system (ILS) and the interlibrary loan interface in an efficient way. Without the ability to utilize these library systems, staff could not successfully work remotely. Leaders had to quickly supply their team members with whatever training was necessary to support the mission of the library and meet the needs of the staff.

TRAINING AND SUPPORT

Plans were immediately put in place to deliver equipment to team members in order to provide training and support for working remotely. A training schedule for learning how to use equipment and various software was incorporated into each staff member's work schedule. Remote technology such as Microsoft Teams, Microsoft Office Suite, and the virtual meeting tool Zoom became the default means for communication, training, and support. Library leaders at each academic institution collaborated to develop training methods. Training involved teaching staff members how to communicate with patrons using various software. Some libraries established a chat feature for their library because of the need to work remotely. Staff members also needed to learn how to work in DOCLINE, which is a telemedicine platform supported by the National Library of Medicine. Specifically, the ability to delete journal titles in DOCLINE using a database spreadsheet, which each staff member has access to, was important to ensure continued assistance for patrons. In addition, staff members learned how to operate Alma (an integrated library system) remotely from home, how to use Microsoft Office to upload work and to utilize a spreadsheet with journal titles, how to find journals that were accessible via PDF files, and how to complete all the Alma modules, tutorials, and more.

Because team members had different levels of experience, training was offered as needed. Some of the training had to be one-on-one and personal; other training took place as a group, with all staff members training together. Navigating training and getting staff prepared to work remotely during the pandemic, especially staff members over the age of 55 with minimum to no technological knowledge or experience, was difficult. Some staff members struggled with working remotely, as well as documenting tasks and information on assignments. Coaching and one-on-one mentoring provided by library leaders and supervisors to individual team members became the most effective and efficient way to support the team and ensure tasks were completed.

Weekly virtual one-on-one meetings with team members provided opportunities to give encouragement and build confidence. They created a safe space to discuss specific challenges each staff member was having. It was also a way to highlight and identify staff members who were able to quickly transition to their new work environment. Working with staff members as a group and individually provided useful information. In particular, the transition to working remotely made leaders aware of the limitations of staff members' skill sets. Despite the fact that staff members have been working for years at the circulation desk, checking students into study rooms, checking books in and out, making copies, and just interacting with the public daily, many still did not have the necessary skills to work in a virtual workspace. The process and the work became very challenging, and staff members shared how much they missed and looked forward to the traditional way of serving patrons. Consequently, leaders resolved to develop a more robust and intentional plan for enhancing staff skills. As part of the yearly review, library leaders evaluated and assessed each member of the team directly.

Spending time with staff members turned out to be an effective way to gain valuable information about staff members' abilities. It was an opportunity to identify what skills they'd already mastered and which skills needed to be developed or enhanced. Library leaders also discovered which staff members were ready and eager to learn new things. These staff members had the ability to develop new skills quickly and take the lead on specific projects. This made it possible for library leaders to give staff members—particularly those who may have been hesitant to share their talents and skills—an opportunity to contribute ideas that could improve library services and support additional training. Springshare LibGuides and PowerPoint slides were created and shared during virtual meetings and on the library Web site. Although the transition process was intimidating and challenging for everyone in the beginning, things became more manageable once everyone had the tools they needed to work remotely.

LIBRARY TEAM WELL-BEING

In our conversations, managers recognized that poor health and well-being can potentially affect both workers and organizations in negative ways. This was supported in an article from the *Journal of Management*, in which the author shared the following: "Experiencing poor health and well-being in the workplace may [cause people to] be less productive, make unwise decisions, and be more prone to being absent from work" (Danna & Griffin, 1999, p. 358). Working remotely adversely impacted the well-being of the library staff, and the effects and outcomes of the pandemic heightened the workers' mental health challenges. Once initial work assignments and training were completed, library leaders addressed the mental health needs of the staff.

Each day, leaders noticed that their team members were dealing with various issues. They were experiencing physical health concerns, wellness issues, family struggles, financial challenges, grief due to the loss of friends and family members, and other mental health concerns as a result of the quarantine and other mandates from the pandemic. Staff members began sharing how they were feeling and what they were experiencing during the pandemic. Their experiences along with the devastating information being broadcasted daily in the news was causing so much stress and anxiety for everyone. Furthermore, due to the circumstances of the pandemic, there was nowhere to go, which made the whole experience of working remotely that much more challenging.

To keep everyone focused on self-care, it became necessary for library leaders to work with team members on their personal well-being. Leaders had to use relevant skills and resources to assist with personal and mental health issues that team members were experiencing because of the pandemic. The Better Health Channel Web site states that "Wellbeing is not just the absence of disease or illness. It's a complex combination of a person's physical, mental, emotional and social health factors" (The Department of Health State Government Victoria Australia, 2021, para. 1). It further states that "Wellbeing is strongly linked to happiness and life satisfaction. In short, wellbeing could be described as how you feel about yourself and your life" (The Department of Health State Government Victoria Australia, 2021, para. 2). This idea reinforces the need to check in with staff members to see how they are feeling. If everyone is sad and dissatisfied with life, things would only get worse for leaders and their staff. Thus, it is important for everyone to be intentional about self-care and their well-being within the work environment.

Library leaders found various ways to help staff members focus on their well-being. Assistance to staff was given professionally and creatively. They partnered with the Human Resources office to offer counseling sessions to staff members who were dealing with mental health and grief challenges. Staff members needed to know that not only were their supervisors concerned, but the company was also vested in ensuring they were well and being heard. Leaders then began creating new ways to assist staff members, such as scheduling time during the day to practice the techniques learned from professional development webinars and hands-on classes that were offered and sharing articles with useful tips for library practice. Staff members were often encouraged to incorporate meditation and breathing exercises throughout the day to deal with stress and anxiety. For example, one company offered a virtual workshop to library employees during the lunch hour on how to practice chair yoga. Chair yoga was one of the highly recommended activities for working remotely. Sharing resources in order to meet the needs of the staff was of utmost importance. Materials were distributed through Microsoft Teams, e-mails, and Zoom meetings. Prioritizing mental health and well-being is crucial to preparing to work remotely.

Other techniques and skills were obtained from staff members who attended training on specific professional development skills, such as time management, with the goal of ensuring that a positive work-life balance was taking place. Library leaders learned that staff members struggled with walking away from their computers when it was time to finish working. Indeed, staff members felt like they did more work at home than they did in the office because working remotely made it more difficult to shut down work and be present at home. Nevertheless, work-life balance and time management skills are crucial, which is seen with the findings that workers spend one-third of their waking hours at work, and do not necessarily leave the job behind when they leave work (Conrad, 1988). Staff members' honest feedback and courage to share what they needed helped library leaders personally address the well-being of each staff member as they communicated through one-on-one discussions, virtual meetings, and coaching.

COMMUNICATION: COMPASSIONATE AND CONSISTENT

The COVID-19 pandemic took a toll on everyone physically, mentally, and emotionally. There was a lot of uncertainty and anxiety about what the future of the library would be when we returned to our various locations in person. Communicating compassionately and consistently with the team became an important daily task for library leaders. Leaders' communication with their team went beyond sharing day-to-day information. Library leaders shared information about what other libraries were doing as they continued to support staff and work with patrons remotely. Communication also began to develop about plans to return to library locations and prepare to work in person. It became essential for library leaders to schedule specific discussion times to plan and learn what changes needed to be made for specific areas of the library when the announcement was finally made about returning to the building physically.

The space to communicate with the staff also allowed the team to share their concerns and frustration. Due to the uncertainty, the team needed space to communicate what was working and what they felt they needed to be successful and safe upon returning to work daily. They also needed space to share what wasn't working and their concerns about information that wasn't being shared or information that was confusing. Open communication helped gauge how the team was feeling and helped keep the team focused and encouraged. As leaders, we had to practice ways to show compassion and be consistent as we communicated with our team members. Communication also had to include appreciation for all that the staff members were doing during these challenging times, such as remembering to say thank you, being flexible with the way things were done, and communicating trust and respect for each staff member.

FEARLESS LIBRARY LEADERS

Jack Kornfield, in his book *Buddha's Little Instruction Book*, says, "If your compassion does not include yourself, it is incomplete" (1994, p. 12). This quote should be shared with every library leader. Library leaders were experiencing the same issues and concerns as their staff. The process of finding the best self-care was not easy. The demand placed on library leaders didn't allow for much flexibility, as it did for staff members. The various activities and Zoom programs became overwhelming and not always feasible for leaders. Library leaders had to be intentional about their time management and self-care. Through discussions and surveys, some leaders shared that they had to take a step back and evaluate what activities and programs were important and find activities they enjoyed to help them manage the many demands that were placed on them. Library leaders worked remotely well over eight hours a day due to the high demands that were placed on them to ensure library services were available and stable, and they often took on additional tasks and responsibilities while also keeping up with goals and professional development. Communicating with colleagues for support and information helped to keep many library leaders moving forward.

SURVEY RESPONSES FROM LIBRARY LEADERS

To gather additional information on how library leaders managed during the pandemic, a survey was created and sent to various library listservs. Sixteen leaders who responded to the survey were library directors, managers, and supervisors from academic libraries. The survey consisted of 10 questions that asked leaders to share information about their experience supporting their team during the pandemic and how they practiced self-care. Questions were designed to be short yet specific. The survey was as follows:

1. Library Leadership Title
2. Gender
3. Age
4. What type of library do you supervise/manage?
5. How many people do you supervise?
6. What type of staff do you supervise?
7. How long have you been in leadership?
8. What was the level of difficulty supporting your staff remotely?
9. How did you handle your well-being working remotely during the pandemic?
10. Share some specific ways you supported your staff.

Analyzing Survey Data

The demographics of the survey were interesting. Most library leaders who took the survey were library directors or heads of a department. There were more female than male directors. Everyone who completed the survey worked in an academic library, and survey respondent ages ranged between 30 and 50 years old. The majority of the leaders were over 50 years old. The type of staff supervised varied and included support staff, faculty, administrative librarians, professional librarians, librarians' assistants, paraprofessional staff, and grant employees. Leadership years of experience ranged from 3 to over 20 years.

Some parts of the survey were on managing staff. Fifty percent of the respondents shared that managing their staff during the pandemic was manageable. The survey also showed that 18.8 percent of the leaders felt it was a tedious task to lead their team during the pandemic, and 31 percent of the leaders said it was easy. These results were not surprising. A large percent of leaders shared that it was easy managing their staff during the pandemic. Based on the years of experience of leaders who responded to the survey, we can perceive that the leaders were seasoned and had spent more than a couple of years working with a team.

The survey assessed the leaders' personal well-being by asking the following question: "How did you handle your well-being working remotely during the pandemic?" It was encouraging to see honest responses to this question. Most answers described specific ways that library leaders were dealing with the pandemic, such as exercising, walking, yoga, and spending time with family. For example, one person responded, "spending time with family; doing needed chores around the house, such as painting a couple of rooms, refinishing pieces of furniture." Others mentioned enjoying not commuting to work, saying, "I was healthier than I am now, since I am commuting again." Overall, many mentioned that their quality of life improved by being able to work from home, such as in this response: "I felt relaxed working from home. I could balance home concerns and work concerns better!"

The survey asked leaders to share the specific ways in which they supported their staff. Responses from the survey were as follows: "Monday morning check-ins, offered online training sessions. Computer equipment for staff or a PC before departing to work from home and that they had adequate connectivity." Another commented, "When we returned from working remotely, a Library Re-Entry Plan was created with all of the specifics for safety in each department and each floor of the library."

Overall, how library leaders handled their own well-being while working remotely during the pandemic revealed that leaders took time to acknowledge how they were feeling and developed a plan to ensure that they practiced self-care. For example, they "scheduled time for self-care on my calendar." Another example from the survey mentioned trying to "integrate fun things like music, videos, reading, and more." Library leaders shared that once they evaluated their activities and created a plan, the main challenge was to incorporate the plan into a schedule to be sure that it was followed. It was important for library leaders to practice what they were expecting from their staff members. As library professionals, we have experienced and learned a lot during the COVID–19 pandemic. We may not have enjoyed the life lessons that we were taught, but we survived and continue to learn from the experience.

Leaders also shared that working remotely allowed time for professional development and additional training to sharpen skills. Signing up for additional training during the pandemic offered many leaders the opportunity to learn new things and attend training and meetings that would have been difficult to attend if they had to travel. This supports the idea that remote or hybrid conferences can be a successful and sustainable way to ensure everyone has an opportunity to participate in discussions and training. Leaders also shared their appreciation for all the organizations that offered webinars and training at no or low cost. Like staff members, library leaders also had financial concerns and challenges.

CONCLUSION AND LESSONS LEARNED

A January 2022 *Library Journal* article announced the annual Librarian of the Year award. The headline and the announcement read as follows: "the winner of *LJ*'s 2022 Librarian of the Year award, sponsored by Baker & Taylor, is all library staff" (Peet, 2022, para.1). This award to all the library staff of the United States of America was representative of the importance of library staff during the pandemic and beyond in terms of being flexible and adaptable during this challenging time. Library professionals have been through many critical situations, stepping in and stepping up to assist during a global pandemic as well as other national events, such as riots and social justice demonstrations, and surviving and often working through natural disasters, such as hurricanes and tornadoes.

The article in the *Library Journal* goes on to say that "all have demonstrated accomplishments that reflect their commitment to free access to information, service to all areas and constituencies, and strengthening the library role in the community" (Peet, 2022, p. 3). All the trials and tribulations that library staff members encountered have strengthened our personal beliefs in who we are and the value we bring to our community. The experience has also given us the opportunity to pause to develop and enhance how we work with one another and focus on the importance of our well-being.

It is honorable and exciting to talk about and document all that we were able to learn and all the skills that we were able to gain while we worked remotely, but it is also the approach we used to handle all the challenges and life changes that took place and continue to take place during the pandemic. Things have changed for libraries and the way we will work moving forward. We know that there is continued discussion and requests to offer some of the options that were allowed during the pandemic. Some of the requests are being considered or have been adopted, acknowledging that we are still in the wave of the COVID-19 pandemic. Library leaders have also adopted practices to help support staff members and ensure that the skills that were learned continue to be developed. For example, the process of documenting the work done each day serves as a blueprint for leaders to review and support the work that staff members are doing each day in their various departments and for specific projects they are working on. It also helps to assess when staff members are proactively signing up for any professional development training to enhance knowledge and skills they think they may need. This document can also be used as a tool for staff performance evaluation.

The COVID-19 pandemic will continue to affect us. We learned that being intentional about the well-being of the library team is important. Implementing and continuing ideas to maintain consistent support, resources, and tools for the well-being of the library staff is essential. Library leaders at various academic institutions support and advocate for activities such as a monthly chat-and-chews, lunch-and-learn sessions, mindfulness meditation time during the week, and at least one work-from-home day for staff who may be interested. This will help staff members to see that we have learned much from our time working remotely and we do care about their well-being. As academic library leaders, we must do our best to continue compassionate and consistent communication with our staff members.

Making staff feel valued and needed is the key to building a team that will be ready to work with you during any time of crisis. Library leaders are still trying to find ways to deal with staff well-being during the pandemic and smooth the transition for the staff's return to the physical library. This will be a revolving issue due to the constant changing nature of the pandemic. Library staff are concerned with returning to work in person, while some staff members would like to continue to work from home indefinitely. We will need to pay attention to what we learned and be intentional about the implementation of things that worked and did not work and continue to develop ways to show our team members that we care and that we are in this together.

REFERENCES

Conrad, P. (1988). Health and fitness at work: A participants' perspective. *Social Science Medicine, 26:* 545–550.

Danna, K., & Griffin, R. W. (1999). Health and well-being in the workplace: A review and synthesis of the literature. *Journal of Management, 25*(3), 357–384.

The Department of Health State Government Victoria Australia. (2020, May 7). *Wellbeing.* Better Health Channel. Retrieved from https://www.betterhealth.vic .gov.au/health/healthyliving/wellbeing

Kornfield, J. (1994). In *Buddha's little instruction book.* Bantam.

Peet, L. (2022). Collective support: LJ's 2022 librarians of the year. *Library Journal.* https://www.libraryjournal.com/story/Collective-Support-LJs-2022-Librarians -of-the-Year

10

Maintaining Comics and Gaming Programming during Institutional Change

Zach Welhouse and Kelly Stormking

INTRODUCTION

Pop culture events, including board game nights and comic conventions, are opportunities to build community and cultivate joy (Laddusaw & Brett, 2020). When the COVID-19 pandemic struck, Oregon State University Libraries and Press (OSULP) staff had recently started similar programming. We adapted to the unprecedented changes by transferring program elements online, researching alternatives, and strengthening our community relationships. Although we were not able to sustain every element of our pre-crisis dreams, the documentation will be invaluable in planning future pop culture events.

Our response to the uncertainty surrounding our temporary library closure and the early stages of the COVID-19 pandemic are most relevant to other public research university libraries. However, elements of our response may benefit any library interested in maintaining pop culture programming during times of institutional change.

In February 2020, librarians were preparing the Valley Library for its first Free Comic Book Day, encouraged by the successes of a pilot game night and Free Comic Book Day events a new hire had overseen at their previous institution (Welhouse, 2020). As the primary library at a R1 research university of close to 35,000 students, the event had the potential to be pretty big. Volunteers were excited to connect their hobbies to our collections and engage with students in a more entertaining manner than everyday operations.

Although we canceled Free Comic Book Day, we maintained momentum from a distance. We continued the comic collection development project that was previously intended to launch on Free Comic Book Day. We also stayed in touch with industry contacts and investigated online comic conventions. Although we decided the online convention model wasn't right for our community, the research provided us with ideas for future projects.

Existing online gaming infrastructure made it easier to start online gaming projects and explore sustainable routes for offering similar services in the future. We hosted online gaming events, researched opportunities for digital role-playing, met virtually with the OSU Gaming Club, and shared the results online with a LibGuide.

The difficulties of the COVID-19 pandemic have made adaptation challenging, but finding space within drastic institutional change for joyful activities has been helpful. Our experiences can be used to develop similar programs. In this chapter, we will discuss techniques for investigating virtual pop culture events for your library, strategies for developing online alternatives for historically physical collections, and methods for maintaining joyful, sustainable relationships remotely with stakeholders, including library staff.

LITERATURE REVIEW

Libraries are increasingly recognized as third places, community hubs that require no expense to visit and where everyone is welcome (Oldenburg, 1999). With tool libraries, seed libraries, and more, libraries are increasingly becoming expansive access centers. Board games are an avenue for education in academic institutions and can be integrated into instruction along with opportunities for play (Cross et al., 2015; Pope, 2021). They build communication, problem-solving, and collaborative skills (Bayeck, 2020; Rogerson et al., 2018). The pandemic has proven the significance of social interaction and supportive communities for resilience and overall well-being. Comics likewise serve many roles in libraries, including as objects of academic study, pleasure reading, and art (Wood, 2018). Over one in four public libraries have hosted events based on comic books or related media (Schneider, 2014). Phoenix's (2020) review of comic programming in libraries concludes, "Librarians are rarely asking anymore, 'Should we carry comics?' but, 'What can we do to make our comics even more accessible?'" (p. 53).

Many academic libraries have circulating game collections for students' recreation and as objects of study. Nicholson (2008) concludes a study of gaming in school libraries by acknowledging "there is a wide variety of gaming experiences available, and all sizes of libraries in all types of settings can find appropriate gaming activities for their space, time, and budget" (p. 55). A 2017 survey of 119 academic, public, and school libraries reveals that 49 percent maintained a circulating collection, while 71 percent offered programming around tabletop games (Slobuski et al., 2017). Other libraries, like Penn State Behrend's Behrend Library, use their game collection to specifically promote student-faculty interactions and reduce library anxiety (Diaz & Hall, 2020, p. 255). Swiatek and Gorsee's (2016) overview of gaming in academic libraries in France goes beyond tabletop gaming to explore video games, live-action role-playing (LARPing), murder mystery parties, and gamification of various tasks, such as library employee training.

Increasingly, youth mental health has become a topic of national concern, not only due to the impacts of the pandemic, but from numerous stressors such as climate change, poverty, and social injustice. The American Academy of Pediatrics (2021) released a statement 2021 declaring a national emergency for youth mental health, with suicide as the second-leading cause of death. Any opportunity to address the mental health of communities, and youth in particular, should be at the forefront of libraries and library planning, especially for academic libraries with student populations. Due to the impacts of the pandemic, 75 percent of youth ages 18 to 24, the age range of the majority of students served by academic libraries, noted one or more negative mental health symptoms, and nearly 25 percent have contemplated suicide (Bladek, 2021; Czeisler et al., 2020). Establishing services and resources to support the well-being and mental health of students is of increasing importance and should be integrated into academic libraries as a permanent, essential feature.

Board games and comics offer patrons a chance to de-stress away from their ever-present Zoom windows. De-stressing and wellness activities can be offered by libraries through pop culture items, whether through casual displays, circulating collections, or hosting events (Diaz & Hall, 2020). Collections also offer an opportunity to collaborate with local enthusiast organizations and game and comic bookstores (Robson & DeWitt-Miller, 2020; Wood, 2018). Gaming programming such as "a Gamers' Night in the library can be an effective way to get new students into the building and, more importantly, interested in our resources and services in a fun and exciting new way" (Donnelly & Herbert, 2017).

BOARD GAME COLLECTION DEVELOPMENT AND EVENTS

Pre-pandemic

The Valley Library's board game collection was started in 2016 by staff in the Library Experience and Access Department (LEAD) with funding from a donor gift. The collection has since grown to nearly 350 board, card, and lawn games, supplemented by additional donor funds and game donations from individuals and local gaming stores. All games are available for check-out to students, staff, and community members for one week. Since the collection was designed to promote community and student wellness, it does not have overdue fines. However, lost items do incur the item's cost. Titles are available in multiple languages, and in various genres. Games have also been incorporated into academic courses and into the course reserves collection.

Everyday maintenance of the board game collection requires 5 percent of a library technician's primary duties. These duties include weighing games for easy check-in and maintaining the board game collection portion of the staff wiki, which includes information on purchasing, cataloging, replacing missing pieces, and promotion. Keeping a written record of our internal processes provides an easy reference when the project lead isn't around and maintains institutional knowledge as employees' positions change.

To assist users with browsing, all titles are listed in a plastic binder and on LibraryThing. The Web site allows staff to add tags for the number of players, play time, and age range, along with a brief description. Games are housed behind the circulation desk but are visible to passersby. They're also highlighted on a rotating basis in window displays and included in displays with books and other media. In 2019, the board game collection circulated 2,410 items compared to 720 items in 2020.

In addition to lending games from our collection, we use our collection in programming. Our early experiments included informal casual gaming, small game nights during finals week, and tabling at other campus events. Our first larger event was Welcome Week Game Nite 2019, which coincided with campus-wide activities for students returning for fall classes. We partnered with the Corvallis Public Library and divided the main floor of the library into several stations. Each board game station had a theme, such as social deduction, casual party games, or complicated game mechanics. Video games, including *Rock Band*, *Mario Kart*, and virtual reality, were also available along with a display of graphic novels. 550 students attended; repeating Game Nite in future years seemed obvious.

With the success and popularity of Game Nite, additional smaller gaming events were investigated. This led to a new partnership with the student-run OSU Gaming Club. The first mini-game night was held the first week of March 2020. The OSU Gaming Club joined the Corvallis Public Library as sponsors to show off the newly expanded library game collection, multiple video game stations, and snacks. Although not as widely attended, this was intended to be the first of many smaller game nights.

Pandemic Effects

Due to the COVID-19 pandemic, Welcome Week Game Nite was not held in 2020 or 2021. However, the popularity of this event indicates our patrons would appreciate another one when safety and staff capacity allow.

At the start of the pandemic, game lending halted as staff scrambled to navigate safety measures, service changes, and the library closure. Once the library started reopening, staff discussed if board games could be reestablished as a lendable resource, in the face of looming health and safety concerns. Could the games be cleaned enough? How long should they lend for, if people may be spending more time isolating at home? When they are returned, what process should be used for the safety of the staff and the community? Is lending worth the risk? It was determined that it was not worth the risk or stress in the initial weeks of the pandemic. Although lending was paused, library staff used this as an opportunity to explore other gaming options outside of the physical board game collection. Limited resources and services inspired creativity, and ultimately, expanded the existing collection offerings into new realms.

To address the gap in board game access, library staff developed a Virtual Gaming LibGuide (https://guides.library.oregonstate.edu/virtual-gaming). This guide highlighted virtual gaming alternatives for community members interested in gaming as well as showcasing the existing collection. Initially focused on highlighting virtual versions of existing physical games, the guide expanded to include free tools for virtual role-playing, online puzzles, trivia events, and gaming applications.

The Virtual Gaming LibGuide gave staff a location to publish the results of their investigations into virtual gaming events. Not every investigation was successful or sustainable. Discord was researched and tested as a potential platform for hosting virtual events. Ultimately, it was not used, as the time investment for already stretched staffing was too much to be feasible. Attempts were made to collaborate across library departments, but the new stressors placed on staff demonstrated that many gaming events required extensive time to plan, set up, host, and assess.

Establishing a detailed online alternative to the board game collection—listing various apps, online role-playing platforms, virtual trivia nights, and local gaming organizations on campus—not only provided an alternative to gaming during the pandemic but also expanded the reach of the board game collection. By including virtual gaming options with the physical board game collection, academic libraries can reach more of the community; providing various formats and alternatives for the physical gaming collection establishes a more inclusive collection. Academic libraries with board game collections should consider establishing virtual options as a permanent feature of their gaming collection. Whether that is through a LibGuide, a list of local gaming resources, or online gaming events, more expansive board game collections are essential in establishing more sustainably inclusive collection practices.

When we resumed lending physical items, they followed our pre-pandemic circulation rules. One-week board game checkouts automatically renewed for up to three weeks, unless they had a hold. This flexibility served our patrons well, as many of them were strictly social distancing or off-campus. All items were quarantined for seven days upon return, following the library policy at the time. As campus authorities eased health restrictions, patrons continued to benefit from gentle fine and renewal policies.

With the immense stress of the pandemic weighing not only on students, but also library staff, we explored gaming as a tool for commiserating and bringing joy while socially distanced. This created a space for librarians across positions to play together, breaking out of departmental silos. What had initially started as a way to test virtual game options turned into multiple staff gaming breaks. It is easy for library employees, in their passion for working with communities, to overlook themselves and their own self-care. The impact of the pandemic on library staff and mental health cannot be overlooked (Goek, 2021; Salvesen, 2021; Waltz, 2021). Rebecca Millter Waltz (2021) notes that library staff have been struggling even prior to the pandemic and identifies various ways of addressing distress through engagement and organizational transformation to support flourishing humans. Gaming and its ability to connect people through fun is another tool for supporting the well-being of employees (see Table 10.1).

Staff in the Library Experience and Access Department (LEAD) held multiple virtual gaming breaks during work time for staff using Jackbox Games on Zoom. Incorporating paid breaks centered around connection and joy for staff supports both individual staff well-being and employee community. This is no replacement for necessary workplace practice and policy changes that are required to support library employees during times of crisis but serves to complement and reinforce care for the library employee community through pockets of relaxation and joy during the workday.

Although the start of the pandemic halted board game lending and events entirely, the creativity and dedication of staff led to new, permanent expansion of gaming services. Transitioning to online alternatives, as seen in the Virtual Gaming LibGuide, not only provided virtual games for the community but also expanded the marketing of the existing game collection. Expanding historically physical collections to virtual spaces, or providing virtual alternatives, is recommended for a more expansive, inclusive collection. This should continue as a sustainable practice for libraries into the future. If a library is limited by time or staffing, developing a brief virtual gaming guide is a relatively quick option. For libraries interested in expanding their current gaming offerings, hosting virtual gaming events is a means through which to take game collections in the virtual realm a step further.

Gaming builds community, connection, and joy. The pandemic has shown us that continuing gaming events in the future is a wonderful feature for student well-being, as an alternative respite from schoolwork. Although in-person, large gaming events cannot take place during the pandemic, this does not mean they are not valued. Seeking alternatives to these events has introduced new means for gaming in libraries and provided time to reflect

Table 10.1 Host an Employee Game Break

Theme	Description(s)	Example	Resource
Coordinate	Establish protocols for keeping the collection clean and maintaining functioning games	Board game collection policies and procedures documentation Circulate game safe cleaning wipes with games Maintain collection of backup pieces for replacements	*Best practices for preserving and circulating games:* Robson, D., Phillips, J., & Guerrero, S. (2018). Don't just roll the dice: Simple solutions for circulating tabletop game collections effectively in your library. *Library Resources & Technical Services,* 62(2), 80. https:// doi.org/10.5860/lrts.62n2.80 Many publishers will send replacement pieces upon request. Alternatively, consider 3D printing replacements.
	Create online alternatives and supplemental options for physical collections	Host virtual board game or trivia nights; arrange guest speakers Establish an online guide of virtual gaming resources	*Extensive list of virtual games:* www .bit.ly/quarantinegamessorted coda.io /@kelsey/board-games Contact publishers for guest speaker resources.
	Utilize collection for staff morale with game breaks	Staff meeting game breaks Informal gaming events during the workweek	
Communicate	If there is a change to how your collection will be checked out, communicate this to the community in as many ways as possible	Use social media, posters, displays in the library, signs at the checkout desk, e-mails, word of mouth, community listservs, contact gaming community groups, etc.	

(Continued)

Table 10.1 (*Continued*)

Theme	Description(s)	Example	Resource
	Advertise new offerings frequently and often	Establish a library communications plan, subsection focused on gaming	
		Include board games in traditional library displays	
Collaborate	Build resilient relationships with local board game and comic groups	Check your campus for student-led gaming organizations or courses on game design and development	
		Look for local gaming groups (Facebook, meetups, Reddit, etc.)	
		Identify local gaming events and conventions for partnerships	
		Connect with game stores and gaming cafés	
		For academic libraries, check with public libraries that may also have collections or an interest in building their own	
	Reciprocate and appreciate relationships	Advertise gaming events for local groups in the library, such as by the game collection or at the circulation desk	*Diamond Comics' Free Comic Book Day partnership program for librarians:* https://freecomicbookday.com/Article /206876-Free-Comic-Book-Day -Library-Partner-Program
		Host gaming events with local groups and invite members to participate directly in the planning process with library event coordinators	
		Thank partners throughout the process (i.e., through e-mails, in-person recognition, and thank-you cards)	
		Innovate together to explore future partnership opportunities outside of board games	

Incorporate student employees	Establish students coordinators for maintaining rotating gaming displays through various themes Promote leadership at events through hosting or teaching games Play test games with student employees (i.e., at staff training events, meetings, employee parties) Encourage student employees to share ideas and get creative	*Beginners guide for game nights*: Pappas, John. *A beginner's guide to hosting a board game night.* (2017, May 25). Programming Librarian. https://programminglibrarian.org/blog/beginner's-guide-hosting-board-game-night *Join library-related gaming organizations:* Games & Gaming Round Table of ALA https://www.ala.org/rt/gamert *Participate in International Games Week:* http://ilovelibraries.org/gaming *Participate in Free Comic Book Day:* https://freecomicbookday.com/Article/206876-Free-Comic-Book-Day-Library-Partner-Program
Continue	Research what other libraries are doing and explore new ideas Plan future, recurring events Evaluate budget and explore grants for maintaining and building physical board game collection	Gaming event ideas: • Fall Welcome Week/school start • monthly game nights • parents weekend events • charity gaming nights and International Games Week • Free Comic Book Day celebration	

(Continued)

Table 10.1 (*Continued*)

Theme	Description(s)	Example	Resource
	Embed assessment and reflection, dedicating staff time to this process	Audit physical collection for missing, broken pieces	
		Expand community involvement in game selection process (i.e., suggestion box in person and online)	
		Review collection for accessibility, equity, diversity, and inclusion (assess for various game formats, levels of complexity, languages, ages, international, ease of transportation, etc.)	

on and assess in-person gaming activities. Both in-person and virtual gaming events should continue, offering the community more ways to engage and including a wider community.

COMIC BOOKS

Pre-pandemic

With the success of Welcome Week Game Nite, OSU librarians began planning in the fall of 2019 for Free Comic Book Day (FCBD) 2020. It would be a pilot event that built on Game Nite's momentum. Plans for the event highlight the project lead's prior FCBD experience as well as lessons drawn from some of the "hundreds of libraries across the United States and Canada" that "now host or participate in a convention in some fashion" (Phoenix, 2020, p. 153; Slobuski et al., 2020; Wood, 2018). The lead describes the general format of library FCBDs in an internal planning document:

> The basic model for Free Comic Book Day is a room, several piles of free comics, a friendly librarian, and a display of library books. Attendees are welcome to select a set number of free comics, read from the curated collection, and enjoy snacks.

> Other libraries—including Zach's previous institution—have done considerably more. Some of the events at library FCBDs include art events, costume contests, guest speakers, snacks, webchats, tutorials, card games, board games, photo booths, film showings, role-playing games, video games, and raffles (or prize-drawings, depending on local laws).

As with other pop culture programming, student interest and volunteer capacity would determine which events would be successful (Slobuski et al., 2020). The literary heart of the event would be a partnership with a local comic book store. The store would sell us at-cost copies of promotional comic books from Diamond Comic Distributors' nationwide Free Comic Book Day event, which we would distribute to patrons along with donations from publishers and community members. Many publishers provide contact options on their Web sites for soliciting donations. Diamond also hosts a FCBD Library Partner program that sends free comics to libraries without access to a nearby comic book store.

As event planning gained steam, we decided on an agenda: Board game demos overseen by volunteers from the comic book store, viewing a documentary on creating comics available through Kanopy, crafts, *Dungeons & Dragons*, a zine creation station, video game stations, cosplay, and a room filled with free comics.

Our internal workflow began with a proposal to the Library Administration, Management, and Planning group (LAMP). The proposal connected the programming to OSULP and OSU goals, indicated preliminary staffing requirements (including volunteers), provided a time line, and requested a budget. The budget included promotional comic books, snacks for attendees, and a list of measurable outcomes.

The organizing team agreed Valley's comic collection hadn't been updated in a while, and a comics-focused event would be the perfect time to engage in further collection development. As Goldsmith (2005) explains, "Collection development continues to be a professional activity that differentiates the library's mission from the missions of other agencies that deal with graphic novels." Our mission, in this case, was to diversify our collection and remind campus stakeholders of our openness to purchase a variety of resources.

We polled seven campus cultural groups, as well as librarians and instructors, asking which comics, graphic novels, manga, and similar visual works they would like to have in our collection. Purchases were tracked on a spreadsheet, with preference given to requests made by the OSU community, finishing limited series we had already started, and short series.

We also contacted publishers for prize support and tracked their responses in a spreadsheet. Many publishers offer library outreach through regular newsletters, making convention support a streamlined process. However, no packages were ever mailed due to the frightening and confusing early days of the pandemic, the temporary closure of the Valley Library, and the subsequent cancellation of Free Comic Book Day 2020 (national and local).

Pandemic Effects

By the end of March 2020, the Valley Library closed to the public and students shifted to remote classes. Because of the resulting budgetary uncertainty, the comic purchasing project was temporarily placed on hold. After nonessential purchases resumed, the Resources and Acquisitions Department decided to complete the order in the lead up to the rescheduled event.

As it became apparent the event would not happen in the near future, an earlier purchase was requested in order to create a fun, welcoming display "for students coming back in the Fall." Although students didn't return immediately in the fall, the comics circulated as part of our home delivery program.

Although the library was closed to the public, we continued to provide access to materials. Overdue fines were suspended and extant items were renewed. Home delivery, a service we originally developed for students taking hybrid or online classes, was extended to everyone. If an item was available for checkout, we would mail it. It was a confusing time, and upper-level decisions changed daily. Many patrons called or e-mailed for clarification, and we wanted them to feel supported.

The Free Comic Book Day event was quickly rescheduled for "when things return to normal," which hasn't occurred as of the time of publication. Oregon's mask mandate, which requires individuals to wear masks in all indoor public spaces, coupled with the prevalence of contagious COVID-19 variants, have encouraged us to direct our programming moxie elsewhere.

As part of the Valley Library's investigation of online gaming substitutes, one librarian investigated the possibility of online comics programming. Through online fandom events (e.g., WisCon in May 2020; Emerald City Comic Con; San Diego Comic Con's Comic Con Online; Manga in Libraries webinars) and one-off industry webinars, we got a feel for what was happening outside the academic sphere. These events were enjoyable but didn't capture the same atmosphere as an in-person event. The topics were creative, and the speakers were delightful, but our students were already reporting reduced engagement and fatigue from virtual webinars. Adding more screens to the mix, even loaded with fun, didn't seem like the way to go.

Although the online Free Comic Book Day plans fell through, we continued to read vendor newsletters, participate on comic librarian Twitter, and monitor the ALA Graphic Novels and Comics Round Table (https://twitter .com/libcomix) for opportunities. The results have been shared at staff meetings and in informal conversations to maintain enthusiasm and signal engagement to library administration.

TAKEAWAYS

Through adapting and reflecting on the ongoing pandemic, our library has developed new practices regarding our pop culture events, services, and resources. These reflections and takeaways can be utilized to strengthen this particular element of our library's programming for longevity as well as improved accessibility. Lessons learned from our experiences can be extended to other academic institutions and used in tandem with additional reflective tools for assessment. Not everything is going to work. Don't take it personally. Reuse what you can, but be gracious and understanding.

The benefits of having detailed documentation and policies, especially when facing crises and change, cannot be overstated. Our well-established protocols, thorough maintenance guides, and gentle philosophy toward fines aided in adapting the board game collection for the pandemic. Shifting staff roles coupled with the hardships of the pandemic have illuminated gaps in previously established procedures, but reliable, detailed documentation eased the stress of navigating the new state of the library. Approaching circulation with an inclusive collection philosophy not only mitigated pandemic stress but also elevates belonging and joy as an established library value.

Table 10.2 includes insights gained from our experiences at the Valley Library as well as potential ideas gathered from other libraries.

Table 10.2 Pandemic Lessons for Comic and Board Game Collections

What You Need		
Computers	All staff will require access to a computer to participate	Cameras and mics not required, but suggested for more expansive interaction
Video Conferencing Platform	Must have a screen-sharing feature	Discord Google Hangouts Zoom Skype
Virtual Game	Jackbox Games is recommended as the games they offer can be purchased and installed on one computer and then shared. Keep an eye out for sales and occasional free releases.	Drawful (Jackbox Games) Quiplash (Jackbox Games) Fibbage (Jackbox Games) Pictionary
Setup		
Date	Establish date and time	Recommended: having multiple dates and different times to cover the variety of work schedules of various employees; 30 minutes to 1 hour for game play
Instructions	Provide game play instructions to staff in advance	Utilize game instructions frequently; available online for staff to reference, or share via e-mail a few days or week before
Reminder	Share and explain game directions before the game starts	Review shared instructions before the game begins to ensure all players are prepared and to allow time to clarify details or answer questions
Prepare Tech	Install and prepare game in advance on host's computer	Recommended: testing the game with a friend to understand all features and flow of play beforehand

Important Notes

- Games can be entirely virtual, in-person, or hybrid.
- Poll staff for best fit, and include various formats for each event.
- If there are a variety of format requests, consider hosting multiple events.
- During the pandemic, many games were available from Jackbox Games for free or available at a greatly reduced price.
- With lucky timing, there are occasional sales where games can be purchased for far cheaper.
- There are a variety of virtual games that can also be played for free.
- Pictionary is a recommended option due to ease of play.

CONCLUSION

The Valley Library explored creative alternative solutions to gaming services in response to COVID-19 with the closure of the library. Experience from navigating impacts of the pandemic on library resources and services has provided insights into establishing sustainable game library collections.

The future of libraries is in "holding a community together. Librarians have shifted from caretaking a collection to truly caretaking the community itself" (Lankes, 2020). Reflections from the pandemic on library purpose and how best to serve communities, has illuminated the breadth of resources libraries can and should offer. Board game collections provide not only entertainment, but also a tool for facilitating communication, learning, and joy. Introducing services such as these into the digital realm strengthens existing collections while expanding the reach of such resources to potentially meet a wider range of students and foster connection.

REFERENCES

American Academy of Pediatrics. (2021, October). *AAP-AACAP-CHA Declaration of a National Emergency in Child and Adolescent Mental Health*. http://www.aap .org/en/advocacy/child-and-adolescent-healthy-mental-development/aap-aacap -cha-declaration-of-a-national-emergency-in-child-and-adolescent-mental-health/

Bayeck, R. Y. (2020). Examining board gameplay and learning: A multidisciplinary review of recent research. *Simulation & Gaming, 51*(4), 411–431. https://doi .org/10.1177/1046878119901286

Bladek, M. (2021). Student well-being matters: Academic library support for the whole student. *The Journal of Academic Librarianship*, 47(3), 102349. https:// doi.org/10.1016/j.acalib.2021.102349

Cross, E., Mould, D., & Smith, R. (2015). The protean challenge of game collections at academic libraries. *New Review of Academic Librarianship*, 21(2), 129–145. https://doi.org/10.1080/13614533.2015.1043467

Czeisler, M. É., Lane, R. I., Petrosky, E., Wiley, J. F., Christensen, A., Njai, R., Weaver, M. D., Robbins, R., Facer-Childs, E. R., Barger, L. K., Czeisler, C. A., Howard, M. E., & Rajaratnam, S. (2020). Mental health, substance use, and suicidal ideation during the COVID-19 pandemic—United States, June 24–30, 2020. MMWR. *Morbidity and Mortality Weekly Report, 69*(32), 1049–1057. https:// doi.org/10.15585/mmwr.mm6932a1

Diaz, S., & Hall, R. (2020). Out of the class and onto the board: Building student-faculty relationships and easing library anxiety through board game nights. In S. Crowe & E. Sclippa (Eds.), *Games and gamification in academic libraries* (pp. 251–264). Association of College & Research Libraries.

Donnelly, J., & Herbert, B. (2017). Calling all gamers: Game night in the academic library. *College & Research Libraries News*, 78(7), 388. https://doi.org/10.5860 /crln.78.7.388

Goek, S. (2021, April 9). The impact of COVID-19 on library staff: Supporting health and well-being, public libraries online. *Public Libraries Association*. http://publiclibrariesonline.org/2021/04/the-impact-of-covid-19-on-library -staff-supporting-health-and-well-being/

Goldsmith, F. (2005). *Graphic novels now: Building, managing, and marketing a dynamic collection.* ALA Editions.

Laddusaw, S., & Brett, J. (2020). Con-vergence: Bringing libraries and popular culture conventions together. *Journal of Library Outreach and Engagement, 1*(1). https://doi.org/10.21900/j.jloe.v1i1.350

Lankes, R. D. (2020, April 30). The "new normal" agenda for librarianship. *R. David Lankes.* https://davidlankes.org/the-new-normal-agenda-for-librarianship/

Nicholson, S. (2008). Finish your games so you can start your schoolwork: A look at gaming in school libraries. *Library Media Connection, 26*(5), 52–55.

Oldenburg, R. (1999). *The great good place: Cafes, coffee shops, bookstores, bars, hair salons, and other hangouts at the heart of a community.* Marlowe & Company

Phoenix, J. (2020). *Maximizing the impact of comics in your library: Graphic novels, manga, and more.* Libraries Unlimited.

Pope, L. (2021). Board games as educational tools, leading to climate change action: A literature review. *Journal of Sustainability Education.* http://www.susted.com /wordpress/content/board-games-as-educational-tools_2021_05/

Robson, D., & DeWitt-Miller, E. (2020). Taming the beast: Game collection management in an academic library. In S. Crowe & E. Sclippa (Eds.), *Games and gamification in academic libraries* (pp. 65–81). Association of College & Research Libraries.

Rogerson, M. J., Gibbs, M. R., & Smith, W. (2018). Cooperating to compete: The mutuality of cooperation and competition in boardgame play. *Proceedings of the 2018 CHI Conference on Human Factors in Computing Systems. Association for Computing Machinery, New York, NY, USA, Paper 193,* 1–13. https:// doi.org/10.1145/3173574.3173767

Salvesen, L., & Berg, C. (2021). "Who says I am coping": The emotional affect of New Jersey academic librarians during the COVID-19 pandemic. *The Journal of Academic Librarianship, 47*(5), 102422. https://doi.org/10.1016/j.acalib.2021.102422

Schneider, E. F. (2014). A survey of graphic novel collection and use in American public libraries. *Evidence Based Library and Information Practice, 9*(3), 68–79. https://doi.org/10.18438/B83S44

Slobuski, T., Robson, D., & Bentley, P. (2017). Arranging the pieces: A survey of library practices related to a tabletop game collection. *Evidence Based Library and Information Practice, 12*(1), 2–17. https://doi.org/10.18438/B84C96

Slobuski, T., Johnson, E., Boehme, G., & Hays, L. (2020). Where do we go from here?: Expanding the reach of your gaming events. In S. Crowe & E. Sclippa (Eds.), *Games and gamification in academic libraries* (pp. 235–246). Association of College & Research Libraries.

Swiatek, C., & Gorsse, M. (2016). Playing games at the library: Seriously? *LIBER Quarterly: The Journal of the Association of European Research Libraries, 26*(2), 83–101. https://doi.org/10.18352/lq.10161

Waltz, M. R. (2021). In support of flourishing: Practices to engage, motivate, affirm, and appreciate. *International Information & Library Review, 0*(0), 1–8. https:// doi.org/10.1080/10572317.2021.1990564

Welhouse, Z. (2020). No comic shop? No problem: Developing free comic book day programming. *The Booklist, 116*(21), S8.

Wood, M. Z. (2018). *Comic book collections and programming: A practical guide for librarians.* Rowman & Littlefield.

11

Other Duties (and Places) as Assigned: How Analog Approaches Are Impeding Progress in Online Librarianship

Heather Blicher, Rebecca Neel, and Joy Howard

POSITIONALITY STATEMENT

This chapter discusses a variety of issues in academic librarianship that, the authors posit, stem from the inequities inherent in historically feminized professions. Thus, recognizing that our personal and professional identities frame our perceptions of this topic, it is important to note that all three authors identify as female and currently work in postsecondary academic institutions. Two authors are librarians, while the third is teaching faculty in the field of education—another historically feminized profession. Additionally, as geography also plays a role in both the notion of positionality (Holmes, 2020) and the arguments within this chapter, we feel it relevant to note that the two librarian authors are geographically bound to their institutions of employment and that all three authors teach online courses and/or have direct work experience in distance and online learning (DOL) environments.

INTRODUCTION

The "other duties as assigned" clause in position descriptions has achieved ubiquity among academic librarians, often soliciting an understanding smirk or eye roll at its mention. Librarians and library staff all assume other duties on occasion for the sake of maintaining workflows and services during staffing shortages or when adjusting to new technologies and professional trends. In short, we grow the job as needed. But it is vital to take a step back and question at what point these "other duties" reach critical mass and necessitate the creation of a new position that requires specific expertise and experience. The COVID-19 pandemic spurred a rapid push toward online learning and librarianship (i.e., online collections, embedded librarianship, and online instruction) and initiated a surge of other *online* duties as assigned for librarians who otherwise would not have considered themselves part of the online-focused segment of the profession. Librarians who already specialized in online librarianship—those with accumulated knowledge and a highly defined skill set resulting from years of focused service to online populations—approached the pandemic-initiated shift in responsibilities by pivoting to act as supports. During the quarantine stages of the pandemic, distance and online learning librarians offered webinars, discussion forums, and workshops for colleagues who were new to online work and intended these training opportunities to fill the remote services gap the pandemic created. The initial intent was to share practical ideas and knowledge as a quick fix to stitch together services in the short term. We argue that this quick-fix approach cannot sustainably support the long-term need for what we now know is a permanent shift toward online learning, research, and general information-seeking practices. While specialized librarians shifted to meet the needs of institutions in the short term, academic institutions must acknowledge and support this work as a foundational necessity moving forward and create infrastructures to support distance and online learning services and positions.

Distance and online learning (DOL) is not a new concept. Community colleges and research universities alike have shifted to embrace and even emphasize online programs and course offerings over the past three decades. Strategically, DOL programs increase enrollment by attracting students that would otherwise not consider enrolling due to scheduling or geographic limitations. The pandemic merely expedited what we have come to call the analog-to-digital shift in education (in other words, the transition from physical to digital education practices and resources) and indiscriminately transformed all librarians into *online* librarians in some form or another. However, simply transferring analog practices and theories of librarianship to a digital setting does not constitute *online librarianship*, just as directly transferring physical teaching and learning paradigms to a digital setting does not constitute *online learning*. Instead, DOL librarianship exists as a formal, practice- and research-based professional subfield, developed with digital modes of information sharing and consumption as points of departure. Thus, as Hodges et al. (2020) note, quick, reactive, and ill-developed analog-to-digital transitions exacerbate existing misconceptions that online education constitutes a subpar or less effective mode of teaching and learning. Hence, while librarians often embrace the jack-of-all-trades mentality as a product of necessity and an indication of adaptability, this does not mean we should accept or normalize "emergency remote teaching" (Hodges et al., 2020) or services that were hastily instituted under quarantine as standards for DOL librarianship. Just as librarians have intentionally developed and strengthened face-to-face services according to professional standards, so too should we intentionally create and support standards based DOL work. To accomplish this work, we propose that academic libraries require both dedicated, experienced DOL librarians *and* progressive organizational structures that embrace the post-traditional work environments needed to fully support modern (i.e., post-pandemic) students.

STANDARDS AND THE VALUE OF EQUITY AND EXPERTISE

The Association of College and Research Libraries' (2016) Standards for Distance Learning Library Services (The Standards), provide personnel, facility, service, and resource benchmarks for academic libraries serving DOL students, staff, faculty, and administrators. The Standards assert, as a point of departure, that all members of a college or university community are entitled to equivalent resources and services as those available to their on-campus counterparts. Accordingly, libraries should also ensure that delivery of resources and services meets the "unique needs" of the online community. Recognizing the institution-specific nature of these "unique needs," The Standards place the onus on libraries to enact distance community needs and outcome assessments, and to incorporate DOL support into their strategic plans and mission statements. Prioritizing DOL innovation and support compels libraries to thoughtfully design equitable services and environments for online library users.

For DOL programs to be truly successful, an intentional focus on equity is vital. While librarians can adapt in-person skills to DOL services, is it equitable to DOL students to simply state that all librarians are now "online" rather than developing the skills and services specific to this population? This approach is reminiscent of pre-COVID library environments that valued physical desk coverage above virtual chat coverage. In other words, serve the students physically in front of you, then attend to the ones waiting online. As one author is experiencing currently, management can often be more concerned with the *appearance* of services—meaning visible desk coverage—even when no reference interactions are logged, rather than putting that time and effort into less visible DOL services. If libraries continue to view DOL services as secondary or less optimal to traditional, on-campus services, they are relegating online library users to a secondary status. This is a particularly problematic approach when considered against trends in Integrated Postsecondary Education Data System (IPEDS) circulation data.

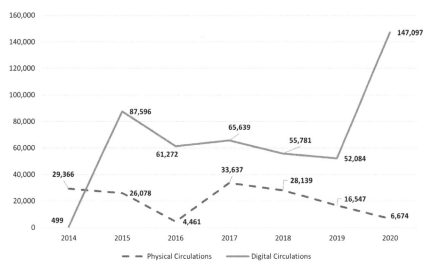

FIGURE 11.1. 2014–2020 IPEDS physical and digital circulation data for J. Sargeant Reynolds Community College

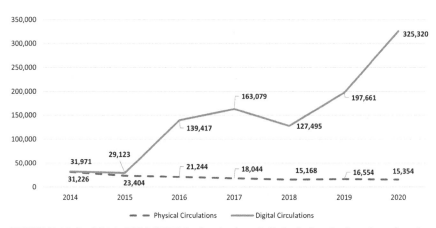

FIGURE 11.2. 2014–2020 IPEDS physical and digital circulation data for the University of Southern Indiana

As depicted in Figures 11.1 and 11.2, both the authors' institutional data reflect steady and significant decreases in physical resource circulation between 2014 and 2020. Meanwhile, digital circulation has substantially increased, reflecting a large-scale analog-to-digital shift in how users choose to interact with information (U.S. Department of Education, 2020a; 2020b). Thus, if online services truly are less optimal in practice, then these services and the positions that provide them need to be redesigned to proactively meet users' changing needs.

Embracing DOL-focused library positions that design and provide equitable resources and services requires the development of intentional, sustainable organizational infrastructures. These infrastructures should support DOL as a distinct and complex field similar to technical services, research services, and access services. As two authors have experienced firsthand, a single DOL librarian cannot achieve all that is required even when collaborating with neighboring departments and librarians, nor can a group of DOL librarians be efficient without a qualified, designated leader. To compare the missing DOL leadership position to one widely accepted at many institutions, the Head of Technical Services works across the library or library system to provide leadership in all aspects of cataloging, acquisitions, and resource management. Top-down leadership is necessary in technical services for the sake of consistency and standardization. Without uniformity of resource description and access parameters, library users would not be able to rely on stable access to essential resources and services. By extension, without a comprehensive and uniform approach in technical services, higher education institutions could not function in 21st-century scholarly information environments. Likewise, without a leadership position in DOL librarianship, the lack of centralized decision making yields a casual and unreliable approach to DOL with equally disruptive effects on library users.

THE ISSUE OF MOBILITY

Approaches to the successful administration of DOL services vary across institutions due to the diversity of populations and resources. Nevertheless, we assert that there are two systemic impediments to the widespread development of robust DOL support programs, namely the lack of both geographic and upward mobility within academic librarianship. In organizational structures, in job postings, and in the very history of the profession, these are the two significant obstacles to the comprehensive adoption of sustainable and scalable DOL service infrastructures across academic libraries. Moreover, both of these impediments are products of the gendered nature of the profession. It is, therefore, integral to the building of an equitable infrastructure for DOL services to examine the geographic demands and hierarchical setting of DOL positions.

The issue of geographic mobility in librarianship is particularly complex considering the mantra throughout library science programs is that graduates should expect to move to different cities or states to find librarian jobs. And we do this, over and over again, each time seeking to enhance our skills and/or job opportunities. This is not geographic mobility. This is geographic constraint—and it transfers the power of choosing where one calls home from the individual to the employer. Additionally, for librarians whose work is entirely online, geographic location is functionally arbitrary. A host of employers, including Dropbox (Dropbox Team, 2020), Ford (Krisher & Rugaber, 2021), and even the State of Massachusetts (Decosta-Klipa, 2021), have adjusted job location norms to allow employees partial or full remote status on a permanent basis as a result of pandemic work experiences. Nevertheless, as higher education institutions begin return-to-campus activities, librarians with online responsibilities are being physically called back to campus along with their colleagues who primarily work on-site. Likewise, many new job postings for online learning, systems, and digital asset librarians still require an on-campus presence.

In short, what current and potential library employers are indicating is that a librarian's place is unequivocally in the library. In a historically feminized profession like librarianship—refer to Sloniowski (2016) for a critical feminist discussion of labor in librarianship—this sentiment sounds dangerously close to—and as functionally unfounded as—the patriarchal notion that a woman's place is in the home. We offer the following example from one author's experience of this sort of geographically restrictive position design. At a former institution, the DOL librarian was housed in the campus's online division, which included instructional designers and online course support positions. After the initial pandemic surge of emergency remote instruction, the institution made all positions within the online division fully remote—with the exception of the librarian position, which was relocated to the library as an on-campus position. The act of singly denying the librarian position geographic mobility could have been motivated by a variety of institutional factors and was, perhaps, not an intentionally patriarchal move on the part of decision makers. Nevertheless, the decision both reflects and perpetuates the exploitation and control over feminized labor upon which Dewey intentionally constructed modern librarianship (Biggs, 1982; Sloniowski, 2016). In short, systemic inequities still occur despite modern intentions.

Some proponents of required, on-campus work maintain that face-to-face interactions improve relationship building and communication among staff, or that shared responsibilities (e.g., every librarian works the reference desk) constitute some manner of fairness. Nevertheless, these ideas are grounded in a reliance on physical paradigms—i.e., place-based notions of information sharing (see Ettarh [2018] for a discussion of the professional impact of vocational awe and the notion of the library as a "sacred place"). In effect, librarians are trained from graduate school onward to embrace poverty, to accept jobs in new places to advance careers, to incur debt for relocation, to accept salary cuts and years lost toward tenure or promotion, to lose access to short-term disability, benefits, and personal support systems, all for the good of the cause. How can we champion equity and inclusion on campus when we readily sacrifice these ideals in vocational awe? Normalizing remote work options will not solve every issue of labor exploitation or inequity within the profession. However, it will eliminate arbitrary, employer-imposed, geographic constraints and their associated financial burdens. Additionally, organizations that remove location requirements from DOL positions increase the pool of qualified, experienced job candidates by including candidates external to their institutional zip code (Clark & Chamorro-Premuzic, 2021).

A lack of geographic mobility, however, is not the only gender-based obstacle facing both librarians and the profession at large. Broadway and Shook (2018) offer an overview of gendered issues in librarianship, which includes a discussion of the ramifications of the post-hierarchical organizational structures common in libraries. On the surface, post-hierarchical structures aim to minimize superfluous levels of bureaucracy. However, eliminating formal leadership roles means eliminating the potential for upward mobility, or put simply, job growth with corresponding pay. Herein lies the difficulty of creating leadership positions in DOL library services. Organizational structures that refuse to devote hierarchical (as opposed to lateral) leadership positions to DOL support undermine the strategic potential for service development by devaluing expertise in the area. The lateral leadership roles many DOL librarians assumed during the pandemic allowed libraries to quickly adapt resource and service delivery during emergency remote semesters. However, emergency-implemented lateral leadership structures were not intentionally or thoughtfully designed with sustainability, growth, or wage equity in mind. They were an emergency means to an end. That said, as the profession adjusts to the "new normal," libraries will not attract or retain specialized DOL librarians without offering pay raises for increased responsibilities. Consequently, without these centralized, qualified DOL leadership positions, libraries run the risk of delivering inconsistent and insufficient DOL services and resources to campus stakeholders.

WHERE DO WE GO FROM HERE?

The DOL labor and service inequities outlined in this chapter stem from the gendered nature and history of librarianship. Post-hierarchical organizational structures and vocational mindsets, respectively, enable and normalize exploitative compensation practices. From library school onward, librarians are indoctrinated and resigned to the expectation of wearing many hats for the sake of the public good. (Refer to Popowich [2018] for a Marxist analysis of libraries in neoliberal society.) Nevertheless, in devaluing our own labor—i.e., accepting other duties as assigned on an individual rather than organizational level, we are devaluing both the expectations and entitlements of our DOL user base. As a profession, we have an opportunity to address this narrative and the resulting practices and policies in the wake of post-pandemic social changes. However, this requires a confrontation of commonly accepted norms in the field and the internal inequities that arise in the analog versus digital approach to information resources and services.

There's no checklist for dismantling systemic inequity, but we can offer some ideas to initiate your thinking on this process. Though circumstances will vary according to institutional culture and history, the following suggestions may serve as a baseline for administrators to establish reformative pathways to successful DOL services:

1. Normalize digital communication and service delivery methods.
2. Conduct a thorough survey of library personnel, services, and resources that specifically support online learning.
3. Develop an action plan for improvement.

Normalize Digital Communication and Service Delivery Methods

Online interactions and information consumption are no longer supplementary or specific to distance users. Distance and local users alike rely on digital information resources for research. Live chat and video conferencing apps enable librarians to interact with users and successfully meet their digital information needs regardless of user or librarian location. Moreover, digital communication methods within the workplace increase opportunities for staff with speech or hearing disabilities to participate in formal or informal workplace conversations. For example, video conferencing software like Zoom and Microsoft Teams now offer live automatic captioning and give participants the ability to contribute input via text or audio. Integrating digital communication methods into standard workplace exchanges (e.g., meetings or quick chats) encourages familiarity and innovation with these resources and promotes inclusive communication practices.

Organization-wide familiarity with current and emerging digital communication and service methods also decreases the likelihood of workflow disruptions during emergency shutdowns. In their discussion of remote work management, Rysavy and Michalak (2020) note that communication through online tools had already been adopted in their pre-pandemic work environment. This allowed team members to transition to work from home quickly during the pandemic as they were already accustomed to digital collaboration. Methods of digital communication enacted during emergency remote work included asynchronous daily check-ins with Flip-Grid, chat with Slack over the course of the day, and virtual face-to-face Zoom meetings a couple of times per week. Rysavy and Michalak also acknowledge the importance of synchronous, face-to-face interactions in building and maintaining healthy communication practices among staff and offered, "Sometimes projects/big ideas/questions just simply need to be talked out" (2020, p. 538). In these scenarios, team meetings were held via Zoom, and the authors suggest that these virtual meetings offered the opportunity to improve interpersonal relationships. Rysavy and Michalak's (2020) experiences support the notion that in-person interactions simply for the sake of being in-person are not necessary for effective workflows, and in this scenario, normalizing digital communication had a positive effect on the team. Apart from digital communication platforms, the teams also leveraged cloud-based file storage systems, which afforded workers the ability to easily access and collaborate on documents regardless of physical location. Likewise, centralized decision making regarding digital communication and file management expectations kept the team organized and effective.

Conduct a Thorough Survey of Library Personnel, Services, and Resources That Specifically Support Online Learning

Normalizing the use of digital communication methods is a terrific first step toward creating inclusive environments for library staff and users. Nevertheless, the creation of *equitable* environments and services for DOL users requires more from the library than simply embracing live chat and video conferencing apps. Services like instruction, research assistance, and technology troubleshooting must be designed and delivered with the DOL population in mind rather than simply replicating existing on-site services in an online environment. The same applies to the information resources offered by the library. The ACRL Standards for Distance Learning Library Services (ACRL, 2016) offer guidance for libraries and academic institutions in this regard.

When considering services and resources:

- Do on-site and DOL users all have direct access to library staff?
- Do services and resources meet ADA, Web Content Accessibility Guidelines (WCAG), Section 504, and Section 508 accessibility standards?
- Are on-site and online library services standardized, assessed, and equitably distributed?
- Are DOL services operating efficiently and effectively?
- Are DOL users adequately represented in assessment and strategic planning endeavors?

When considering personnel:

- Does the library currently have DOL expertise on staff?
- Is there a librarian or group of librarians on staff responsible for researching emerging DOL strategies and advocating for DOL user needs?
- Are DOL services centrally coordinated, or are they inconsistent across library units?
- Do DOL experts have hierarchical authority, or do they occupy lateral leadership roles?

As learning and research across the P-20 spectrum increasingly depend on online resources and services (in both pandemic and non-pandemic times), libraries must adapt technical services, research services, and access services to equitably and effectively meet the information needs of DOL users. Consequently, the many resource and service considerations for consistent, successful DOL programs, as evidenced by the diverse requirements listed in The Standards (ACRL, 2016), unequivocally require both intra- and inter-departmental coordination of staff and operations. Likewise, per The Standards, DOL librarians in this sort of coordinating capacity should receive equivalent status and pay that is comparable to other coordination or leadership positions in the library. If budgets or organizational hierarchies do not currently support equitable pay or status for DOL librarians, then those structures should be analyzed and reconfigured for equity.

Develop an Action Plan for Improvement

After surveying and analyzing DOL resources, services, and staff, consider methods for improvement based on measurable goals. The Standards for Distance Learning Library Services Worksheet (Haber, n.d.) provides a template for assessment and progress planning that takes into account both library and institutional considerations that factor into meeting The Standards. It is important to note that, oftentimes, we must ask difficult questions to maximize improvement potential as an organization. For instance:

- What work is the library engaged in that could be reduced or altered based on current needs?
- Where are we spending the most time and money? Why?
- What work are we focusing on that is no longer a priority to the institution or students?

These questions have the potential to yield some answers with uncomfortable implications for library staff at all levels of the organization. No one wants to hear that their efforts are obsolete or no longer necessary, especially if they have been engaging in and enjoying specific tasks for years. Conversely, questioning and reimagining processes, spaces, and resources can create opportunities that allow institutions to dismantle the historically restrictive and exploitative environments within libraries and establish a more equitable workplace and institutional culture. All said, if analysis of operations, goals, and resources indicate the need for change, the library ultimately owes it to its user community to adapt workflows and redirect efforts.

Large-scale project changes and institutional reorganization can seem daunting, but there is a wealth of theory and documented experience upon which we can build our action plans for improvement and successfully manage change. Soehner (2014) outlines a successful change management program, implemented as part of the University of Utah's Marriott Library's "evolution[ary]" processes, which involved the combination of library IT departments and services to eliminate resource and service duplication and to streamline processes and communication. Library leadership utilized Kotter's (2007) influential eight steps to organizational transformation to guide the analysis of the current situation and ultimately develop a successful action plan for repositioning personnel and services. The Marriott Library's change processes, though successful, were not without issue and Soehner (2014) provides helpful details regarding unforeseen points of contention regarding staff perceptions and overall communication.

Kotter's (2007) oft-cited eight steps for transformational change—with 9,362 citations per Google Scholar as of March 2022—provide a valuable, loose blueprint for organizations looking to communicate, enact, and embed vision-based change at an institutional level. That said, broad steps such as "institutionalizing new approaches" (p. 99) imply that institutional leadership has, in fact, decided on an appropriate and effective approach to change. Nevertheless, many of us (institutionally speaking) may very well agree that a change is needed, but the path to enacting that change may be fraught with seemingly insurmountable social, technological, or systemic obstacles. Likewise, the awareness of the need for change may be so recent that the available paths to achieving change may be totally unknown or untested. In these scenarios, an exploratory, iterative approach may be in order. The plan-do-check-act (PDCA), also known as the plan-do-study-act (PDSA), approach offers a structured, iterative, and institution-specific approach to issues of quality control. One particularly functional and appealing aspect of the PDSA approach is the variety of action steps available in a given scenario. Langley et al. (2009), for example, note that iterations of a PDSA cycle may result in adoption, abandonment, adaptation, or expansion of a given approach. This structure complements Kotter's (2007) eight steps by reinforcing the idea of continual change as progress, applying the scientific method to decision-making processes, and embedding flexibility into institutional actions.

One author's institution recently began the large-scale process of shifting library resources and workflows to emphasize digital resources, systems, services, and users. The library began by analyzing structured user feedback and trends in resource usage to ascertain if a change was needed. The pandemic certainly increased digital demand, but that demand had been growing for years, so change was deemed essential. The library's strategy follows Kotter's (2007) eight steps, has been relatively successful at the first four (i.e., identifying issues, establishing a leadership group, and creating and communicating the overall vision with stakeholders), and is now at the point of engaging stakeholder action and planning specific, short-term improvements, which is where PDSA cycles have proven useful. Some of the initiatives within the larger process include transitioning to exclusively hosted systems and platforms (including migration to a new ILS) to minimize access downtime for users, formalizing a digital-first acquisitions policy, and exploring controlled digital lending (CDL) mechanisms. One of the more disruptive changes was the migration from a legacy ILS to a modern system. The migration resulted in the automation of workflows that had previously required considerable staff time. Between the reduction of ILS-related tasks and the trending decline in physical circulation, front desk staff experienced considerable decreases in daily workload. As a result, library administration has begun redistributing personnel (both current and future hires) from front-facing positions to resource management and metadata-focused positions to support digital infrastructures and is currently in the "study" phase of a PDSA cycle. Likewise, a "plan" stage has begun for exploring ways to integrate front desk staff into CDL workflows, which are still in the "plan" phase as well. In this scenario, the PDSA approach has given the library the flexibility to investigate, test, and redesign processes and approaches if needed, while Kotter's eight steps provide a high-level framework and direction for successful change navigation.

CONCLUSION

Though higher education was already making permanent transitions toward online learning, the COVID-19 pandemic expedited that process at many institutions with the onset of emergency remote work and instruction. The global pandemic has passed the two-year mark, and new variants of the virus carry continual threats of lockdowns and cancellations worldwide. At this juncture, it is vital to recognize that a proactive library is more effective for its users than a reactive library, and we must work toward building sustainable infrastructures for supporting all learners and researchers at a distance—in both emergency and non-emergency environments. To this end, academic libraries must pivot library operations and organizational structures in a manner that values and liberates both library staff and users. Libraries must acknowledge and support the expertise of DOL-focused librarians and integrate DOL considerations into operations across all library units. These DOL considerations should extend not only to library users but also to librarians and staff whose work can be completed successfully regardless of geographic location. In short, creating a sustainably effective modern library requires an intentional shift in organizational mindset that elevates and embraces DOL services, resources, and strategies from the inside out. Steps toward sustainability include:

- Iterative analysis of institutional data to proactively support changes in users' information habits
- Institutionalizing digital services and tools as means of equity
- Prioritizing and formalizing DOL in strategic planning efforts

- Critically questioning and reconfiguring organizational hierarchies to value DOL expertise and initiatives
- Eliminating workplace restrictions that are outdated, arbitrary, or oppressive

Physical resources and on-site services will always have a place in libraries. Nevertheless, if we are to meet our users' increasingly digital information needs, physical paradigms should no longer dictate our processes and approaches.

REFERENCES

ACRL (Association of College and Research Libraries). (2016). Standards for distance learning library services. Retrieved from https://www.ala.org/acrl/standards/guidelinesdistancelearning

Biggs, M. (1982). Librarians and the "woman question": An inquiry into conservatism. *The Journal of Library History, 17*(4), 409–428.

Broadway, M., & Shook, E. (2018). The pink collar library: Technology & the gender wage gap. *Lady Science, Libraries & Tech Series*. Retrieved from https://www.ladyscience.com/essays/the-pink-collar-library-technology-and-the-gender-wage-gap

Clark, D., & Chamorro-Premuzic, T. (2021, April 21). Reshaping your career in the wake of the pandemic. *Harvard Business Review*. Retrieved from https://hbr.org/2021/04/reshaping-your-career-in-the-wake-of-the-pandemic

DeCosta-Klipa, N. (2021, March 5). Massachusetts is planning to have around half of state employees telework permanently. *Boston.com*. Retrieved from https://www.boston.com/news/local-news/2021/03/05/massachusetts-remote-work-government-employees/

Dropbox Team. (2020, October 13). Dropbox goes virtual first [Blog]. Retrieved from https://blog.dropbox.com/topics/company/dropbox-goes-virtual-first

Ettarh, F. (2018). Vocational awe and librarianship: The lies we tell ourselves. *In the Library with the Lead Pipe*. Retrieved from http://www.inthelibrarywiththeleadpipe.org/2018/vocational-awe/

Haber, N. (n.d.). Mapping to the ACRL standards for distance learning library-services. Retrieved from https://www.ala.org/acrl/sites/ala.org.acrl/files/content/standards/Standards_for_Distance_Learning_Library_Services_Worksheet2018.xlsx

Hodges, C., Moore, S., Lockee, B., Trust, T., & Bond, A. (2020, March 27). The difference between emergency remote teaching and online learning. *EDUCAUSE Review*. Retrieved from https://er.educause.edu/articles/2020/3/the-difference-between-emergency-remote-teaching-and-online-learning

Holmes, A. G. D. (2020). Researcher positionality—A consideration of its influence and place in qualitative research—a new researcher guide. *Shanlax International Journal of Education, 8*(4), 1–10.

Kotter, J. P. (2007). Leading change: Why transformation efforts fail. *Harvard Business Review, 85*(1), 96–103.

Krisher, T., & Rugaber, C. (2021, March 17). Ford Motor Co. tells 30,000 employees they can work from home indefinitely. *Associated Press*. Retrieved from https://

www.chicagotribune.com/business/ct-biz-ford-motor-work-from-home
-20210317-7dtnwjehebggnkpkm7utugwqoa-story.html

Langley, G. J., Moen, R. D., Nolan, K. M., Nolan, T. W., Norman, C. L., & Provost,
L. P. (2009). *The improvement guide: A practical approach to enhancing
organizational performance.* John Wiley & Sons.

Popowich, S. (2018). Libraries, labor, capital: On formal and real subsumption.
Journal of Radical Librarianship, 4, 6–19.

Rysavy, M. D. T., & Michalak, R. (2020). Working from home: How we managed
our team remotely with technology. *Journal of Library Administration, 30*(5),
532–542.

Sloniowski, L. (2016). Affective labor, resistance, and the academic librarian. *Library
Trends, 64*(4), 645–666. https://doi.org/10.1353/lib.2016.0013

Soehner, C. B. (2014). Change management in libraries: An essential competency for
leadership. *2014 IATUL Proceedings.*

U.S. Department of Education, National Center for Education Statistics. (2020a).
University of Southern Indiana: Academic libraries. *Integrated Postsecondary
Education Data System (IPEDS).* Retrieved from https://nces.ed.gov/ipeds
/datacenter/Facsimile.aspx?unitid=151306

U.S. Department of Education, National Center for Education Statistics. (2020b).
J Sargeant Reynolds Community College: Academic libraries. *Integrated Postsecondary Education Data System (IPEDS).* Retrieved from https://nces.ed.gov
/ipeds/datacenter/Facsimile.aspx?unitid=232414

12

Retooling the Academic Librarian Hiring Process

Diane G. Klare and Andrea M. Wright

INTRODUCTION

Prior to COVID-19, the process for hiring academic librarians was not a focus for reflection or innovation. Most libraries simply lifted the structure for hiring teaching faculty and applied it within the library. This process was not designed for efficiency. In fact, some of the more grueling aspects—multiday final interviews, which last from breakfast to dinner—seemed valued for their difficulty. Hiring may be one of the few areas of academic libraries where "But we've always done it this way" was rarely uttered simply because so few were pushing to change those practices.

When COVID-19 emerged in 2020, there was simply no way to continue with the academic librarian hiring process as it had been. Travel was difficult and dangerous. But the pandemic also spurred adoption of and improvement to technologies that would enable remote communication and work. This forced reckoning of a stale process, along with the new tools available, would enable us at the United States Air Force Academy's McDermott Library to reconsider our goals, craft new methods, and develop a streamlined process. Ultimately, this new approach was so successful, we decided that we will continue to use it even after the pandemic is over.

THE SITUATION

McDermott Library was committed to moving forward on staffing needs during the early months of the COVID-19 pandemic despite the inability to travel, which rendered obsolete the use of standard interview protocol practiced in the past. Previous practice typically started with preliminary interviews using video conferencing software (e.g., Zoom or Skype) followed by on-site visits for the finalists. Making smart use of communication software tools to overcome travel and in-person meeting issues was particularly important because we had several vacancies to fill. These vacancies had occurred as a result of an internal reorganization, previous retirements, or librarians moving on to other opportunities. Library leadership used these openings to update job descriptions and fill needs identified in the library's inaugural strategic plan. This plan had been adopted shortly before the pandemic began in the spring of 2020.

At the time, the strategic plan had not anticipated a need to hire library personnel in a fully virtual environment. The closing of the library facilities and the Air Force Academy campus presented immediate challenges that required complete telework and online instruction in March 2020 due to the significant rise of COVID-19 cases. However, there remained a sense of urgency with library senior management to fill these vacancies in order to reduce the workload on the remaining library personnel. Just as we were exploring new delivery methods and tools for nearly all of our library services, we realized that this was an opportunity to leverage technology already available at the United States Air Force Academy to move the hiring process forward during this time.

Due to the dearth of literature on hiring academic librarians pre-COVID-19 and because the pandemic upended so many standard processes, there were no rules for us to break, only unsustainable traditions to improve upon. This freed us to pull in ideas and best practices from outside academic libraries that could increase our efficiency while simultaneously making our process more transparent and accessible to candidates. Our job ads already included a salary listing and evaluation criteria. Now we could move beyond the listing and reflect on what we needed and wanted from each stage of the hiring process before reconsidering how to obtain those objectives.

COMMITTEE MAKEUP AND INITIAL APPLICATION REVIEW

One of the very first decisions we were able to reexamine was the makeup of the search committee. The adoption of newer technologies (see Table 12.1) that facilitated document sharing, real-time communication without geographic constraints, and centralized data gathering allowed us to become more creative in our committee selection. The ability to think outside the normal limitations of having only committee members affiliated with the institution enabled us to focus on the qualifications that would best serve the committee in reviewing and selecting candidates. This was particularly helpful when the library was seeking to hire a Head of Special Collections and Archives. This is a specialized role, and there were no other McDermott Library personnel in Special Collections and Archives eligible for the committee, so we sought an appropriately skilled committee member who was affiliated with another service academy. Not only did this enable us to have an expert on the committee for reviewing candidates, but it also established a connection between the final selectee and an experienced colleague who would better understand the unique opportunities and challenges of Special Collections work at a service academy.

With the competing time obligations of the search committee members and potential for the committee members to be in multiple time zones, it was vital to find software that would ease coordination and collaboration in a user-friendly manner. Scheduling software was critical throughout the search process to allow all committee members to coordinate the search team meetings and find common availability which could then be presented to the candidates for the interviews themselves. Because candidates and the committee members could now be scattered across several time zones, it was important to use software that could be customized for time zones without requiring special accounts or affiliations to access.

Even with the expanded committee access provided by new technology, we still focused on making the search committees as small as possible—no more than four members, with a minimum of one Air Force Academy faculty member. Some committee meetings and all interviews with candidates would need to be synchronous, and we knew how difficult it would be to find mutually agreeable times to meet between class schedules, standing meetings, and other institutional commitments. The streamlined process we gained from leveraging all this technology within the committee itself also helped us recruit faculty members. One faculty member who served on a search was also committed to cadet flight instruction beyond their classroom teaching load. Their ability to work around their existing schedules, join meetings from any location, and conduct reviews with online tools ensured that their service would be efficient, while still impactful.

We leveraged online forms to streamline the initial review of applications. Based on the approved hiring rubric, the committee chair created an online form that each committee member could use to independently score each candidate against the required criteria. Because the form was online, members could review and score applications when and where it best served them. Once all the scores were entered by the committee members, the chair of the committee was able to download the scores directly into a spreadsheet, subtotal sections, and create pivot tables to quickly and easily identify outlier scores, ensure completion of all sections, and generate a final ranking of the candidates based on the scores. The resulting numerical rankings were shared and used to guide the committee discussion on which candidates to bring forward for the semifinalist round. Soliciting search committee input in this way drastically reduced the time spent in committee discussions to determine the next stage in the selection process. Moreover, the scores were fully documented and became part of the hiring record required by Human Resources to validate the selection process.

By combining the use of scheduling software, video conferencing, and forms/spreadsheets, the preliminary committee meetings were relatively short and efficient, making good use of everyone's time so that the committee could move to the next step in the overall search process. While the committee chair had to spend time developing the polls and forms, using the various software platforms was ultimately a time-saver because it eliminated the strings of e-mails and manual data analysis. It also tightened the overall hiring calendar considerably compared to legacy practices. Most importantly, it kept everyone safe and avoided COVID-19 concerns since it was all accomplished remotely.

FIRST-ROUND INTERVIEWS

For many academic libraries, the first round of interviews had transitioned from the telephone to conferencing software well before COVID-19. As we were rethinking the entire hiring process during the pandemic, the enhancements to the first-round interviews were focused more on improving accessibility and equitability than changing modality.

One efficiency we gained in the first-round interviews was scheduling with candidates using single-slot sign-up in scheduling software. First, we created an online poll using the scheduling software with all of the time slots that committee members were available for the interviews. To ensure confidentiality to all candidates taking a single poll, we changed the poll settings to "hidden poll," which meant that only the poll owner could see participants and their selection. We also utilized the poll settings to limit the number of votes per option to first come, first served and to limit participants to a single vote. This meant that candidates could only choose one slot and that slot would immediately become unavailable to future participants.

The link to the scheduling poll was included within an e-mail message to each potential first-round candidate. Messages were drafted and sent at the same time so that contact order would not privilege one candidate over the others in terms of options. We also explicitly stated that slots were available on a first come, first served basis in the body of the e-mail so candidates would know that options could change if they delayed. We aimed to send the scheduling message a little more than a week in advance of the interview slots. Not only did this allow us to finalize the schedule for the committee, but it also enabled us to provide the interview questions to the candidates several days in advance.

Providing the first-round interview questions in advance of the meeting was a key change we wanted to make while retooling the hiring process. It was an accessibility enhancement in that candidates could read the full questions in advance rather than trying to hear fairly long questions over sometimes spotty Internet connections. It also meant that candidates didn't have to parse and track long or complex questions in real time. As the slots were scheduled, the official invite and a PDF of the questions were sent to the candidates so that each one received the questions the same number of days ahead of their specific interview. During the interview itself, the committee members did read aloud the questions to ensure that everyone was on track and allow follow-up questions from the committee, as needed.

We also felt that providing the first-round interview questions in advance would enable us to get a better sense of the candidates. With the questions in hand, candidates could prepare as much, or as little, as they wanted. Examples and answers would be the best possible ones the candidate could give rather than just the ones that first came to mind. It also put the onus on candidates to pace their answers since they knew exactly how many questions we had, how much time was allotted for the interviews, and how many questions they themselves wanted to ask during that time.

An important consideration for first-round interviews, in particular, is that conferencing software can provide candidates with needed access flexibility as long as the interviewing institution does not impart unnecessary restrictions or fail to provide complete information. Requiring video for participants can be a burden when trying to find a suitable location with the necessary bandwidth requirements. Providing the dial-in phone numbers and allowing video-in without requiring the camera to be turned on enabled candidates to meet our schedule limitations in the best way available to them.

FINAL-ROUND INTERVIEWS

Perhaps the most impactful modification that we made to the hiring process in response to COVID-19 was to transition the entire final-round interview process—normally referred to as an "on-site interview"—to completely online. Initially, this was the only way to hold the final round as the Air Force Academy base was under restricted access. But even as non-Department of Defense visitors have been allowed on to base once again, we have decided to maintain the fully online interview process. Our experience has been that this online process benefits the institution, the library, and the candidates by eliminating expenses, reducing time commitments, and expanding participation options.

The cost-saving to the institution is probably the most straightforward benefit. There are no flights, hotels, or meals involved. Thousands of dollars were saved in each search by eliminating these costs. While the United States

Air Force Academy handles all of the arrangements and costs on behalf of the candidate, policies which require candidates to front costs associated with their interview have equity issues that can prevent the best candidates from applying and completing the interview process. By eliminating these costs entirely, we removed a potential barrier should funding policies change in the future.

A fully online final interview also saved time for everyone involved. After much discussion and planning, our final interview "day" lasted four to five hours, with breaks. We focused on what information we needed from candidates to make a final decision and how to efficiently gain it. We also considered how to best share information about the institution and the position with the candidates so that they could make a decision as well. In order to achieve those ends, the final-round online schedule included the following:

- *Brief welcome and logistics review with search committee chair*: A 15-minute welcome meeting with the search committee chair to review the schedule for the day and answer any preliminary questions regarding logistics.

- *Interview session with the search committee*: Structured like the first-round interview. Questions were provided approximately two weeks in advance of the interview date.

- *Open session available to all campus and library personnel*: The "job talk" portion of the interview. Several of our open positions were for Research Librarians, so their sessions were designed as a teaching demonstration with a specific prompt provided in advance. The sessions were advertised to the entire campus, with special emphasis on library personnel, liaison departments (if applicable), and potential close collaborators, such as the Academic Success Center and Center for Educational Innovation. The session also included a question-and-answer component.

- *One-on-one meeting with library director*: An opportunity to discuss larger library goals and details of the position (e.g., tenure and promotion).

- *Informal session with select library personnel*: This session was specifically designed to fill in the gaps created by not having meals and other informal encounters during an on-site interview. No library administrators and no search committee members were involved in the session. Instead, it was an opportunity for the candidate to learn more about working at the Air Force Academy and living in Colorado Springs.

- *Brief wrap-up with search committee chair*: A chance to ask remaining questions and discuss next steps.

While four to five hours of video conferencing is not insignificant, the overall time saving from holding the final interviews online is noteworthy for everyone involved. For on-site interviews, finalists often need two to four days of leave from their current position and away from home in order to travel and complete the interview; our finalists needed one day of leave at most, and there was minimal impact on their personal situations as they were not away from home overnight. The campus participants, especially the search committee, also saved a significant amount of time. There were no airport pickups, hotel shuttling, or evening meals. Online meetings make it possible for participants to join from wherever they are working at the moment.

The flexibility offered by having final interviews online also expands participation options. Much like the ability to recruit search committee members from outside institutions, an online final round makes scheduling with the committee much easier. Online open sessions meant that other faculty could join from any online location and come and go as needed without interrupting the presentation. We recorded the open sessions to make them available to library personnel and campus faculty, by request, if they were unable to attend the session live. Remote workers could participate in any portion of the interview. The online open sessions also presented candidates with a chance to demonstrate various technologies and tools that enhance online presentations. For example, most video conferencing software now includes live captioning. When utilized in a live session, this adaptive technology enables attendees with hearing difficulties to engage more fully.

The transition to a fully online final round was not without its compromises. While the online invitations included a link to the Air Force Academy's professionally done online tour, the library was a very small portion of that tour. A custom overview of Clark Special Collections and Archives, with extensive photos and narration, was still not the same as seeing the area in person. And, of course, candidates did not get a chance to see the town in which they would be living if selected for the position. It is possible that these losses could impact our ability to recruit candidates in the future, especially when travel becomes safe and commonplace again, but we hope that the benefits to the candidates—efficiency and transparency—will balance out with those concerns.

FINAL SELECTION

Just as document sharing and forms for centralized data gathering provided significant efficiencies during the initial selection process, they also streamlined the steps required to conclude the selection process. They again eliminated protracted e-mail exchanges, reduced required meetings or phone calls, and increased transparency for all committee members.

In order to gather internal feedback from non-committee members, after each finalist presented their open session to the library and faculty audience, attendees were given the opportunity to provide comments using one of two methods. One was to send an e-mail to the committee e-mail address that was associated with the committee file-sharing platform. This not only sent the message directly to all members' inboxes, but it also automatically created a dedicated subfolder that only held messages to the committee address, making it easy to track and collate responses.

The second option, an online form, was the preferred format for non-committee members to provide feedback. The form, whose direct link was contained in the notification e-mail, was designed with specific prompt questions to direct comments toward candidate attributes we were seeking in our ultimate selectee. The form included a drop-down menu for users to select the finalist by name prior to providing input so that the same questions were asked each time but responses could be easily sorted in the resulting spreadsheet. Much like the e-mail method, individual responses could be sent directly to each search committee member's inbox for review. Similar to the application review form, this data was also centralized into a spreadsheet that could then be downloaded and sorted by the committee chair for search committee members to read through prior to the online meeting to select the top candidate.

The search committee also collected feedback from the professional references for each finalist using an online form. We created separate forms for each candidate after developing a template to confirm the salient questions we wanted to ask of the references. Direct e-mails with an embedded link to the form were sent to the reference contacts provided by the finalists along with a brief explanation regarding the purpose of the e-mail and a return date deadline. One of the advantages of the online form was that it would generate automatic e-mails with the full responses included whenever a form was completed and submitted by a specific reference. These notifications facilitated following up with any late references to ensure the committee received timely feedback prior to the final selection meeting. Again, all the feedback data was consolidated into a spreadsheet and shared with the committee before the final meeting.

The direct written comments from the professional references had the added benefit of eliminating issues often inherent in phone interviews. There was no need for committee members to organize a phone call with each reference, saving committee time. The form was available for references to complete at their convenience before the deadline. Perhaps most importantly, this system did not rely on a committee member to take notes and report back their interpretation of the call to the full committee; instead, each member was able to read the exact response of each reference.

The single drawback to the form was that it was designed with no character limit for responses. Consequently, when these comments were lengthy, the consolidated spreadsheet would become unwieldy and proved hard to follow onscreen. Thus, the individual response e-mails with the responses embedded proved easier to read initially, while the spreadsheet served best to quickly compare ranking questions and identify trends in the consolidated comments. Since the committee members were all receiving responses—both internal and external—as they were submitted and the central spreadsheets collected all the information for organization, the selection meetings went very quickly.

TECHNOLOGY SUMMARY

Technology is constantly changing, though COVID-19 seemed to hasten the pace of technological enhancements and adoption. Further, institutional contracts and restrictions can limit what specific technology tools are available to readers. We expect that these tools, and the features available within them, will continue to evolve well into the future, so we have purposefully avoided listing specific platforms in the chapter so far. At the same time, we recognize that knowing exactly what we used and the functionality needed throughout this process will make it easier for readers to adapt these ideas to their own institution. Therefore, we are providing a summary table (see Table 12.1), which

Table 12.1 Technology Used by the United States Air Force Academy's McDermott Library in 2021 Hiring Actions

Purpose	Software Used	Functionality
Committee scheduling	Doodle	• Time zone adjustment • Consolidated responses
Committee document sharing	SharePoint Site	• File library • Links to online forms • Shared e-mail distribution
Committee meetings	Zoom	• Screen sharing • Video and call-in options • Device agnostic
Application review	Microsoft Forms	• Online access • Answer restrictions (e.g., must be a number between 0 and 10) • Spreadsheet consolidation and download
Candidate scheduling	Doodle	• First come, first served slots • Hidden participants • Time zone adjustment
Candidate interviews and open sessions	Zoom	• Screen sharing • Video and call-in options • Recording capability • Device agnostic
Open session feedback	LibWizard	• Response e-mails to members • Online access • Anonymous • Spreadsheet consolidation and download • Library branding
Professional references	LibWizard	• Response e-mails to members • Online access • Spreadsheet consolidation and download • Library branding

includes more details on the specific technology used throughout the retooling process.

FINAL THOUGHTS

After applying this approach to multiple searches, we believe that our new approach to hiring librarians has worked quite well. Despite concerns that the inability to bring people on-site to the Air Force Academy to provide them with a sense of the working environment, the campus, and the surrounding area might result in a candidate declining an interview invitation or even a job offer, this has not been the case. The distillation of the previous multiday affair to key interactions over a half day with staff, faculty, and the search committee has worked well from multiple perspectives.

The search committee members from outside the library appreciated the ability to house all documents in one shared online document library. These same members have confirmed that the move to online scheduling, forms for scoring against the rubric and reviewing references, and holding all meetings—including the candidate open sessions—remotely have worked to their advantage. These tools saved committee members' time, reduced paper waste, and allowed search committee members to contribute fully despite the ebbs and flows of the pandemic as the positivity rate changed on an almost daily basis. Using an online form to gather professional reference feedback and then making it available on a spreadsheet with side-by-side comparisons is a practice already being adopted by the home department of one of the non-library members. These same positive sentiments regarding the reduced time line for hiring and equitable accessibility regardless of location have been expressed by participants from within the library as well.

As a follow-up, we recently held a meeting with our newer librarians who had been selected through our online interview process. We were interested in hearing about the process from the candidate's perspective and identifying any further improvements we might consider adopting to make the process more inclusive going forward. Overall, they indicated that they were appreciative of our new approach, noting the more equitable and convenient aspects of this process. Of particular note was their appreciation for receiving the interview questions before the semifinalist and finalist rounds. There was little nostalgia over the inability to attend the obligatory "social" meals that were part of the earlier protocol. Instead, the informal meeting held with library personnel who were not on the hiring committee provided a welcome alternative to gain the practical perspectives of relocating to a new campus and community. Although it wasn't the same as a visit on-site that would have occurred as part of the process prior to the pandemic, the various meetings, virtual campus tour, and other slides and documents such as the library's strategic plan, gave them a relatively good sense of the library overall.

Based on the new librarians' suggestions for improvement, we will be adding language that describes best practice for participants to our introductory scripts for virtual open sessions. These will include asking audience members to turn their camera on (if feasible), introduce themselves, and indicate their primary role at the Academy when they ask a question during the question-and-answer portion. As candidates, our new librarians found it disconcerting to be asked a question from a disembodied voice and struggled with the inability to connect the person with their role at the Air Force Academy. We determined that we would also be well served by providing more information on the surrounding area, such as staff-favorite attractions and restaurants, key shopping areas, neighborhoods, and outdoor activities, to finalists. Not only would this provide candidates with a better sense of Colorado Springs, but incorporating staff picks would also give them some insight into the library personnel as potential colleagues.

The Air Force Academy's McDermott Library does not plan on moving back to the pre-COVID-19 legacy practices. Clearly, the impact of the pandemic is broad, having caused many changes to all aspects of academia and beyond. It gave us the ability to overcome the objection "But we've always done it this way" because the established process was impossible to continue. This gave us the chance to reflect on the fundamental goals of the hiring process, reconsider how we could meet those goals, and identify ways to utilize technology to benefit everyone who participated in our searches. We retooled our librarian hiring process from beginning to end, sometimes with small enhancements, other times with drastic new approaches.

Having the proven ability to be agile, creative, and adaptable against unexpected circumstances outside of the library's direct control is a positive outcome. Attracting and hiring the best and the brightest is one of the foundational and necessary pillars of academic libraries in today's fast-moving world, and we have continued to do that with our new system. The ramifications of the COVID-19 pandemic brought about a remarkable test of the flexibility and resourcefulness of academic libraries. The libraries that can leverage forced change to abandon stagnant practices and adopt processes that are efficient, accessible, and equitable will be the same libraries that remain relevant in the future. We plan on making sure the McDermott Library at the United States Air Force Academy is one of them.

Approved for public release: distribution unlimited. PA USAFA-DF-2022-50.

13

The Archive Is Temporarily Closed: Teaching Students Alternative Methods for Finding Archival Materials Online

David Sye

INTRODUCTION

Libraries and archives have always played a crucial role for historians and history students, as they search through materials to find primary sources for their research. In the context of historical research, a primary source refers to a source of information created during the time period studied, such as letters, newspapers, pictures, etc., to name a few. Many college history departments, whether at the undergraduate or graduate level, require students to complete a research project based primarily on primary sources (Jones et al., 2012). To find these sources, students often travel to other locations to visit archives and special collections (Barrett, 2005, p. 329). Overall, it is very common for history students to visit a physical repository to search for sources.

As a result of the COVID-19 pandemic, many archives and museums temporarily closed or otherwise limited in-person access. Even the National Archives and Records Administration (NARA) closed all research rooms nationwide, with limitations easing up in June 2021 (Ferriero, 2021). This posed a challenge for historians and students, impacting how and what they can research. Graduate students at my own institution, Murray State

University, write an extensive research article based on original primary source material as part of their capstone course. As the subject librarian for history, I worked with this cohort and delivered an instruction session that focused on archival research and accessing digital materials during this time.

Near the onset of the pandemic, historians Alan MacEachern and William J. Turkel explained that "historical research is never strictly about accessing everything we need, but about accessing what we can, and stopping when time, resources, and the availability of sources tells us to" (2020, para. 3). With this in mind, it became imperative to focus on finding digitized primary sources when working with history students. This chapter will first examine traditional approaches to teaching archival literacy, then illustrate the challenges posed by the COVID-19 pandemic. After establishing this context, we will explore solutions and the future of using digitized/digital primary sources for research.

RECENT DEVELOPMENT OF ARCHIVAL LITERACY PRACTICES

In recent history, various social, political, and intellectual movements advocate for more inclusive presentations of the past, including "peoples from all backgrounds, the way they lived and worked and played, and what they did and said in their most intimate moments" (Bridges et al., 1993, p. 731). Today, those movements are actualized in resources such as *The Inclusive Historian's Handbook* and the *Interpreting History* book series from the American Association for State and Local History. As researchers strive to present a more inclusive representation of the past, archival materials have expanded to include more than just written documents. This is in addition to an increase of written documents produced. For example, Ritchie (1988, as cited in Bridges et al, 1993) explains that at the time, the number of physical documents the federal government produced every four months is equal to all those produced between the Washington and Wilson presidencies, a 124-year period.

The increase of archival material necessitated a review of archival literacy practices. Based on a 1992 survey conducted by the Joint Committee on Historians and Archivists, a collaboration between the American Historical Association (AHA), the Organization of American Historians (OAH), and the Society of American Archivists (SAA), library/archival specialists were systematically used in training graduate history students 37 percent of the time (Bridges et al., 1993, p. 737). Also, the need for library/archival specialists to be involved in teaching research skills for history was emphasized in 1993, as Bridges et al. (1993) explained that increased interaction between historians and archivists could help history faculty as they work with students on core components of research skills. At the time, graduate history students were not acquiring archival research skills through formal training or archival literacy sessions, but rather through trial and error in the archives. This, of course, creates a very time-consuming experience. Overall, this group agreed that historians and students who know how archival systems work can more efficiently access and use archival collections (Bridges et al., 1993).

In the past decade, there have been several efforts to discuss and codify archival literacy competencies. From the researcher perspective, in 2013, the American Historical Association published *Historical Research in Archives: A Practical Guide*, which offers up ideas for working in modern archives (Redman, 2013). Building on the ideas introduced in 1993, Redman (2013) acknowledges the role technology now plays in the archival research experience and offers guidance on such, including an emphasis on using online finding aids and catalogs to effectively take advantage of a collection's holdings. After testing out keywords associated with the research topic, he suggests assessing if the collection(s) are mainly personal or institutional papers, are centered around a theme or geographic location, and if results lead to a more expansive finding aid or just an item record (Redman, 2013, p. 8).

Morris et al. (2014) highlighted that, at the time, there were no standard identified archival research competencies for college history students. Therefore, they sought to collect information on history faculty expectations that they could use to create a list of archival research competencies. In the end, they created a list of 51 competencies. These competencies are organized into six categories: accurately conceive of primary sources; locate primary sources; use a research question, evidence, and argumentation to advance a thesis; demonstrate acculturation to archives; follow publication protocols; and have advanced skills (Morris et al., 2014, pp. 404–407). The following year, the research team sent out their list of competencies to history faculty, archivists, and librarians at a sampling of 123 universities in order to determine the effectiveness of each competency. There was no consensus on competencies to delete; however, many were moved to the "advanced skills" section, and a note was added that they were not required skills for undergraduate history majors. Many respondents commented on a lack of competencies related to online archival sources, so some were modified accordingly (Weiner et al., 2015).

SAA has two guides relevant to students searching for primary source materials. In *Using Archives: A Guide to Effective Research*, Schmidt (2016) focuses a great deal on the in-person archives experience. She briefly mentions digital collections in the "Finding and Evaluating Archives" section, discussing the convenience and that digitized materials are sometimes fulltext searchable. She also advises to "be aware that digital collections often reflect just a fraction of the total holdings of a repository" and that it can be unclear whether items represent a complete collection or not (Schmidt, 2016, p. 5). In 2018, SAA approved guidelines for primary source literacy that librarians, archivists, and teaching faculty can employ, and they include five sets of learning objectives. One set pertains to finding and accessing primary sources, and these points do address some aspects of research in a digital environment. The guidelines emphasize using effective strategies to locate primary sources, distinguishing between databases and online resources, understanding that certain records may never have existed or may not be collected or accessible, and understanding the policies and procedures that affect accesses to primary sources. (SAA-ACRL/RBMS Joint Task Force, 2018, p. 5).

Overall, the evolution of archival research standards and guidelines do begin to address finding digital and digitized material. In a normal setting, these standards and competencies would develop gradually, as researchers steadily increased their use of digital archives. The COVID-19 pandemic, however, abruptly forced researchers to transition to online and remote research, accelerating the need to seriously consider competencies that singularly focus on and prepare students for digital archive use.

CHALLENGES POSED BY THE PANDEMIC

The need to develop alternate methods for finding archival materials right now stems from the drastic changes brought on by the COVID-19 pandemic. During this time, students were thrust into a learning environment that may or may not have fit their learning needs. At the same time, options to conduct in-person research were limited.

One of the most impactful factors necessitating students to find primary source materials online was the closure and restriction of access to physical repositories during the first year of the COVID-19 pandemic. While we know the National Archives and Records Administration (NARA) shut down its public facilities, it is important to consider how different types of archives across the nation responded as well. Although a study looking at archives and special collections at different types of institutions (academic libraries, public libraries, historical societies, museums, corporations, etc.) was not conducted during 2020, there are multiple national studies we can pull data from that can help paint a picture of how widespread archival closures were. *The State of State Records*, published by the Council of State Archivists (CoSA), included a section on access and engagement for financial year (FY) 2020. As part of the upcoming Association of College and Research Libraries (ACRL) Value of Academic Libraries (VAL) Report, Bullington et al. (2021) share COVID-19 protocol information from academic libraries in the United States and Canada. The 2020 National Visitation Report from the American Association for State and Local History (AASLH) provides information on history museums, historical societies, and other history organizations.

The 2021 CoSA report covered FY2020 and included responses from state archive and records programs in most U.S. states and territories;

responses were not received from California, Delaware, Hawaii, Guam, and the Northern Mariana Islands. Most states have a joint archives and records management program, while others are separate or have only a state archive (CoSA, 2021, p. viii). The survey asked, "Did your facility close to the public due to the COVID-19 pandemic?" Out of 48 responses from state/territorial archives, 42 facilities (87.5 percent) were closed to the public at some point. At the time of the survey (responses seem to have been received in October 2020), 14 facilities remained closed, 26 reopened with restrictions, and 2 had fully reopened. (While the Pennsylvania survey response said it was open with restrictions, a note stated that the State Archives were not open yet and it was just the state records center that reopened.) (CoSA, 2021, pp. C1–C3). This means that researchers in ~83 percent of U.S. states and territories faced reduced access to archival material maintained at state/territorial archives due to the pandemic even toward the end of 2020. Examples of restrictions after reopening include in-person visits by appointment only, reduced research room hours, reduced capacity, and critical-need research only (CoSA, 2021, pp. C1–C3). Data collected each year is compared to previous survey results, administered biennially. Compared to FY2018, the total number of in-person visits to state archives was down from 141,312 to 65,952 visits, a ~53 percent decrease. Remote communications also decreased, with telephone interactions decreasing by ~30 percent and e-mail decreasing by ~40 percent (CoSA, 2021, p. 9).

The VAL committee distributed its survey to various institutions at the start of 2021. Responding libraries answered questions regarding how library services, resources, employees, patrons, and spaces were affected due to the COVID-19 pandemic. Responses came from academic libraries representing 43 U.S. states and six Canadian provinces. Relevant to barriers to historical research, one question asked "Are Special Collections materials accessible?" A total of 217 libraries responded to this question, and 41 percent allowed in-person access via appointment only and 13 percent closed access at some point during the pandemic. In addition, 5 percent of libraries still allowed in-person drop-in visits and 32 percent shifted to online access only. About 9 percent of responses were categorized as "other," which included methods such as material requests where library personnel would scan requested items (Bullington et al., 2021, p. 11). Overall, this shows that while academic libraries made efforts to make their special collections accessible, there were still restrictions students/researchers had to adhere to.

While university special collections and state archives are certainly go-to archives for historical research, students may also visit institutions such as museums and historical societies if they are nearby. For example, during my MA in History studies in Indianapolis, I visited the archives at the Indiana Historical Society to access a collection of letters from a past state governor I was researching. Therefore, AASLH's National Visitation Report can help us look at another group of archives students may use. A total of 968 history institutions responded, with over half (57 percent) representing smaller museums that report an annual budget of less than $250,000 (AASLH, 2021, p. 4). One portion of the survey asked how the pandemic affected their operations and staffing in 2020. On average, they were fully closed for 22.5 weeks and partially closed for another 14 weeks. This means that institutions limited access for approximately 9 months (AASLH, 2021, p. 6). When you consider that institutions began reacting to the pandemic in March, access was restricted during the entirety of the pandemic in 2020.

In discussions with history faculty, students, and other researchers during the 2020 fall semester, we all figured that archives would be closed or limited based on anecdotal stories. As this data comes out, it shows how truly widespread these archival closures were. They were not necessarily a local problem. So, what did students miss out on by not having in-person access to archives? With archives closed, students lost out on direct assistance they could receive from archives and special collections staff. Even with digital collections available online, depending on the ability for employee remote work as well as furloughs or layoffs, students may not have been able to receive assistance. For example, when asked about staff turnover during 2020, ~35 percent of history institutions reported furloughs or layoffs of some kind (AASLH, 2021, p. 7).

Academic libraries, which are a likely stop for history students doing research of any kind, also had limited in-person interactions. Only 36 percent of libraries reported that they allowed reference desk consultations in-person, and only 29 percent offered subject librarian consultation in-person. Over 90 percent, however, offered virtual reference options (Bullington et al., 2021, p. 6). One thing to consider, though, is that because of the rapid shift in mode of services provided, students may not have been aware of them. Therefore, just because libraries and archives were offering virtual reference opportunities does not necessarily mean students were taking advantage of such methods. Additionally, one must consider a degree of hesitancy as students may not be comfortable visiting a library or archive in person.

Although there are many archival materials available online, they only represent a fraction of what is available in physical repositories for students and researchers. Therefore, with widespread closures, relevant primary source material may be missed. While no statistics exist regarding how much of all archival material is digitized, we can look at a large institution that makes information about their collections available to get an idea. Take the Smithsonian Institution, for example, which in addition to museum objects also has a large collection of archival materials and library volumes. Only ~17 percent of its total collection of archival material and ~3 percent of library volumes are digitized (Smithsonian Institution, 2018). The Smithsonian Institution has a large budget and a Digitization Program Office, so when we consider what resources are available in special collections at university libraries or local historical societies, they may have even smaller proportions of their collections available online.

SOLUTIONS TO CHALLENGES

When confronted with the challenge of severe limitation of physical access to archival materials, a common solution is to access materials digitally. While it seems simple enough, this exposes additional challenges. Students are often unprepared to meet the intricacies of digital archives. This can lead them to irrelevant sources, or even cause so much frustration that they give up on their course of research. Therefore, the challenge is how to teach students skills to successfully conduct historical research in an online environment. At the beginning of the 2020 fall semester, my colleague in the history department working with the History MA cohort reached out to me, bringing up this predicament. Noting that students would have to rely extensively on digitized primary sources, I was asked to cover any databases they could use and teach how to assess digital repositories for their research needs.

We scheduled a time for me to deliver an instruction session for the graduate students' research seminar class, and I planned to incorporate digital literacy components into a context of conducting historical research. The session was delivered online via Zoom. One of the benefits of delivering these sessions over such a platform is the ability to share screens easily. While I could easily show examples on my screen, the ability for others to share their screen means that we can use students' examples. It also helps when students are struggling, perhaps navigating a particular online archive in this scenario, and we have the opportunity to all look at their screen and come up with a solution. After the session, I reflected on how well I prepared the students, digging into literature and standards on archival literacy. I also sought to collect information on how these students, as well as upper-level undergraduate students, searched for and used digitized primary sources for their research projects.

Instruction Sessions

Library instruction sessions are a valuable tool for reaching out to students directly to teach them new skills and strategies. Duff and Cherry (2008) studied the impact of archival orientation sessions in undergraduate research. They found that following archival orientation sessions, students' average confidence level in finding archival material increased from 4.1 to 6.0 on a scale of 1 to 10 (Duff & Cherry, 2008, p. 521). Overall, a clear path forward was to teach students skills toward digital archival use via instruction sessions. For them to be effective, it is important to reflect on what works well and what new concepts we need to incorporate into instruction.

After instructing on the use of databases the library subscribes to, such as newspaper collections from ProQuest and our own digital collections, I talked with the students about how to identify other collections that might be relevant for their research. First, we sought to explore what types of institutions collect and digitize materials, which would therefore have a digital archive or repository. I separated institution types by common and unique. Institutions that are very likely to have some sort of collections or archive are college/university libraries, public libraries, museums, historical societies, and government agencies—NARA, Library of Congress, State Archives, Local/County Archives, etc. Other, more unique institutions include professional organizations, religious organizations, hospitals/health systems, and businesses/corporations. Some examples given were the American Library Association (ALA) archives, Archives of the Archdiocese of New York, the Mayo Clinic Archival Collections, and the Ford Motor Company Archives. This mostly aligns with Schmidt (2016), who lists types of archives, although some are lumped under "special collections."

Students may be tempted to type their topic name + "digital collections" into Google to try to find primary sources. While occasionally there might be a topic-specific special collection, that typically will not lead to all collections that might be helpful. With that in mind, I came up with tips and questions to ask that would help students locate digital collections. Materials are sometimes maintained by institutions in the locale the materials were created or represent, so students should ask, "What geographic locations are connected to my research?" This could lead them to special collections at universities and public libraries in a given region. The same thing goes for any organizations associated with a topic, as sometimes organizations will archive their own material or even donate all their materials to a special collection. Another question to ask is, "What key people are connected to my research?" Then, they should think about where they are from and analyze related geographic locations. One recent example is the Joe Biden Senatorial papers collection. While it would make sense if the collection was located in Washington D.C., perhaps at the Library of Congress, the collection is actually housed at the University of Delaware due to his ties to the state.

Once students find a potential collection to use, they will want to be able to quickly see if it contains necessary digital materials to complete their research. Because there is a vast amount of archival material on the Internet now, it is important to have strategies to efficiently *test* a digital collection. One method I taught my students, which aligns with AHA's guide for research in the archives (Redman, 2013), is to type key terms related to the topic or research question into the archive's search system and see what comes up. Students will want to look for "names, places, ideas, and keywords" associated with their research (Redman, 2013, p. 7). Additionally, students should be aware of certain pieces of information that specific aspects of the search system can tell them. This includes looking at things such as resource type and date range filters. For example, if the collection does not have a category for the types of materials needed, or the dates are outside what you are looking for, it is a sign to pass up the collection.

The initial instruction session for the graduate student cohort was well received. Students seemed more comfortable seeking primary sources in an online environment than before the session. Most of what I taught was rooted in some previous literature and guidelines. As the use of digital materials in history research will continue to increase, however, it is important to consider if there needs to be a more specified look at using digital archives. As the SAA and AHA both have guides on how to use archives, mainly focusing on physical archives, it may be worth a look to establish standards or guidelines specifically for digital archives as we learn from the pandemic.

Digital Archival Literacy

Helle Strandgaard Jensen (2020) coined the term "digital archival literacy," which combines critically thinking about digital archives with the skills involved in utilizing them. Jensen argues that "the shift from analogue to digital archives is a shift in medium which establishes a new set of logics for the production, content, distribution and uses of archives" (Jensen, 2020, p. 2). Incorporating such concepts into effective archival instruction will not only reinforce the skills needed to navigate digital archives but also allow them to analyze and assess such an environment as the need for finding archival materials online grows.

Jensen (2020) breaks down this framework into the following topics: understanding archives, the archive as medium, when digitization becomes popularization, the economy of digital archives, questioning systems design, and responsible users. These are presented as a "framework for supporting a professional reflection on the 'everyday use' of digital archives and the powerful forces that shape online content and availability" (Jensen, 2020, p. 2). So how do we go from professional reflection to teachable concepts? When discussing digital archival literacy in an instructional capacity, there are four conceptual areas that can be emphasized: availability of sources, bias in representation, aspects of the search system, and responsible usership. In this section, I will summarize the main ideas of these areas, then suggest supplemental instructional activities. Further discussion of the framework for professional reflection and teachable concepts can be found in Jensen (2020) and Sye (2022).

Summary of Components

With regards to availability of sources, students need to consider and acknowledge how digital repositories differ from their physical counterparts.

In a physical archive, most materials owned by the archive are accessible after the initial accession process. Materials may exist, but the digitization process is separate. For example, let us revisit the digitization of the Smithsonian Collections. Out of its total 163,000 cubic feet of archival material, only 62 percent are even prioritized for "digital image creation." Out of the prioritized collections, only 28 percent have been digitized (Digitization, 2018). This goes hand in hand with bias in representation of materials online. Digitization, most importantly the selection process, is a human element. Therefore, the availability of sources is subject to a level of bias. Popularity and usage statistics often drive digitization in addition to pressure /demand from any stakeholders (Jensen, 2020). Depending on the archive, stakeholders may include entities such as governing boards, donors, institutional alumni, staff, and community members.

Most digital archives feature a search system, allowing users to enter terms to find relevant materials. Not only should students be exposed to different components of search systems, but just like bias in representation, they also need to be aware of the human processes that go into establishing subject categories, search fields, and adding metadata to records. Students need to consider multiple ways relevant materials may be described in an online environment. Additionally, we must teach students to be responsible users of digital archives. Jensen (2020) states, "if historians . . . want to make their (scholarly) interests matter in the creation of new digital archives, they have to become users who are actively engaged in the discussion about digital archives" (p. 11). This refers to the archival labor involved in making materials available online. So, when using digitized materials, students and researchers should properly credit or reference the repository. A simple way of accomplishing this is to accurately cite digitized sources, including proper URLs and other relevant information.

Instructional Activities

To supplement discussing digital archival literacy with students, I provide examples of questions/exercises that challenge them to think about these concepts. The following questions and exercises could be addressed either as one complete assignment or broken up into individual sections. In addition to supplementing digital archival literacy, these questions also reinforce effective research planning skills.

- General Plan for Research
  - Develop a research question or a narrowed research topic.
  - What types of materials can help me answer my question?
  - When would these materials have been created? Who would have created these materials?

- Digital Availability and Representation
  - Reflect: What materials can I expect to find, or not find, online?
- Locating a Repository
  - What geographic locations are connected to my research?
  - What organizations are connected to my research?
  - What key people are connected to my research? Where are they from/who are they associated with?
- Test a Collection
  - Identify a digital archive or collection that is relevant to your research question/topic. Is there a finding aid or any information about the scope of the collection?
  - What dates are included?
  - What different search fields are available in the search system?
  - What material type filters are available in the search box or results page?
  - What subject categories are available in the search box or results page?
  - Find a source that will be helpful for your research. What subject categories, tags, or other metadata can be used to identify other relevant materials?
  - Do the contents of the digital collections suggest that there may be additional relevant materials not digitized? Explain.
- Responsible Usership
  - Find a source that will be helpful for your research.
  - Provide an accurate bibliographic citation for the source. (Make sure it reflects the fact it was found in a digital collection.)
  - Examine the digital collection and archival institution. Is there any information about their digitization process?

These questions are merely suggestions for students to reflect on when approaching online historical research. As history students become more dependent on finding primary sources online, librarians, archivists, and history faculty may come up with additional or modified questions to reinforce digital archival literacy.

LOOKING TOWARD THE FUTURE

The COVID-19 pandemic certainly accelerated digitization and usage of digital archives, and this trend will continue even after such a limiting situation. In addition to facilitating effective historical research in a traditional capacity, teaching students how to effectively use digital archives will prepare them for other research activities. This involves the use of born-digital materials as historical artifacts; increased opportunities for comparative historical research (as materials from different parts of the world become more accessible without having to expend large amounts of time and money to use them); and applications for digital humanities.

As society shifts to digital methods of creating and sharing information, historians and other researchers will have to rely on born-digital sources. These sources have no analog counterpart, meaning that researchers can only access them through the use of a digital archive/repository. I often like to share a comparison of U.S. Presidential Libraries administered by NARA. Let us look at the Dwight D. Eisenhower Presidential Library, which is a physical building located in Abilene, Kansas. The library and museum contain materials related to Eisenhower's military service and presidency. These materials originated in physical form and are mainly stored on-site, though archivists have digitized some of the most popular items (National Archives and Records Administration [NARA], 2021a, 2021b). Now take a look at the Barack Obama Presidential Library, which is planned to be the first fully digital presidential library. When you think of presidential papers from someone like Eisenhower or even George Washington, one envisions things like written letters or documents, either by hand or by typewriter. In the modern age, presidential "documents" originate as things such as e-mails, tweets, and PDF files. NARA (n.d.) estimates that 95 percent of the records of the Obama administration were born-digital. While digital preservation is beyond the scope of the chapter, due to born-digital materials' nature of existing in a digital format, searching for such sources in historical research will require a similar skill set to finding digitized archival material.

While the world will never get close to digitizing everything, it is clear that archival material is becoming increasingly accessible online. Researchers, specifically college students, have typically been limited by not having the time or resources to travel to archives. Online material allows them to overcome these obstacles. There is also a potential for increased comparative history research, as they will not have to travel to different corners of the world to find primary source materials for research. Another avenue for research is digital humanities (DH). Many tools and DH methods require material to exist in a digital form. Even for something as simple as building a digital exhibit, it is useful to know how to find digitized materials so they can be easily incorporated and displayed. With other activities such as digital text analysis becoming more popular, students need to be able to effectively find digital materials.

Overall, to meet current and future research needs, librarians, archivists, and history faculty need to focus on teaching new methods for finding archival materials that emphasize navigating an online environment. As libraries and archives pivot to online services and digital collections, students must be able to utilize them effectively.

REFERENCES

AASLH (American Association for State and Local History). (2021). History organizations in a year of disruption: A national visitation report. http://download.aaslh.org/Research/2021+National+Visitation+Report.pdf

Barrett, A. (2005). The information-seeking habits of graduate student researchers in the humanities. *The Journal of Academic Librarianship, 31*(4), 324–331. https://doi.org/10.1016/j.acalib.2005.04.005

Bridges, E., Hunter, G. S., Miller, P. P., Thelen, D., & Weinberg, G. (1993). Toward better documenting and interpreting of the past: What history graduate programs in the twenty-first century should teach about archival practices. *The American Archivist, 56*(4), 730–749. https://doi.org/10.17723/aarc.56.4.p42334g65g366866

Bullington, J., Farne, S., Gersch, B., Murphy, J. A., Sanford, L., & Zaugg, H. (2021). COVID-19 protocols in academic libraries in Canada and the United States. *ACRL VAL Report.* https://lawdigitalcommons.bc.edu/lsfp/1340/

CoSA (Council of State Archivists). (2021). The state of state records: A statistical report on state archives and records management programs in the United States. https://www.statearchivists.org/HigherLogic/System/DownloadDocumentFile.ashx?DocumentFileKey=e6efd7ac-7b02-f372-b4bb-6744db0ab09c

Duff, W. M., & Cherry, J. M. (2008). Archival orientation for undergraduate students: An exploratory study of impact. *The American Archivist*, 499–529. https://www.jstor.org/stable/40294528

Ferriero, D. S. (2021, May 24). An update for researchers from the archivist [Blog Post]. *National Archives News.* https://www.archives.gov/news/message-from-archivist-to-researchers-05-24-2021

Jensen, H. S. (2020). Digital archival literacy for (all) historians. *Media History.* https://doi.org/10.1080/13688804.2020.1779047

Jones, K. W., Barrow, M. V., Stephens, R. P., & O'Hara, S. (2012). Romancing the capstone: National trends, local practice, and student motivation in the history curriculum. *The Journal of American History, 98*(4), 1095–1113. https://doi.org/10.1093/jahist/jar538

MacEachern, A., & Turkel, W. J. (2020, March 31). A time for research distancing [Blog Post]. *Active History.* http://activehistory.ca/2020/03/a-time-for-research-distancing/

Morris, S., Mykytiuk, L. J., & Weiner, S. A. (2014). Archival literacy for history students: Identifying faculty expectations of archival research skills. *The American Archivist, 77*(2), 394–424. https://doi.org/10.17723/aarc.77.2.j270637g8q11p460

NARA (National Archives and Records Administration). (n.d.). About the library. *Barack Obama Presidential Library.* Retrieved from https://www.obamalibrary.gov/about-us

NARA (National Archives and Records Administration). (2021a, July 12). About us. *Dwight D. Eisenhower Presidential Library, Museum & Boyhood Home.* Retrieved from https://www.eisenhowerlibrary.gov/about-us (Accessed December 16, 2021)

NARA (National Archives and Records Administration). (2021b, July 19). Online documents. *Dwight D. Eisenhower Presidential Library, Museum & Boyhood Home.* Retrieved from https://www.eisenhowerlibrary.gov/research/online-documents

Redman, S. J. (2013). Historical research in archives: A practical guide. *American Historical Association.*

SAA-ACRL/RBMS Joint Task Force on the Development of Guidelines for Primary Source Literacy. (2018). Guidelines for primary source literacy. *Society of American Archivists.* https://www2.archivists.org/sites/all/files/Guidelines ForPrimarySourceLiteracy-June2018.pdf

Schmidt, L. (2016, March 26). Using archives: A guide to effective research. *Society of American Archivists.* https://www2.archivists.org/usingarchives

Smithsonian Institution. (2018, September 1). Digitization of Smithsonian collections. Retrieved from https://www.si.edu/newsdesk/factsheets/digitization-smithsonian -collections

Sye, D. (2022). Innovating digital literacy for history students during COVID-19 and beyond. *Journal of New Librarianship*, 7(1), 10–16. https://doi.org/10.33011 /newlibs/11/2

Weiner, S. A., Morris, S., & Mykytiuk, L. J. (2015). Archival literacy competencies for undergraduate history majors. *The American Archivist*, 78(1), 154–180.

14

The Impact of the COVID-19 Pandemic on Hiring and Onboarding in Academic Libraries

Roslyn Grandy, Lauren M. Fletcher, Faythe Thurman,
Rachel Whitney, and Kimberly MacKenzie

INTRODUCTION

The COVID-19 pandemic has forced academic libraries to navigate myriad changes in all facets of day-to-day operations. At the beginning of the pandemic, libraries sought first to pivot resource offerings and maintain the levels of service they are accustomed to providing their constituents in accordance with quarantine and physical distancing measures. As the pandemic progressed, it became clear that they would also need to make significant changes to their internal processes and staff interactions (Alexander, 2021). One area of academic library work that has been impacted by the upheaval of the pandemic is the hiring and onboarding of new employees.

Librarians are accustomed to being flexible and doing more with less. These skills make them "uniquely equipped to adapt to the altered job landscape and to make the best of it" (Zulkey, 2021, para. 31). As academic libraries have had time to adjust to the ever-changing "new normal," information about the academic employment landscape has been shared and commiserated over by employers and job seekers alike, which is how the authors of this chapter came to know one another. This chapter combines the anecdotal experiences of five authors who started new academic library jobs in 2020–2021 with published and gray literature on best practices for hiring and onboarding during a pandemic.

THE IMPACT OF THE COVID-19 PANDEMIC ON THE ACADEMIC LIBRARY JOB LANDSCAPE

The emergence of COVID-19 in the United States in March 2020 created a period of uncertainty surrounding hiring that changed by the minute. Many academic libraries initially postponed scheduled interviews for open positions with the hope that they would be able to return to business as usual soon. In the following months, hiring freezes were implemented by some administrations. Other institutions waited with bated breath to see how virtual learning, economic relief packages, and general pandemic anxiety would influence admission numbers and, in turn, budgets. A fortunate few continued with job searches without interruption. During this period, private undergraduate institutions were more likely to be protected from budget cuts compared to their public counterparts (Frederick & Wolff-Eisenberg, 2020).

The American Library Association's (ALA) JobLIST noticed a significant drop in postings in March, and those levels remained throughout the summer. Of note, "entry-level and mid-level positions contracted the most" (Ford, 2021, para. 6). This situation was particularly difficult for graduates and prospective graduates who need entry-level positions. One library and information science (LIS) program saw their job placement rate decrease from 80 percent in 2019 to 60 percent in 2020 (Ford, 2021). Toward the end of the summer, the job market started to recover, as indicated by a slow but consistent rise in job postings to the ALA JobLIST (Association of College and Research Libraries [ACRL], 2020). In this difficult job market, LIS graduates have needed to adapt, and some have even pursued opportunities outside of the field instead of waiting for a full recovery at some unknown point in the future (Ford, 2021). The academic library job market has certainly improved but may never return to pre-pandemic levels. Sharing experiences, innovations, and new best practices will help both job seekers and employers have success moving forward.

INTERVIEWING: CANDIDATE LESSONS AND RECOMMENDATIONS

Traditionally, the hiring process for academic library positions involved up to a dozen first-round screening interviews, which typically lasted a half hour and were conducted via phone or web conferencing software. The final round of interviews usually involved two to four candidates at an on-campus all-day or multiday interview. These interviews may include several components, such as presentations, tours, meals, and meetings with the search committee, university leadership, library leadership, human resources, and potential colleagues. Prior to the pandemic, virtual methods were used often in screening interviews but were not the standard for academic library final-round interviews (Hodge, 2019). Because of social distancing requirements, travel and quarantine restrictions, and other factors, many libraries transitioned to virtual formats for the final interview, though this was not the case for every library.

One result of the virtual environment was that average interview duration was shortened. Among the five authors, we participated in seven final-round interviews from March 2020 to December 2021. Of these, five were completely virtual, one was hybrid, and one was in-person. The average duration of our final-round interviews was 6.1 hours. A 2015 study reported that the average length of final-round academic library interviews at the time was 10.2 hours spread across multiple days (Reed et al., 2015). This study also revealed that applicants reported an average of 3.15 months from the time they submitted a job application to the time they accepted the position (Reed et al., 2015). Our average time from application to offer or rejection was 4.5 months. This above-average length of the interview cycle reflects the uncertainty and delays caused by the pandemic in relation to hiring new employees.

Virtual interviews have both advantages and disadvantages. They require less time and travel on the part of the candidate, but they make it difficult for the candidate to pick up on nonverbal cues of interviewers or experience the campus or location the way that the in-person format allows. Making it through a day of video meetings also requires the development of a different set of skills and type of stamina. Candidates need access to a quiet room with a stable Internet connection. They are also susceptible to video conferencing fatigue from staring at a computer screen for a significant amount of time.

Technology skills are even more essential now, as those who do not demonstrate a strong command of video conferencing tools will be at a distinct disadvantage. In the library world, this is especially true; a candidate who is late for an interview because they had difficulty joining the virtual meeting does not inspire confidence for a role that often requires assisting patrons with technology issues (Zulkey, 2021). Interviewees should make it a point to check and practice with the needed technology before the interview and to sign in to each interview meeting early, as well as develop a backup plan in case of problems, such as bad connectivity or power outages (Chan Zuckerberg Initiative, 2021; Laker et al., 2021; Landry, 2018). Having the meeting application on more than one device, if possible (i.e., a laptop and a smartphone), is preferable, as one author experienced firsthand:

> During one virtual interview, my landlord happened to be doing electrical work, so the internet went out. I had to go outside to get cellular service and finish the interview on my phone using mobile data. I was so glad that I had downloaded the Zoom app in advance so that I could transition fairly easily.

For those who take part in virtual interviews, the "soft skills" are what may make or break their success (Williams, 2019). Virtual soft skills are somewhat different than those employed at an in-person interview (Landry,

2018). For the virtual interview, a candidate's on-screen appearance and presentation is key. If the interviewee wants to make a good impression, they should experiment with different webcam placements and angles. It is recommended to find a neutral, uncluttered area, with clear walls or perhaps a few pictures (Chan Zuckerberg Initiative, 2021; Laker et al., 2021). Candidates should make sure that the area is well-lit and that their faces can be clearly seen without shadow or backlighting (Landry, 2018; Zulkey, 2021).

Professional dress despite being at home is also important. Dressing up for an interview can help project confidence, and even improve a feeling of self-confidence (Landry, 2018; Zulkey, 2021). Because it can be harder to read body language through an online platform, the candidate may not know how their message is being received (Levine, 2021). This is especially true during a presentation, when only some of the audience's screens are visible or when their video is turned off. To make a connection with the audience, it is important to look directly into the camera, to simulate eye contact, and to reduce potential distractions (Kay, 2021; Laker et al., 2021). Candidates should take their time answering questions and not hesitate to ask for clarification as the virtual environment can lead to misunderstandings (American Association of Law Libraries [AALL], 2021). As the pandemic continues, it is important for job candidates to become comfortable presenting virtually. They can maximize their chances for success by taking the time to test technology tools and create the best on-screen presence possible.

Best Interview Practices for Candidates

- Test technology well in advance
- Ask about needed accommodations
- Have a backup plan in case of technology failure
- Choose a spot with a clear background
- Check the lighting; avoid sitting in shadows
- Dress as if the interview were in-person
- Log in a few minutes early for every meeting
- Look directly at the camera
- Have your CV or résumé easily accessible
- Do not hesitate to ask for a question to be repeated
- Use your breaks to move away from the computer screen

INTERVIEWING: EMPLOYER LESSONS AND RECOMMENDATIONS

Filling open positions during a pandemic has required search committees for academic library positions to modify their processes. For in-person or hybrid interviews, clear guidance about masking, physical distancing, and the logistics of eating and breaks needs to be given in advance of the interview. With myriad web conferencing and communication tools now available, it is imperative that the search committee decide on the platforms that they will use internally as well as with candidates during virtual interviews. One hiring manager felt that scheduling virtual interviews was easier than in-person due to the lack of travel and the need to "book" meeting space (Kay, 2021). The search committee should send out the schedule and all meeting links ahead of time and correspond with the applicant to ensure a working knowledge of the chosen platform (AALL, 2021). One university offered candidates detailed instructions on how to fully utilize their video conferencing software in terms of screen sharing and using polling tools to collect audience feedback (Rogers-Collins, 2020). If any candidate meetings will be recorded, the search committee should let them know in advance that their application materials and recorded presentations will be shared with involved parties and how long the materials will be kept by the institution.

Prior to the interview, the search committee should offer the candidate a chance to test connectivity and audiovisual settings. For those candidates with limited Internet access, the search committee needs to be understanding and work with the candidate to find solutions that work for all parties involved. The University of Leeds offered all candidates a no-questions-asked second chance if they were unable to attend their scheduled virtual interview (Kay, 2021). During the interview, it is suggested that committee members follow general virtual meeting best practices: mute cell phones, limit distractions, be aware of background noise and sound quality, reduce background clutter, and mute yourself when not speaking (AALL, 2021).

Because building rapport is difficult in the virtual environment, several institutions implemented novel techniques such as icebreaker sessions to ease the stress of the interview process (Jewkes et al., 2021; Zulkey, 2021). Gretchen Corsillo, director of the Rutherford Public Library (NJ) stated, "It's okay to acknowledge that everyone is feeling very stressed and it's taking a toll on everyone's mental health. It'd be helpful [for interviewees to know] that they'd be working in a compassionate environment and they're not going to be left to fend for themselves" (Zulkey, 2021, para. 29). Building in breaks for both the applicant and search committee members gives all those involved time to regroup and take a breath (Wros, 2021; Zulkey, 2021).

Another pandemic-era strategy employed by an institution needing to fill multiple positions at once was a pre-interview informational webinar. The webinar provided interested applicants information regarding the position and the institution and left time for a Q&A session. The session was recorded and made publicly available (Jewkes et al., 2021). This novel technique allows candidates to get a better sense of who the potential employer is or to withdraw from the search if the information they hear in the session is not in line with what they are seeking in their next position. For the employer, this eliminates the need to go over basic information in later stages so that the search committee can spend interview time determining if the candidate is a good fit for the position. Another helpful innovation included a virtual walk-through of the library and workspace. This allowed the applicant to "see" the library and ask the search committee or hiring manager questions about the space or culture in real time (Wros, 2021). One author appreciated having this as part of the interview process, saying, "Work is where I spend a lot of my life. I would not have been able to accept the position without seeing the setup of the library as well as the staff area."

In their presentation on the humane job search, Kraus and Baum (2021) emphasized the use of a rubric or matrix for scoring each candidate to ensure a fair and uniform assessment. Additionally, they suggested that after each interview or cycle of the search, committee members assess candidates independently before meeting as a full committee (Kraus & Baum, 2021). One search committee member noticed no difference between candidates who interviewed virtually versus in-person during the pandemic, commenting, "I personally felt like I got just as good of a sense of the video candidates as the in-person candidates, and I wasn't supposed to be evaluating them on anything other than the content of their answers anyway" (Library Think Tank, 2021). Arch and Gilman (2021) discourage searching for candidates who "fit" the library's organizational culture, as evaluating candidates using metrics that have nothing to do with a candidate's ability to perform the job introduces bias into the hiring process. Standardizing interview questions and processes helps lower the chance of implicit bias from the search committee and ensures that candidates are evaluated equally.

As candidates often meet with institutional staff who are not on the search committee, standards of behavior and technology norms should be agreed upon prior to the interview. Ultimately, the search committee and other parties a candidate meets with throughout the process should strive to make the applicant feel comfortable with the technology, people, and environment; acknowledge their feelings and basic necessities; and show empathy and kindness, as this fosters a healthy start to relationships with future colleagues (Kay, 2021; Zulkey, 2021; Rogers-Collin, 2020; Kraus & Baum, 2021).

Best Interview Practices for Employers

- Send links and agenda ahead of time
- Take time to test connectivity and links
- Provide basic instructions for preferred video conferencing platform
- Make eye contact and smile

- Start the interview with an icebreaker
- Employ video conferencing best practices
- Be attentive and limit distractions
- Replicate aspects of in-person interviews, such as building rapport and showing the workspace
- Be empathic and understanding
- Ensure you are being equitable and fair to all candidates

ONBOARDING: EMPLOYER AND EMPLOYEE RECOMMENDATIONS

Onboarding is a pivotal time during which employees are introduced to the institution's culture, processes, and their colleagues. Onboarding during a pandemic creates unique challenges. One librarian noted that training a new employee to conduct expert-level searches of medical literature virtually was much more difficult than hiring the employee virtually (Harnegie, 2021). It is vital that virtual onboarding addresses different learning styles and that employees become well-versed in all technologies needed to fulfill their responsibilities (Alexander, 2021). The transition to a virtual onboarding process requires supervisors to adapt their existing training materials. Information that was previously acquired by going next door to ask a colleague now needs to be explicitly documented. A comprehensive onboarding handbook detailing both remote and in-person work practices should be made available online (Smith, 2020). Identifying point people for new employees to reach out to for different needs is important (Alexander, 2021). Virtual onboarding also includes ensuring employees have received all equipment needed to work from home in advance of their start date, including laptops, webcams, and monitors, as well as instructions on how to set up the technology (Dill, 2020).

Dill and Nutefall (2021) gave advice for those starting new supervisory roles:

> Be authentic, especially right now. Authentic leadership allows full expression of oneself, including sharing some of your life/interests outside of work [to foster] trust and openness. Being open about potential struggles (finding housing, doctors, etc.) can help build strong connections. (p. 238)

They also encourage asking new colleagues the following questions: "What three words would you use to describe the campus culture? What's the one unwritten thing, something that everyone knows after they've worked here for a while?" (Dill & Nutefall, 2021, p. 237). Answers to these questions provided valuable insights into the history and daily operation of the institution. Some employees spoke to the importance of celebrating your first day as you might in person, with rituals such as wearing a special outfit or taking a photo or video conference screenshot (Dill, 2020). Other advice given to new hires is to communicate early and often, engage in scheduled reflected practice, seek regular feedback on progress, schedule consistent meetings with colleagues, and remember to pace yourself and take breaks (Carlos & Muralles, 2021; Cruz, 2021).

Many people who began new roles virtually during the pandemic reported a sense of loneliness and isolation (Carlos & Muralles, 2021; Dill, 2020; Levine, 2021; Smith, 2021). Assigning a mentor to a new employee provides them with someone they feel comfortable asking a variety of questions and allows them to have a starting point for building connections among their new team members. It is important to find creative ways to build formal and informal connections, including touch-base meetings, virtual coffees, and happy hours (Cruz, 2021). Replicating the small interactions that would occur in person fosters a supportive work environment. At one author's institution, the hiring of a new librarian prompted the scheduling of meet-and-greets with the library staff, as well as biweekly watercooler sessions to facilitate bonding among team members. In addition to these watercooler sessions, several crafting lunch sessions were scheduled and held via Teams. These sessions allowed people to pop in and out and work creatively on a project, share something they have been working on, and build morale and interdepartmental connections.

Several new employees have joined UConn Library during the pandemic. This prompted two librarians to implement a program called Coffee Connections (Lim & Cowan, 2021). Any library employee can fill out a form that asks whether they would like to strengthen a connection with someone they already know or create a new connection with a colleague they do not know well. Participants have the option to select whom they would like to be connected with or to be randomly assigned someone. To facilitate easier discussion during these conversations, multiple copies of a team-building card game called Building Blocks were made available to participants. They also received an e-mail with conversation prompts and icebreakers. Nearly half of the library staff have participated in the program so far and reported that the program helped to remove awkward communication barriers and sparked collaborations that would not have otherwise happened. While building trust and communication among teams is not a new concept, the pandemic environment requires novel strategies as colleagues are often not together at the same location. A structured program that makes forging these connections less intimidating is a valuable tool when onboarding new employees.

Onboarding Best Practices

- Employers:
  - Communicate early and more often than in person
  - Create a detailed virtual onboarding guide

- ○ Assign a mentor to work with a new hire
- ○ Identify a point person for different topics
- ○ Create opportunities for socialization of new hires
- Employees:
  - ○ Get creative with ideas to build connections outside of work meetings
  - ○ Commemorate your first day or other milestones
  - ○ Make time for breaks and step away from the computer
  - ○ Seek feedback regularly

DIVERSITY, EQUITY, AND INCLUSION CONSIDERATIONS

The pandemic environment has shone a light on several issues regarding diversity, equity, and inclusion in hiring processes and the labor market. The presence of systemic racism in the United States has become more salient since March 2020. In the early days of the pandemic, anti-Asian sentiments and violence fueled by ignorance became rampant (Tavernise & Oppel, 2020). One author interviewed at an institution in a large metropolitan area just as COVID-19 was becoming more prevalent in the United States. They were told by the hiring manager to avoid moving to a certain area of the city due to "the Chinese and the coronavirus." The author did not accept a second interview invitation after hearing this concerning comment in the first interview. The rates of infection and COVID-related deaths were consistently higher among Black and Hispanic populations compared to whites (Greenhouse, 2020). This physical toll was compounded by the mental weight of the murders of Breonna Taylor and George Floyd and the ensuing Black Lives Matter protests and counter-protests. One librarian commented on how these events affected her onboarding processes at a new job:

> To begin with, I expected some anxiety and other emotional labor in the process of my acculturation in my new institution . . . the fear of not being enough, not accomplishing enough, or fears of not meeting the expectations of peers or the community can be very isolating. I had/have all of these fears and starting my new job during this coronavirus pandemic, during Black Lives Matter protests, during a point in our society where we need to stand for what is right ever more fiercely, adds a whole other set of additional fears of working in a public institution where its mission is to provide equitable access to information. (Carlos & Muralles, 2021, p. 5)

Black, Indigenous, and people of color (BIPOC) are still dealing with various effects of the pandemic, and hiring managers need to take this into account at all stages of the hiring process, whether that involves humane interviewing procedures, sensitivity training for search committee members, or increased empathy and reassurance during onboarding.

Lockdowns and remote work have also highlighted the difficulties women have faced during the pandemic. Many women were forced to leave their jobs or cut back hours due to childcare, remote schooling, and elder care responsibilities. There were 1.4 million fewer women in the labor force in 2021 versus 2019 (Kamal, 2022). There is also evidence that women are shouldering more of the burden of simultaneously juggling work and home responsibilities. Women working from home during the pandemic are interrupted more frequently than men, both by colleagues and family members (Hall, 2021). Three university employees "expressed feelings of inadequacy and, at times, anguish over how our professional and maternal roles are being compromised in different, painful ways" (Couch et al., 2021, p. 269). There is a need for hiring committees to avoid judging candidates if family obligations interrupt a virtual interview or result in an interview being rescheduled. Supervisors should also check in regularly with new employees with dependents to ensure that their work-from-home arrangements are as functional as possible while their home situation may be in flux.

The pandemic has highlighted socioeconomic and technological disparities among job applicants. Millions of Americans in rural areas still do not have reliable broadband access due to a limited presence of telecommunication companies in their communities (Janse et al., 2021). While virtual interviewing may make job hunting easier for those with family responsibilities or disabilities, its requirements favor those who have both the financial means to purchase technological devices and maintain stable Internet connections as well as the skills and infrastructure to use those devices (Zulkey, 2021). Some public libraries are addressing this need by offering virtual interview spaces "designed to offer the public access to the hardware, software, and bandwidth needed for success" (Sauers, 2021). Internet access is essential for a successful academic library interview, so search committees should be understanding of outages that are beyond the candidate's control.

A positive effect of pandemic-induced changes to the labor market is the opportunity to recruit candidates from not only all ethnic and racial backgrounds but from varied locations as well. One university employee hopes that "jobs advertised in major metropolitan cities, which have previously assumed you must be physically present to do the work, become more open to regional and rural applicants" (Couch et al., 2021, p. 273). Whether just the interview process or the long-term job is completely remote, institutions should strive to advertise jobs not only on national job lists but also through local associations and listservs to ensure representation from rural as well as urban and suburban candidates.

THE FUTURE OF HIRING IN ACADEMIC LIBRARIES

The COVID-19 pandemic has greatly impacted various facets of hiring and onboarding in academic libraries. The long-term effects of the pandemic on these processes are yet to be seen, but several changes and predictions have already emerged. Some job descriptions now include phrases that allude to candidates' ability to be nimble with work modalities. As pandemic waves continue to impact our ability to provide in-person services, many institutions are reluctant to explicitly list work arrangements in job descriptions but will include phrases such as "flexible hybrid work schedule possible" (West Virginia University, 2021) and "demonstrated ability to work well independently and collaboratively with others in a rapidly changing environment, including remotely when required" (Western Kentucky University, 2021). The expectation that candidates can adjust quickly and stay flexible is likely to persist post-pandemic.

Many academic libraries are examining their interviewing processes to make them more thorough, inclusive, and efficient. The structure and work of search committees will likely depend on the persistence of work-from-home arrangements. One librarian found her unit communicated more via Teams compared to their on-site, pre-pandemic level of communication (Howes et al., 2021). A study conducted by Microsoft found that remote work improved existing connections among coworkers but made sharing new information and making new connections more difficult (Jones, 2021). Academic libraries may want to provide hybrid meeting spaces for search committees as well as clear communication about processes and where application materials will be stored. Despite challenges presented by working in a virtual environment, most library professionals predict that virtual interviews at multiple stages are here to stay (Hardenbrook, 2021; Khodarahmi & Gregory, 2021; Sauers, 2021; Zulkey, 2021).

There is debate in the field about the necessity and duration of in-person interviews. On August 6, 2021, a group member posted anonymously about the future of library job interviews on Library Think Tank, a public Facebook group with 47,700+ members. A lively discussion ensued about the perceived need for in-person interviews now that the field has pivoted to virtual hiring practices. Advantages of in-person over virtual interviews mentioned were the chance to pick up on body language cues, to have candid interactions with staff, to see the workspace, and to experience the campus or location. Specifically, the dicussion on Library Think Tank included comments such as the following:

The candidate is interviewing us as much as we are interviewing them, and they should really see what it's like.

I think personally I would want to see the place I'd be working in person, get the vibe of the city it's in, and meet my potential coworkers. I'd feel very uncomfortable going into a job where I'd never really experienced any of those things.

We live in an area that not everyone wants to live in and would never hire someone who hasn't actually visited here.

Other respondents discussed how long in-person interviews pose several barriers that could keep potential candidates from applying. Disadvantages of in-person interviews brought up include the time off work and possible expenses incurred, child and elder care concerns, and difficulties that populations such as international candidates, people with disabilities, and the LGBTQ+ community face when traveling, as mentioned in these specific comments in the Library Think Tank (2021) discussion:

> It is climate change poison, it's high cost, it's running by childcare tabs and drycleaning bills and it is disrepsect [sic] for applicants time and effort.

> Honestly the whole having to travel for interviews always felt so gross and classist to me. Just say you don't want poor people who can't get time off work or single parents and move on.

There was no consensus among respondents on which interview format was preferred. Some feel they present better in person and would avoid virtual interviews at all costs. Others pointed out that many large public institutions have moved to completely virtual interviews, and they expect this to become the norm going forward. There is a general expectation that if an employer wants to interview the candidates in person, the employer should cover the costs of the trip. Another common thread that emerged from this conversation is the idea that candidates should feel empowered to ask for interview format accommodations. Pre-pandemic, most institutions would not have considered candidate preference when establishing the interview format. Offering more flexibility in this area will allow academic libraries to recruit a more diverse applicant pool.

The authors also had differing opinions about whether virtual interviews provide sufficient information for candidates to accept a new job and move to a new location. One author described how this particular issue impacted their experience as follows:

> All rounds of my interview were 100% virtual. I knew that, if offered the job, I would want to visit campus and the surrounding area prior to accepting the job offer. I would have been moving across the country to take this job, and after having previously done that without seeing the area, I promised myself that I would never do that again. I was offered the job and after speaking candidly about my past with the hiring manager we agreed to hold off on my decision on the position until I could visit the area. I paid for all my travel out of pocket. While an expensive trip, the cost was worth the peace of mind.

Another author felt confident moving forward after only meeting future colleagues and seeing the campus virtually, saying:

> The final round of interviews for my current position occurred 100% virtually. The first time I visited the campus was after I had accepted the offer and came

house hunting. Despite the virtual environment, I could tell that multiple people I met with were organized, dedicated to their institution and profession, and possessed emotional intelligence. I was comforted knowing that they prioritized my health and safety by offering a virtual interview. I had no hesitation in accepting the offer and found that the in-person job responsibilities and staff environment matched what I saw in the virtual interviews.

Questions regarding pandemic response are now often included in the interview process from both candidates and employers. One library director asks candidates to "prepare examples of how you can be flexible during a pandemic—and beyond" (Zulkey, 2021, para. 17). Managers want to know that they can depend on the candidate in an environment where policies and circumstances can change on a dime. Institutions also need to be prepared to answer similar questions from candidates. One author gave examples of the types of questions she asked the institution during a job interview:

> Some questions that I asked in my interviews and that I will continue to ask in the future are: How did your institution/library respond in the immediate aftermath of the COVID-19 pandemic? What steps did you take to minimize staff's exposure to the public? What personal protective equipment did you supply your staff and/or patrons?

The way in which an individual or institution responded to the pandemic will provide insight into how they might respond to other difficult situations that arise.

The COVID-19 pandemic has affected the general labor market in many ways. The year 2021 saw unprecedented numbers of employees quitting their jobs, in what has been referred to as the "Great Resignation" (Thompson, 2021). Many of these resignations are driven by workers switching from low-paying jobs or industries to more lucrative careers. However, there is also evidence that the uptick in job switching is driven by discontent with employers, regardless of pay or industry (Gandhi & Robison, 2021). The pandemic has caused many employees to reevaluate their work-life balance and willingness to stay at companies where they do not feel valued. Working through lockdowns has made it evident that institutions have the capacity to be more flexible with employee work arrangements than they have been historically. The post-pandemic employment landscape has seen a shift from a mindset of "You get to work here" to "We get to have employees" (Cohen, 2021). This monumental change will require managers to be increasingly responsive to employee requests and preferences.

It is important now more than ever to invest in employees' long-term job satisfaction. Library workers as a profession are highly susceptible to burnout (Christian, 2015). Academic librarians often simultaneously juggle several responsibilities, including circulation, reference, instruction, outreach, technology troubleshooting, publishing, event planning, committee work, and budgeting. The pandemic environment has required librarians to pivot modalities and services even more in response to national, local, and institutional policy changes. A constant need to be flexible and engage in multitasking can lead to exhaustion and burnout. Long-term academic librarians were found to have a strong commitment to their careers but considerably weaker loyalty to organizations (Millard, 2003). Though employees in academic libraries may be very dedicated to the profession, they will not hesitate to leave an institution when needed.

Communicating how an academic library shows confidence in and appreciation of staff is vital during the hiring process. Upskilling, or investing in the education and professional development of employees, will not only attract talented candidates, but it can also help retain employees who are at heightened risk of burnout due to the pandemic (Cohen, 2021). Henry Albrecht, CEO of Limeade, stated, "Employees want their needs recognized and wellbeing prioritized. When companies invest in upskilling, education, and learning, it shows workers that they're valued" (Cohen, 2021, para. 8). Strategies that are important for retaining workers in academic libraries include funding and time for professional development, tuition reimbursement opportunities, receiving feedback on a regular basis, cross-training for backup coverage in the case of staff absences, and encouraging staff to participate in mentoring programs (Stanley, 2008).

Another personnel issue affecting today's labor market is the increase in retirements already happening among the Baby Boomer generation. Many Boomer employees are in management positions and possess extensive institutional and industry knowledge informed by years of experience. This "silver tsunami" will result in several job vacancies in coming years as well as a need to bridge the skills gap with workers from younger generations who will fill these positions (Young, 2021). The effects of the silver tsunami have been intensified by the COVID-19 pandemic. More than twice as many Baby Boomers retired in 2020 compared to 2019 (Fry, 2020). Several retired earlier than planned to avoid risk of being exposed to COVID-19 in the workplace. Others left due to the stress related to constantly changing guidelines and policies or the sudden need to care for family members.

According to the Current Population Survey, 50 percent of library technicians are 55 years old or older, meaning at or near retirement age (Bureau of Labor Statistics, 2020). The reality of upcoming mass retirements in academic libraries also heightens the need for thorough succession planning. Agarwal and Islam (2015) recommend a combination of extensive policy and procedure documentation, having current employees job shadow departing employees, and documenting workplace practices and history. Specific items that may need to be captured before an employee departs include training documents, signage, outreach handouts, organizational charts, history of the library and collections, and employment records. These documents should be moved to a shared drive or a place that does not require the departing employee's login for access. Proper planning can reduce stress surrounding filling vacant positions as well as ensure continued access to institutional knowledge.

CONCLUSION

After navigating the COVID-19 pandemic for two years, academic library employers and job seekers have weathered a wide variety of changes to employment trends in the field. The experiences shared by both sides can inform and shape a new era of equitable and sustainable hiring practices. As many institutions now face mass retirements and issues surrounding diversity, equity, and inclusion, now is the time to learn from the pandemic to update processes and provide a better hiring and onboarding experience for both employers and candidates.

Virtual hiring poses several challenges but also many exciting opportunities for academic libraries. As one author's supervisor put it, "What if we could find the best candidates for the position period, not just those who are able to come here and interview?" Equipped with current literature and an awareness of the advantages and disadvantages for different interview modalities, employers can increase efficiency while simultaneously attracting a wider range of candidates for open positions. Job seekers can maximize their chances for success in job searching by following recommended best practices and advocating for inclusive and flexible hiring practices.

REFERENCES

Agarwal, N., & Islam, A. (2015). Knowledge retention and transfer: How libraries manage employees leaving and joining. *VINE*, *45*(2), 150–171. https://doi.org/10.1108/VINE-06-2014-0042

Alexander, A. (2021). Virtual onboarding: Lessons from the pandemic. *Public Services Quarterly*, *17*(3), 208–211. https://doi.org/10.1080/15228959.2021.1915913

American Association of Law Libraries (AALL). (2021). Trending: Job searching during the pandemic. *AALL Spectrum*, *25*(3), 7. https://www.aallnet.org/spectrum_issue/

Arch, X., & Gilman, I. (2021). One of us: Social performance in academic library hiring. Proceedings from the ACRL 2021 Virtual Conference. Retrieved from https://alair.ala.org/bitstream/handle/11213/17561/arch_oneofus.pdf?sequence=1

Association of College and Research Libraries (ACRL). (2020). ACRL annual report 2019–2020. *College & Research Libraries News*, *81*(11), 559–586. https://doi.org/10.5860/crln.81.11.559

Bureau of Labor Statistics. (2020). Labor force statistics from the Current Population Survey. https://www.bls.gov/cps/cpsaat11b.htm

Carlos, A. R., & Muralles, D. C. (2021, August 24). Onboarding in the age of COVID-19. *IFLA Journal*. https://doi.org/10.1177/03400352211035413

Chan Zuckerberg Initiative. (2021). A candidate's guide to prepare for a Zoom interview. https://chanzuckerberg.com/wp-content/uploads/2021/05/A-Candidates -Guide-to-Prepare-for-a-Zoom-Interview.pdf

Christian, L. A. (2015). A passion deficit: Occupational burnout and the new librarian: A recommendation report. *The Southeastern Librarian*, 62(4), 2–11. http:// digitalcommons.kennesaw.edu/cgi/viewcontent.cgi?article=1533&context=seln

Cohen, M. (2021, December 11). The "career curiosity" mental shift that the Great Resignation is forcing on employers. *CNBC*. https://www.cnbc.com/2021/12/11 /a-career-curiosity-mental-shift-employers-face-in-great-resignation.html

Couch, D. L., O'Sullivan, B., & Malatzky, C. (2021). What COVID-19 could mean for the future of "work from home": The provocations of three women in the academy. *Gender, Work & Organization*, 28(S1), 266–275. https://doi .org/10.1111/gwao.12548

Cruz, S. (2021, February 19). What's your normal?: A pandemic hire: Thriving as a new academic librarian. *Asian/Pacific American Librarians Association*. https:// www.apalaweb.org/whats-your-normal-a-pandemic-hire/

Dill, E., & Nutefall, J. (2021). Managing self-imposed leadership transitions during unprecedented challenges: Here's your new office! Don't ever come here. *College & Research Libraries News*, 82(5), 237–238. https://doi.org/10.5860/crln.82.5.237

Dill, K. (2020, April 15). It's not just working remotely; hiring and onboarding go virtual, too. *Wall Street Journal*. https://www.wsj.com/articles/its-not-just -working-remotely-hiring-and-onboarding-go-virtual-too-11586963419

Ford, A. (2021, May 3). The library employment landscape. *American Libraries Magazine*. https://americanlibrariesmagazine.org/?p=123175

Frederick, J., & Wolff-Eisenberg, C. (2020). Academic library strategy and budgeting during the COVID-19 pandemic: Results from the Ithaka S+R US Library Survey 2020. *Ithaka S+R*. https://doi.org/10.18665/sr.314507

Fry, R. (2020, November 9). The pace of Boomer retirements has accelerated in the past year. *Pew Research Center*. https://www.pewresearch.org/fact-tank/2020 /11/09/the-pace-of-boomer-retirements-has-accelerated-in-the-past-year/

Gandhi, V., & Robison, J. (2021, July 22). The "Great Resignation" is really the "Great Discontent." *Gallup*. https://www.gallup.com/workplace/351545/great -resignation-really-great-discontent.aspx

Greenhouse, S. (2020, July 3). The coronavirus pandemic has intensified systemic economic racism against Black Americans. *The New Yorker*. https://www .newyorker.com/news/news-desk/the-pandemic-has-intensified-systemic -economic-racism-against-black-americans

Hall, C. (2021, December 13). Women are facing greater interruption challenges with remote work than their male colleagues. *UConn Today*. https://today .uconn.edu/2021/12/women-are-facing-greater-interruption-challenges-with -remote-work-than-their-male-colleagues/

Hardenbrook, J. (2021, February 12). Will COVID end the all-day academic librarian interview? I hope so! *Mr. Library Dude*. https://mrlibrarydude.wordpress .com/2021/02/12/will-covid-end-the-all-day-academic-librarian-interview -i-hope-so/

Harnegie, M. P. (2021). COVID snapshot: How medical libraries and staff adapt to deliver services during a pandemic. *Journal of Hospital Librarianship*, 21(2), 173–183. https://doi.org/10.1080/15323269.2021.1904184

Hodge, M. (Ed.). (2019). The future academic librarian's toolkit: Finding success on the job hunt and in your first job. *Association of College & Research Libraries.*

Howes, L., Ferrell, L., Pettys, G., & Roloff, A. (2021). Adapting to remote library services during COVID-19. *Medical Reference Services Quarterly, 40*(1), 35–47. https://doi.org/10.1080/02763869.2021.1873616

Janse, A. M., Isackson, A., & Chang, A. (2021, November 22). Life without reliable internet remains a daily struggle for millions of Americans. *NPR.* https://www .npr.org/2021/11/22/1037941547/life-without-reliable-broadband-internet -remains-a-daily-struggle-in-nevada

Jewkes, M. D., Swinton, J. J., Cromwell, S., Schramm, D. G., & Brower, N. (2021). Remote hiring innovation during the COVID-19 Pandemic. *Journal of Extension, 58*(5). https://tigerprints.clemson.edu/cgi/viewcontent.cgi?article=1045&context=joe

Jones, S. (2021, September 15). A study of 61,000 Microsoft employees suggests remote work is bad for communication between different teams. *Business Insider.* https://www.businessinsider.com/remote-work-working-from-home-study -microsoft-meetings-2021-9

Kamal, R. (2022, January 4). Quitting is just half the story: The truth behind the "Great Resignation." *The Guardian.* https://www.theguardian.com/business /2022/jan/04/great-resignation-quitting-us-unemployment-economy

Kay, M. (2021). Hiring digital teams remotely. *Information Today, 38*(3), 36–37. https://www.infotoday.com/it/apr21/Kay—Hiring-Digital-Teams-Remotely .shtml

Khodarahmi, M., & Gregory, G. M. (2021). Ready or not, here we come: Job transitions during a pandemic. *College & Research Libraries News, 82*(7), 323–325. https://doi.org/10.5860/crln.82.7.323

Kraus, H., & Baum, R. (2021, April). The humane job search: Recommendations for academic library search committees [Lighting talk]. *Association of College & Research Libraries.* https://opencommons.uconn.edu/libr_pubs/68

Laker, B., Godley, W., Kudret, S., & Trehan, R. (2021, March 9). 4 tips to nail a virtual job interview. *Harvard Business Review.* https://hbr.org/2021/03/4-tips -to-nail-a-virtual-job-interview

Landry, L. (2018, October 3). 9 tips for mastering your next virtual interview. *Harvard Business School Business Insights.* https://online.hbs.edu/blog/post /virtual-interview-tips

Levine, J. (2021, August 16). Summary, July 2021 Core e-forum: Job hunting and hiring during the pandemic. *Core News.* https://alacorenews.org/2021/08/16 /summary-july-2021-core-e-forum-job-hunting-and-hiring-during-the -pandemic/

Library Think Tank—#ALATT. (2021, August 6). Anonymous asks: With the job market really starting to open up, is anyone else planning to call BS on employers [Group post]. *Facebook.* https://www.facebook.com/groups/ALAthinkTANK /permalink/5888888247850613/

Lim, E. J., & Cowan, S. M. (2021). Coffee connections. *University of Connecticut Library.* https://drive.google.com/file/d/1a3-pflj5dWKIAV7t5tfjRncYCRRuRx8G /view?usp=sharing

Millard, D. M. (2003). Why do we stay? Survey of long-term academic librarians in Canada. *Portal: Libraries & the Academy, 3*(1), 99–111. https://doi.org/10.1353 /pla.2003.0015

Reed, J. B., Carroll, A. J., & Jahre, B. (2015). A cohort study of entry level librarians and the academic job search. *The Journal of the New Members Round Table*, 6(1). https://doi.org/10.13016/M2RG9Q

Rogers-Collins, K. (2020, December). Recruiting for an academic librarian position in the age of COVID-19: An inside look at the process. *Library Worklife*. https://ala-apa.org/newsletter/2020/12/08/recruiting-for-an-academic-librarian-position-in-the-age-of-covid-19-an-inside-look-at-the-process/

Sauers, M. (2021, November 1). Acing the interview. *American Libraries*. https://americanlibrariesmagazine.org/?p=126690

Smith, K. (2020, September 15). From public to academic libraries: Changing jobs during COVID-19. *CLIR News*. https://www.clir.org/2020/09/from-public-to-academic-libraries-changing-jobs-during-covid-19/

Stanley, M. (2008). How 'ya gonna keep 'em down on the farm: The problem of retention. *Indiana Libraries*, 27(1), 86–89. http://journals.iupui.edu/index.php/IndianaLibraries/article/view/17109

Tavernise, S., & Oppel, R. A. (2020, March 23). Spit on, yelled at, attacked: Chinese-Americans fear for their safety. *New York Times*. https://www.nytimes.com/2020/03/23/us/chinese-coronavirus-racist-attacks.html

Thompson, D. (2021, December 8). Three myths of the Great Resignation. *The Atlantic*. https://www.theatlantic.com/ideas/archive/2021/12/great-resignation-myths-quitting-jobs/620927/

West Virginia University. (2021). Scholarly Communication Librarian job description. *ALA JobList*. https://drive.google.com/file/d/1u6KFUIOZZT0V-XzGvP2WzWDmqJ8aJcV9/view?usp=sharing

Western Kentucky University. (2021). Core Curriculum Instruction Librarian job description. *ALA JobList*. https://drive.google.com/file/d/1NtPn3ucQvt4Wirv5ilgp66WltoWpZisi/view?usp=sharing

Williams, C. (2019, January). Use your soft skills to stand out in an interview. *Library Worklife*. https://ala-apa.org/newsletter/2019/01/07/use-your-soft-skills-to-stand-out-in-an-interview/

Wros, E. (2021, April 1). The academic library interview: COVID-19 edition. *HLS*. https://hacklibraryschool.com/2021/04/01/the-academic-library-interview-covid-19-edition/

Young, B. (2021, September 30). From the publisher: Silver tsunami. *Georgia Trend Magazine*. https://www.georgiatrend.com/2021/09/30/from-the-publisher-silver-tsunami/

Zulkey, C. (2021, May 3). The virtual job hunt. *American Libraries*. https://americanlibrariesmagazine.org/2021/05/03/virtual-job-hunt-library-jobs/

15

The Virtual Graduate Research Marathon: Remote Library Instruction for Doctoral Candidates

Marina Morgan, Julie N. Hornick, Randall M. MacDonald, and Steven Wade

INTRODUCTION

This chapter will discuss how, during the COVID-19 pandemic and the temporary shift to online instruction, librarians at Florida Southern College sought to preserve meaningful, personalized interaction with graduate students. One element of this service paradigm was based on a model developed over six years of research marathon events hosted by Roux Library, with significant feedback from faculty and graduate students.

Florida Southern College is located in Lakeland and is the oldest private college in Florida. *U.S. News & World Report's* "Best Colleges" guide ranked Florida Southern in the top 10 in three categories in its 2021 edition (U.S. News & World Report, n.d.). Moreover, the college has been recognized in *The Princeton Review*'s prestigious "The Best 387 Colleges" guide for its campus beauty and exceptional architectural heritage (The Princeton Review, 2022). The college is included in the top 20 of the 2022 edition's "Most Beautiful Campus" listing, in part due to featuring the world's largest single-site collection of Frank Lloyd Wright buildings, which were designated a National Historic Landmark in 2012 (National Park Service, 2022).

Florida Southern College, primarily a residential institution, has 149 full-time faculty and over 3,500 students. It offers more than 70 undergraduate majors and 14 graduate programs. The Roux Library and McKay Archives team consists of six librarians with faculty status and six staff. The library provides access to over 600,000 electronic resources, 170,000 print, and 12,000 media resources.

SUPPORTING GRADUATE STUDENTS AT FLORIDA SOUTHERN COLLEGE

A review of the literature regarding support for students revealed that librarians play a key role in providing information literacy instruction for subject-relevant library resources (Bussell et al., 2017). It also showed that virtual learning environments are extensively used in higher education (Allan, 2010). Typically, academic libraries offer in-person or virtual instructional sessions focused on topics such as introduction to citation management software, literature reviews, or research strategies. Other libraries take a holistic approach to library support for graduate students and create environments that foster communication and facilitate academic writing. For example, the University of Utah's J. Willard Marriott Library designed a virtual community for research practice approach for graduate student support (Ziegenfuss, 2021), while Cornell University Library took their existing library workshops and transformed them into a four-day research skills boot camp for graduate students (Eldermire et al., 2019). Another example of graduate student support is the University of Oklahoma Libraries' Research Retreat, which incorporates technology and research workshops for graduate students in various disciplines (The University of Oklahoma University Libraries, 2022).

Graduate students have a greater need for formal research support compared to established academics. They must become comfortable with an academic environment, learn how to navigate unfamiliar databases, become proficient in developing comprehensive literature reviews, and successfully generate new scholarship. Students require librarians' expertise to gain access to a wide range of information resources at different stages of their research. Some students start their graduate program with up-to-date information-seeking experience, while others have only basic research skills, having been out of academia for some time.

Florida Southern College first offered master's degrees in education from the late 1930s through the late 1940s. The graduate program was revived in the 1980s with the development of an MBA program, at which time funding for graduate-level library resources was established. Additional graduate programs in nursing and allied health and the social sciences followed in the 2000s and 2010s, including master's and doctoral programs in education. Among those are a general Doctor of Education (EdD) program and an EdD in Educational Leadership (EdD-EL) program.

The director of the library is an ex officio member of the college's Graduate Council and has observed the formation and development of a number of graduate programs at the college. The director shares information about each new program with other librarians so that a cohesive, program-specific support approach may be developed.

In addition to funding for graduate library resources, traditional library support for graduate students has included general orientation sessions, course-specific instruction, and all manner of individual consultations for in-person and remote students. Librarians serving as departmental liaisons regularly communicate with faculty about resources and services, and the relationships fostered by this dialogue helped ease the transition to remote instruction during the COVID-19 pandemic, as librarians were counted on to remain engaged with students and faculty. Circulation staff members are trained by librarians on how to use and suggest electronic products, a team approach that ensures continuity of support and assistance.

Today, the Roux Library instruction program serves nearly 600 graduate students from master's and doctoral programs in business and accounting, nursing and health science, education, industrial and organizational psychology, and physical therapy. Instruction librarian visits to new student orientations for these programs each year provide students with their first exposure to the library's resources and services. In the 2020–2021 academic year, librarians met with 85 graduate students in consultations, and with 145 students in graduate classes. According to a student survey conducted in the spring of 2021, 70 percent of graduate students surveyed reported that all or most of their professors required the use of library resources, and 60 percent reported that they had received library instruction in class from a librarian.

Roux Library has been an OCLC member library since 1978 and has participated in OCLC-supported interlibrary loan (ILL) services since the late 1980s. ILL services are provided to students, faculty, and staff at no cost, and they are supplemented by librarian-mediated document delivery. The resource sharing librarian has extensive experience with copyright issues and provides guidance to graduate and undergraduate students on these and related topics.

Roux Library also provides support to doctoral students in education who wish to publish their dissertation in ProQuest Electronic Theses and Dissertations (ETD). Students working on their dissertation and recent graduates meet with the metadata librarian to start the process of submitting their dissertation to ProQuest.

ORIGINS OF THE GRADUATE RESEARCH MARATHON

Roux Library's Faculty Research Marathons began in the summer of 2015 and are designed to support faculty research, writing, and study. During a research marathon, the second and third floors of the library are closed

to other patrons, allowing a quiet, distraction-free environment for participants. Breakfast and lunch are served, and faculty are encouraged to share
their progress and successes, and to network with colleagues. The library
offered two-day research marathons at least twice each year until the
COVID-19 pandemic forced the cancellation of in-person events in 2020.
While the early marathon events offered presentations to faculty by guest
speakers throughout the day, feedback received from faculty demonstrated
that they placed more value on quiet, isolated time in which they could
work free from distractions.

In the summer of 2018, the EdD program coordinator approached the
library director about the possibility of adapting the existing Faculty
Research Marathon for the students in her program. She had participated in
the research marathons and believed that her students would benefit from
the same sort of dedicated time for research and writing, skills development,
and fellowship with other graduate students. The librarians were immediately able to see the benefit of offering such a program and began the
planning process.

After several planning meetings, during which possible sessions were
discussed and selected, a format for this reimagined research marathon was
established. The first EdD research marathon was held in October 2018.
Seeing the success of the EdD marathon, the coordinator of Florida Southern's EdD-EL program approached the library about supporting a marathon for his students, and the first marathon for EdD-EL was held in
June 2019.

The structure of the graduate research marathons differs slightly from the
faculty research marathons. While the latter program focuses on providing
quiet, focused time for faculty away from distractions, the graduate research
marathons offer workshops and meeting opportunities throughout the day
in addition to quiet, focused time.

Held over the course of two days, in-person graduate research marathons
began on Saturday at 8:00 a.m. with introductions from faculty, librarians,
the dean of the School of Education, the associate provost, and the provost.
Students introduce themselves and state their goals for the day. Concurrent
workshops begin at 8:45 a.m. Students are free to attend any workshops or
to work quietly on their own. After a break for lunch and socializing, the
workshops resume and continue until 5:00 p.m. After a brief wrap-up, the
marathon concludes at 6:00 p.m. On the second day, participants gather at
noon and work until 6:00 p.m. In addition to workshops and focused work
time, the research marathon schedule also includes opportunities for students to meet and connect individually with their professors, advisers, or
librarians.

Although the EdD and EdD-EL programs are complementary and share
many faculty, the initial series of graduate research marathons was open to
students in one or the other program, not both. Two parallel events were

held each semester, with instructional and informational sessions repeated for each group. Leadership within the School of Education changed for both programs during the pandemic, and in the spring of 2022, students from both programs attended a unified graduate research marathon, a progression the librarians welcomed.

Following each marathon, an anonymous Likert-type survey was e-mailed to all participants, inviting them to share ratings and comments regarding their satisfaction with the marathon they attended. Additionally, at the third graduate research marathon, interviews and focus groups were held as part of a collaborative research study conducted by librarians and School of Education faculty. The interviews and focus groups proved informative and showed that the marathons were providing benefits to the students in several key areas, and, by correlation, to the library and the School of Education.

According to the coordinator of the Doctor of Education program, the first in-person graduate research marathon was "a smash hit," with students expressing their gratitude and appreciation for the opportunity to study in an environment focused on research and scholarship with support from librarians. In the survey that followed the event, students shared that work colleagues and mentors were impressed by the collaborative academic program represented by the marathons. One student brought a work colleague enrolled in another doctoral program so they could benefit from Roux Library's space and time to engage in their scholarly work. Others recognized that this kind of library support was unique and that the collegial and collaborative atmosphere of the research marathon contributed to a weekend of research alongside a community of scholars for the doctoral students. The research marathons have become a point of pride for the School of Education.

BENEFITS OF THE GRADUATE RESEARCH MARATHON

Unsurprisingly, research indicates that doctoral students often experience a sense of isolation, especially as they reach the dissertation stage (Devenish et al., 2009; Fleming-May & Yuro, 2009; Greener, 2021; Janta et al., 2014). This isolation, beyond being detrimental to the well-being of the student, has the potential to lead to non-completion of the degree. Librarians were gratified to find through interactions with students that the research marathons were helping not only to alleviate feelings of isolation they were experiencing but were also helping to build a stronger sense of community, not only with their professors but also with their peers.

Another benefit provided by the research marathons was the alleviation of anxiety on the part of participants. There is a great deal of research in the literature that addresses the feelings of anxiety students at all levels experience when entering an academic library (Carlile, 2007; Mellon, 1986; Parks, 2019; Shelmerdine, 2018; Van Kampen-Breit & Cooke, 2015).

Understanding that anxiety can keep students from fully benefiting from the services the library offers and may contribute to non-completion of degrees, one of the goals of the research marathon was to reduce both that anxiety and the anxiety related to the process of working toward, and completing, their studies and dissertation. Feedback indicated that this goal had been accomplished.

As indicated in the interviews (Giordano et al., 2020), Florida Southern College graduate students appreciated the opportunity to build their skills as researchers through the workshops and information sessions, as described in the following comment: "The research foundation that I got just exponentially grew from the beginning of this program to now in the sessions that we've had." Furthermore, from initially thinking of the library experience in an unflattering way ("I was horrified to go to the library. I don't know why, I just always was."), or being mystified about the function of an academic library ("I just didn't really understand the whole library environment, or what a librarian does or what they have to offer."), participants' perceptions shifted to an understanding that the library is a welcoming space, and that librarians are there to assist them.

Roux Library's mission is to connect students with resources to fully support academic programs and to provide engaged instruction in their use. The in-person research marathons directly support this mission and the librarians' commitment to remain dynamically engaged and visible in the academic life of the college. Both the faculty and the graduate research marathons provide a direct connection to scholars who are receptive to support and assistance, and for whom the librarians can provide a tangible benefit. Informal and survey feedback has indicated that this support is timely, useful, and appreciated, all of which reinforces the positive reputation of the library and librarians on campus.

EVOLUTION THROUGH NECESSITY

At the beginning of 2020, the college community was only vaguely aware of what was happening with the developing COVID-19 pandemic. As reports of the scope of what the world was facing became more urgent, though, the seriousness of the situation was evident. It was no surprise, then, when the campus shut down after spring break and moved to a fully online environment. This precluded any in-person research marathons for the foreseeable future. Given the benefits that students and the library were gaining from the marathons, the librarians did not want to abandon the developed momentum. Furthermore, in the rush to move to virtual learning, librarians had concerns about the (ultimately unfounded) perception that the library would lose relevance in the face of the faculty's valid anxiety about mere survival.

When the college moved to remote instruction during March 2020, the librarians focused on delivering broad-based library services and resources in a manner that was timely and visible, primarily for the benefit of our patrons. While working remotely, librarians explored various modalities for providing services to students and faculty. Online practice sessions were held with library staff using Microsoft Teams and Zoom to determine which platform was preferred as a method of virtual conferencing. GroupMe and Slack for communication between teams were evaluated to determine the benefits of each. In addition to learning platforms that had been unfamiliar to some in the library, there was a need to ensure that library staff would become proficient enough with the available technology in order to effectively provide services to users. Librarians initiated a voicemail and texting service for patrons using a shared Google Voice account. Taking the time to plan scaffolded strategies for communicating with the campus community ensured that the library maintained previous personal connections.

When the fall of 2020 began with the College still in a mainly virtual environment, and with students now accustomed to virtual classrooms, librarians and School of Education faculty considered whether the marathon could also be moved online. The work the librarians had done to become familiar with online and virtual modalities ensured that they would be comfortable making the shift from in-person to online information delivery. In addition, the team did not want to lose the momentum and strong partnerships that had been created with in-person marathons. For these reasons, the decision was made to create the virtual graduate research marathons, which allowed for the continuation of the workshops, advising, and social time the doctoral students had come to value.

Moving to online instruction during the marathon allowed the librarians to provide flexible research skills training and connect with graduate students who would otherwise work in isolation. Simultaneous sessions were offered to introduce students to key resources and skills without losing the advantages of an in-person event. The number of participants in the first virtual research marathon was 30 percent higher than the previous in-person event pre-COVID-19. Ease of access contributed to this increase; one virtual marathon had graduate students attending from all over Florida, as well as Michigan, Texas, and Washington State.

The structure of the virtual marathon closely resembled that of the in-person events, with a key difference being that they were one-day events instead of two. Virtual marathons were held via Zoom and utilized breakout rooms to offer concurrent sessions each hour, as well as quiet rooms that participants could join to approximate the experience of working in the presence of others, as they would at in-person events. A virtual poster session was held to allow students to present the progress of their research. Additionally, the librarians observed during the in-person library events the importance of social interactions and knew it was critical to adapt those for the virtual environment. For this reason, virtual marathons featured a social breakout room in addition to quiet rooms.

During the virtual marathon, librarians facilitated a number of work-shops, including basic and advanced research strategies, individual questions regarding researching, interlibrary loan services, copyright, and publishing dissertations in ProQuest ETD. In addition, School of Education faculty and graduate students delivered presentations on nutrition and relieving stress, writing literature reviews, APA citation style, and preparing to write a dissertation.

Feedback from students who participated in the virtual research marathons indicated that they would recommend the virtual research marathon to others. Students highly rated library workshops, quiet rooms, and individual consultations, with no session having a mean score below 4.25 out of 5. Additionally, when asked how helpful the support they received from academic librarians and faculty was, respondents' answers had a mean rate of 4.95.

Virtual marathons conducted during the first three pandemic-affected semesters remained separate by program (EdD and EdD-EL), but the flexibility offered by Zoom led to a changing philosophy among School of Education faculty. Eventually, the two programs successfully came together in a single in-person, schoolwide marathon held at Roux Library and McKay Archives.

CONCLUSION

As the pandemic continued, initial concerns about the library's perceived relevance quickly subsided, as faculty and students reacted positively to outreach and communication. The virtual graduate research marathons provided a familiar, direct connection for students and faculty, and provided a welcome opportunity for the librarians to engage virtually with our community of scholars. Each of the marathons reinforced the library's importance on our campus and highlighted specific ways librarians support students. This visibility led to increased opportunities for librarians to address the entire faculty during pre-semester symposia and during faculty meetings, and to a gradual return to pre-pandemic general instructional services numbers.

There is no doubt that librarian-faculty relationships cultivated over a number of years eased the transition to virtual graduate research marathons and related support. Clarity of purpose and a shared willingness to serve students in any way possible were also critical.

Once the move was made to a virtual environment, advantages were realized that were incorporated into subsequent in-person events, all of which benefited students, faculty, and the library. The scale of the virtual marathons, with concurrent sessions, demonstrated that we could increase the scope of the in-person event. As a result, in the spring of 2022, a joint marathon was held that included students from both the EdD and

EdD-Leadership programs. Events were held in two adjacent buildings, including a dynamic poster session that was modeled on earlier virtual poster sessions. Although virtual graduate research marathons were not envisioned prior to the pandemic, they strengthened the library's identity and reputation, and librarians met team and personal challenges creatively and with enthusiasm.

REFERENCES

Allan, B. (2010). *Supporting research students*. Facet Publishing.

Bussell, H., Hagman, J., & Guder, C. S. (2017). Research needs and learning format preferences of graduate students at a large public university: An exploratory study. *College & Research Libraries, 78*(7), 978–998. https://doi.org/10.5860/crl.78.7.978

Carlile, H. (2007). The implications of library anxiety for academic reference services: A review of the literature. *Australian Academic & Research Libraries, 38*(2), 129–147. https://doi.org/10.1080/00048623.2007.10721282

Devenish, R., Dyer, S., Jefferson, T., Lord, L., van Leeuwen, S., & Fazakerley, V. (2009). Peer to peer support: The disappearing work in the doctoral student experience. *Higher Education Research & Development, 28*(1), 59–70. https://doi.org/10.1080/07294360802444362

Eldermire, E. R. B., Johns, E. M., Newberry, S., & Cole, V. A. (2019). Repackaging library workshops into disciplinary bootcamps: Creating graduate student success. *College & Research Libraries News, 80*(7), 394–410. https://doi.org/10.5860/crln.80.7.394

Fleming-May, R., & Yuro, L. (2009). From student to scholar: The academic library and social sciences PhD students' transformation. *Portal: Libraries & the Academy, 9*(2), 199–221. http://dx.doi.org/10.1353/pla.0.0040

Giordano, V., Hornick, J., Galbraith, N., MacDonald, R. M., Morgan, M., & Wade, S. (2020, October). The Graduate Research Marathon: Leading the way forward for doctoral candidates in an academic library [Poster session]. *2020 Florida Library Association Annual Meeting, Virtual*.

Greener, S. L. (2021). Non-supervisory support for doctoral students in business and management: A critical friend. *The International Journal of Management Education, 19*(2), 1–8. https://doi.org/10.1016/j.ijme.2021.100463

Janta, H., Lugosi, P., & Brown, L. (2014). Coping with loneliness: A netnographic study of doctoral students. *Journal of Further & Higher Education, 38*(4), 553–571. https://doi.org/10.1080/0309877X.2012.726972

Mellon, C. A. (1986). Library anxiety: A grounded theory and its development. *College & Research Libraries, 47*(2), 160–165. https://doi.org/10.5860/crl_47_02_160

National Park Service. (2022, February 24). List of NHLs by state. https://www.nps.gov/subjects/nationalhistoriclandmarks/list-of-nhls-by-state.htm

Parks, C. (2019). Testing a warmth-based instruction intervention for reducing library anxiety in first-year undergraduate students. *Evidence Based Library & Information Practice, 14*(2), 70–84. https://doi.org/10.18438/eblip29548

The Princeton Review. (2022). Most beautiful campus. https://www.princetonreview.com/college-rankings?rankings=most-beautiful-campus

Shelmerdine, A. J. (2018). Library anxiety: Stories, theories and possible solutions. *Journal of the Australian Library & Information Association, 67*(4), 343–352. https://doi.org/10.1080/24750158.2018.1534281

The University of Oklahoma University Libraries. (2022). 2022 graduate student research retreat. https://libraries.ou.edu/researchretreat

U.S. News & World Report. (n.d.). Florida Southern College rankings. https://www.usnews.com/best-colleges/florida-southern-college-1488/overall-rankings

Van Kampen-Breit, D. J., & Cooke, R. (2015). Do they think we're the frenemy?: Examining student anxiety and service perception in today's academic libraries. *Library Leadership & Management, 30*(1), 1–16.

Ziegenfuss, D. H. (2021). Designing an online graduate community for research practice: Going beyond single purpose design. *Journal of Library & Information Services in Distance Learning, 15*(1), 1–12. https://doi.org/10.1080/15332 90x.2021.1896622

16

Leverage from the Lockdown: Transitioning Information Literacy Instruction during the COVID-19 Pandemic: A Case Study

Judith Toppin

BACKGROUND

The coronavirus spread rapidly across the world after it was first reported on December 31, 2019, in Wuhan province, China. In January 2020, the World Health Organization (WHO) issued a press release stating that the coronavirus was a "public emergency of international concern" (WHO, 2020a). By February, the University of the West Indies (UWI), established a COVID-19 Task Force to address internal readiness and response of the institution to the COVID-19 situation. (University of West Indies, 2020a). The rapid spread of the virus prompted the WHO to issue a further statement in March, at which time the coronavirus was categorized as "a global pandemic" (World Health Organization, 2020b).

INTRODUCTION

The Cave Hill campus of the University of the West Indies is located on the Caribbean Island of Barbados. Geographically, the island is 21 miles long and 14 miles wide, with a land mass of 166 square miles (430 square kilometers). The population of Barbados is approximately 270,000, and the country is ranked 58th in the world by the United Nations Human Development Index (2022), which gives Barbados a literacy rating of 99.6 percent.

The Cave Hill campus was established in 1967 as the third campus of the University of the West Indies, after the Mona and St. Augustine campuses, located on the islands of Jamaica and Trinidad and Tobago, respectively. The Cave Hill campus provides teaching and research support to students enrolled in six faculties: Culture, Creative and Performing Arts, Humanities and Education, Law, Medicine, Science and Technology and Social Sciences. The student population of just over 6,000 includes undergraduate and postgraduate students from Barbados, other Caribbean territories, and various international jurisdictions (University of West Indies, 2020b).

There are six libraries on the Cave Hill campus. The Sidney Martin Library (SML) is the largest, with a staff of eight professional librarians and twenty-four paraprofessionals. Liaison librarians are assigned to each faculty to provide information literacy instruction and research support. The library's holdings include a print collection of approximately 200,000 titles as well as subscriptions to commercial databases, e-books, and audiovisual resources. The SML includes a West Indian collection (WIC), which focuses on building a collection of contemporary and archival resources, including special collection material, on Barbados and the wider Caribbean. The other libraries on campus are the Audine Wilkinson Documentation Centre, the CLR James Cricket Research Centre, The Elizabeth Watson Audiovisual Unit, the Faculty of Law Library, and the Faculty of Medical Sciences Library. Services offered by the Sidney Martin Library include information literacy instruction, reference assistance, interlibrary loan, and thesis scrutiny. Patrons also have access to material on course reserves, rooms for individual or group study, a computer lab, and 24-hour study rooms. Photocopying, printing, and a book binding and repair service are also available. Strong wireless connectivity is available throughout the campus and at all campus libraries.

The holdings and resources of all libraries located on the campuses of the University of the West Indies are jointly accessible through an online, web-based information portal. The portal, known as the UWI Libraries Information Connexion and commonly referred to as UWILinC, provides access to bibliographic listings of print resources. Full-text access is provided to subscription databases that include scholarly journals, e-books, and newspaper articles. The catalogues of all four campuses can also be accessed through the UWILinC portal: https://uwin-primo.hosted.exlibrisgroup.com/primo -explore/search?vid=CAV&lang=en_US&fromRedirectFilter=true

PREPARING FOR THE PANDEMIC

By February 2020, campus administration announced the cessation of face-to-face classes and a transition to an online format (University of West Indies, 2020c). An effort was made to keep lecture rooms, science laboratories, computer labs, and study spaces, including libraries, open and operational. The campus embarked on an education and sensitization campaign to inform the campus community of guidelines and procedures to curtail spread of the virus, including frequent handwashing with soap, use of hand sanitizer, and maintaining a social distance of six feet between persons (University of West Indies, 2020d). Posters outlining these measures were placed on notice boards and highly trafficked locations, such as classrooms and lecture theaters.

The library implemented all health and safety guidelines as outlined by the campus. Hand sanitizer dispensers were placed at the circulation desk, in the computer lab, on each floor of the library building, and at the main entrance to the library where students are required to deposit their bags before entering the building. Initially, the established hours of operation for the libraries remained unchanged; however, concern over the rapid spread of the virus led to an adjustment to operating hours and the introduction of a staggered work schedule for staff (UWI, 2020e). Online reference support, information literacy instruction, and research assistance for postgraduate students were identified as services which the library would continue. A notice was circulated to the campus community to inform everyone of the services that the library would continue to deliver in the event of closure (University of West Indies, 2020f).

Less than two months after the initial announcement by the WHO, the local newspapers reported in a front-page headline on March 11 that two cases of the coronavirus had reached the shores of Barbados (International Monetary Fund, 2021). By March 23, staff were informed via the Office of Marketing and Communication (MARCOMM) that the campus would close the following day (University of West Indies, 2020g, March 23). One week later, the government of Barbados announced plans for a national curfew and implemented legislation that effectively brought all major commercial and educational activity to a halt (Barbados Government, 2020).

INFORMATION LITERACY INSTRUCTION AT CAVE HILL

Information literacy, as defined by the Association of College and Research Libraries (ACRL), "is a set of abilities requiring individuals to recognize when information is needed and have the ability to locate, evaluate and use effectively the needed information" (American Library Association, 2000, p. 207).

The information literacy instruction program at the Sidney Martin Library developed out of the library orientation program when it was recognized that students needed additional assistance on how to conduct research. Library orientation is held in the first semester of every new academic year. Student participation is voluntary and traditionally includes a physical tour of the building, a brief demonstration of the library's catalog, and information on special collections and resources. A handout outlining the range of services is provided to students who attend.

Feedback received revealed that many first-year students required more help and guidance on how to conduct research. Conscious that the young students were entering the university with limited research skills and exposure or experience on how to approach library research, a plan was developed to introduce information literacy instruction sessions (Iton, 2006). This began as a separate component of student library orientation, which focused on developing information research skills (Iton, 2006). The need for an additional instruction session was supported by the results of an unpublished analysis of library orientation at Cave Hill conducted over a three-year period from 2009 to 2011. The survey showed evidence of a low level of student participation in orientation (Toppin & Lewis, 2013). The results of this survey also highlighted the need to inform students on how to develop an effective approach to conducting research.

Prior to this survey, an information literacy competency document was drafted to guide instruction to first-year students. The plan outlined learning objectives and key learning outcomes (Iton, 2008). An instruction template was prepared to guide the approach to teaching information literacy to students. Information literacy instruction grew from its fledgling beginnings as a pilot project out of the Faculty of Humanities and Social Sciences and expanded to include students from all faculties across campus. It has become an integral part of the teaching and instruction landscape for students enrolled in the first-year language program (Iton, 2006). The courses taught in this foundational series are compulsory for all students in the Faculty of Humanities and Social Sciences. Fortuitously, this has allowed the information literacy component to become embedded in courses taught in both semesters and to have a wider reach and greater impact on students' understanding and comprehension. Later, the Foundation Language Program was rebranded as the Academic Literacies Program (ALP).

The scope and content for information literacy instruction followed the guidelines established by ACRL's Framework for Information Literacy for Higher Education and the Information Literacy Competency Standards for Higher Education The SML's information literacy strategic plan adopted the six threshold concepts: 1. Scholarship is a conversation, 2. Research as inquiry, 3. Authority is contextual and constructed, 4. Format as a process, 5. Searching as exploration, and 6. Information has value. The SML plan outlined that information literacy instruction should target students at three levels:

- Level 1. Entry-level, or first-year students
- Level 2. Second- and final-year students enrolled in courses with a research component
- Level 3. Postgraduate students.

LEVEL 1. ENTRY-LEVEL, OR FIRST-YEAR STUDENTS

Prior to the COVID-19 pandemic, most instruction sessions at this level were held in the library's computer lab, which can accommodate about 30 students. A PowerPoint-based instruction template was prepared, which ensured uniformity in scope and concepts for delivery of instruction. Later, a worksheet was added to the instruction module, and the two-hour session was divided to allow the presenter to describe the essential components of the research process, such as developing a search strategy, primary versus secondary sources, and scholarly versus popular resources. The second half of the session gave students the opportunity to gain practical exposure to conducting research using the worksheet as a guide. This was very popular with students since it allowed them to practice searching skills under the guidance of the instruction librarian. (See sample worksheet in this chapter's appendix.) A general evaluation form captured student feedback on the various sections covered and the presenter's ability to teach. Although feedback provided by students was informative, it was felt that a better approach could be used to evaluate student comprehension of concepts.

To address this, an active learning component was introduced using the interactive presentation software Mentimeter, which provided real-time assessment of student knowledge and critical thinking skills. The software facilitated the use of in-class quizzes, which increased student participation, since they could use their cell phones to respond. Students were often visibly thrilled to see their responses assessed in real time. The software offered a range of options for testing students' knowledge and understanding, which made it possible to incorporate short quizzes, multiple-choice questions, and timed team competitions into the two-hour session. This approach to assessing student understanding and critical thinking also gained favorable feedback from lecturers.

LEVEL 2. INSTRUCTION AT THE COURSE/SUBJECT LEVEL

Instruction provided at this level began with the assumption that students had completed one of the compulsory foundational courses and had some exposure and understanding of information literacy. Emphasis was placed on providing students with advanced search techniques, including guidelines on how to effectively evaluate Web sites. Students were expected to apply search techniques and be knowledgeable on the different types of scholarly resources. Techniques used to identify electronic resources of relevance to their subject or topic were also covered at this level. Some sessions were held in the library, while sessions for larger classes were delivered in the lecture theater by the librarian. The sessions were delivered using a PowerPoint presentation followed by a practical demonstration of the online catalog, UWILinC, and a demonstration of effective approaches to advanced search strategies. A handout was provided to students when the practical component was not possible.

LEVEL 3. INSTRUCTION TO POSTGRADUATE STUDENTS

Instruction at this level took the form of a workshop. Topics covered included crafting a literature review, finding relevant resources, using bibliographic management software (EndNote), and formatting theses and research papers. The workshop was conducted in collaboration with the Department of Graduate Studies, who promoted the workshop to postgraduate students. Sessions were well received, which led to requests for the library to deliver other presentations. Presentations were prepared and delivered on academic integrity, using the Web for research, advanced database search techniques, and avoiding plagiarism.

Between 2014 and 2019, over 450 training sessions were held for students, with all instruction delivered by librarians in the Sidney Martin Library. The number of requests received for instruction at the entry level and course levels increased, and, as illustrated by Figure 16.1, is evidence of growing support by faculty for the program.

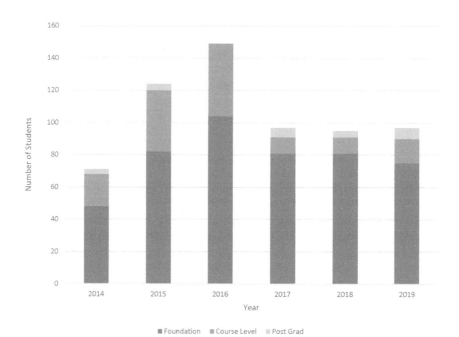

FIGURE 16.1. Information literacy instruction at the Sidney Martin Library from 2014 to 2019

TRANSITION TO ONLINE DELIVERY OF SERVICES

The rapidly deteriorating circumstances resulting from the COVID-19 pandemic required making quick decisions. At the time, the library was not prepared to provide instruction or services online. Initially, the task seemed daunting. After meetings with librarians, it was decided that the library should make a concerted effort to continue to support teaching and learning on campus. In addition to information literacy instruction, other services identified for transition to online delivery were thesis scrutiny, access to databases, and online reference support.

UPGRADE OF COMPUTER HARDWARE AND SOFTWARE

Some of the areas identified as potential hindrances to providing online services were the library's aged computers, the need for upgraded software, and limited server space. Most of these were successfully addressed with the assistance and support of the Campus Information and Technology Services (CITS) Department and Educational Media Services (EDS). Most of the computers used by librarians were upgraded to accommodate installation of the required software (e.g., Microsoft 365 and Microsoft Teams). Once the software was installed and staff members were taught how to use it, the library organized online training sessions and established remote contact with lecturers and students. The library was also provided with a Zoom account to facilitate online instruction during the pandemic.

INSTRUCTION DURING LOCKDOWN

Discussions held with the coordinator of the Academic Literacies Program (formerly the Foundation Language Program) sought to identify an effective approach for delivery of information literacy instruction if the library closed. After considering several options, and conscious of the limitations of access and unavailability of software, it was decided that information literacy instruction should be packaged for asynchronous delivery using a voiceover PowerPoint. Quick training by the Educational Media Services (EMS) Department facilitated the preparation of the voiceover PowerPoint. The PowerPoint, titled *Sharpening Your Research Skills*, was prepared by the coordinator of the library's information literacy program and uploaded to the eLearning platform. Students were encouraged by their lecturers to view the PowerPoint, which was about 90 minutes long. The research worksheet was revised, and an electronic version sent to the ALP coordinator for distribution to the students. (See the chapter appendix for a sample worksheet.) Information literacy instruction to second- and third-year students continued during the closure when requested by the lecturer of a course. The liaison librarians used Microsoft Teams and Zoom to conduct online training sessions. During closure, the *thesis* *c*onsultation *s*ervice held sessions on thesis formatting with those postgraduate students who contacted the library for assistance. The *o*nline *c*hat *s*ervice, although introduced, was suspended after a short period.

APPROACHES TO INSTRUCTION AFTER REOPENING

After campus libraries and the administration offices reopened, most classes continued to be delivered online. The coordinator of the Academic Literacies Program indicated satisfaction with the asynchronous format, since it allowed students who were not physically on campus or in the country to participate online. Additionally, they recommended that an evaluation component be added so that student understanding of the concepts could be assessed. Five questions were prepared to cover topics discussed in each section. A final quiz of 10 questions was prepared to test the students' overall knowledge and understanding. The instruction session was divided into the following sections to facilitate insertion of a short quiz after each section.

- Using the online catalog UWILinC
- Identifying various information resources
- Searching by keyword, subject, and Boolean connectors
- Searching electronic databases
- Avoiding plagiarism

Online instruction sessions continued to be held at the course/subject level and for postgraduate students. An online workshop was held for postgraduate students after the library reopened.

CHALLENGES

Coping with the COVID-19 pandemic was challenging on several fronts. A major challenge arose from the psychological effect that the pandemic had on staff and students. A feeling of uncertainty and fear enveloped many persons, who, in addition to continuing to undertake work activities, also had to confront the effects of the virus on themselves, their families, and work colleagues. Although many people showed tremendous resilience, this was an emotionally stressful time, and it affected work output.

The social distancing protocols, which required six feet to be maintained between persons, meant that the library's computer lab could only accommodate classes of up to 15 persons. Additionally, some sections of the library remained closed (e.g., the 24-hour reading room) to ensure compliance with the campus protocols of cleaning, sanitizing, and social distancing.

Martzukou (2021) discusses the challenges resulting from the rapid switch to an online environment by academic libraries. The permanence of the change and the realization that a return to a traditional approach to instruction is unlikely in the foreseeable future led to uncertainty when planning how the library would deliver remote instruction. The library's lack of access to electronic teaching platforms such as eLearning meant that the library's ability to provide effective instruction and support online teaching programs was limited.

The suspension of the online chat service due to operational difficulties reduced the options available to students should they wish to contact the library for assistance. Allowing students to have remote access to their liaison librarian would have helped in the planning and delivery of instruction. Some librarians resorted to using their own devices to contact students.

Environmental issues were experienced due to increased humidity resulting from the extended closure of the physical building. This has repercussions for all resources, but is of special concern to material in special collections, where a controlled temperature is critical to the longevity of material.

Some students experienced challenges with the switch to online classes, especially those that did not have immediate access to computers or other electronic devices. Unstable Internet connectivity or lack of access to equipment were main areas of concern. While arrangements were made to assist students, such as loaning laptops, the lack of access to print resources proved challenging for many. Students with special challenges were also affected since the library's special needs unit was also closed during the pandemic.

LESSONS LEARNED

For centuries, libraries were regarded and perceived as being the heart of institutions of learning and guardians of knowledge. In turn, libraries were confident that their collections would always be accessible according to their terms and conditions. The emergence of the Internet as an information resource, the development of commercial databases, and the onset of the COVID-19 pandemic resulted in immediate change to the access and availability of critical resources and the valuable printed resources stored in libraries. The stark reality is that libraries can no longer depend on one mode for delivery. This also applies to methods used to deliver library instruction. Attention must be given to developing tools to support research and instruction that can be accessed online. These include guides to collections and resources, videos, and digital learning objects (DLOs). These guides will provide effective support to the library's online instruction and will add significant value to the university's online teaching and research objectives.

A critical lesson learned from the pandemic is the importance of establishing collaborative networks with the academic community. The successful transition of library services to online delivery was largely due to the support and assistance received from other departments on campus who provided workable and cost-effective solutions that could be easily implemented. Support from faculty for the continuation of asynchronous information literacy instruction is heartening and provides much-needed support for the transition to an online format. Collaboration with faculty must be expanded to allow for the development of digital learning objects to support online teaching and learning.

RECOMMENDATIONS

Teaching and instruction will continue to be offered by academic libraries; however, the mode of delivery must adjust to fit the new environment. The experience gained from delivering information services during the COVID-19 pandemic emphasizes the importance of updating and revising the information literacy strategic plan for libraries on the Cave Hill campus. The plan should include integrating information literacy instruction into the curriculum at the course level. An instruction design specialist should support development of online instruction modules. Librarians must become trained in information literacy instruction so that effective support can be provided to the information literacy curriculum.

Libraries must look beyond their traditional audience and explore the opportunity to host seminars and activities that appeal to a wider, even international audience (Martzoukou, 2021). Emphasis should be given to hosting online seminars and providing outreach services to customers, specifically researchers beyond the immediate academic community of students and researchers (Cox & Butler, 2020). The development of research services can provide additional revenue since the traditional forms of revenue obtained though overdue book fines is likely to decrease. Consideration should also be given to establishing an outreach program which targets both primary and secondary students and exposes these potential university students to research skills.

Both Martzoukou (2021) and Cox and Butler (2020) believe that libraries should take a strategic approach to ensuring their survival and sustainability. In a separate article, Cox (2020) suggests that a digitization program is one of the critical areas that will support the survival of academic libraries. He explains that future leverage for academic libraries lies in their ability to expand access to digital content A digitization plan should be prepared to expand access to the resources and collections currently only available in hard copy. The digitization of resources would support the development of digital learning objects (DLOs) and expand access and visibility to material in special collections. These would prove to be invaluable resource support for information literacy instruction. For small libraries in developing countries, much of this expansion hinges on the availability of financial support to allow for the procurement of relevant hardware and software. This is critical if projects such as digitization and the storage of electronic or digitized material is to be expanded.

Cox and Butler (2020) suggest that less emphasis should be given to the physical spaces in libraries and more focus shown to electronic and online storage options. This approach may differ for academic libraries in developing countries since the need for the physical space will continue. In addition to expanding online storage capacity, consideration should be given to repurposing internal library spaces to support alternative forms of instruction and creativity,

CONCLUSION

The rapid spread of the coronavirus impacted our lives and livelihoods worldwide. Curfews and national lockdowns affected workplace functionality and economic productivity and disrupted family life. Libraries prepared for closure and established remote instruction in an environment that had not been experienced in recent memory. Several approaches were considered to ensure continued service delivery. Despite these challenges, the pandemic created a silver lining in the proverbial COVID cloud, which has given life to new opportunities for instruction and information delivery.

Despite the short time frame and limited resources, the transition of information literacy instruction to an online format is one of the success stories of the Sidney Martin Library. While informal feedback indicates that there is room for improvement, the online method of instruction is preferred by students and lecturers. This will encourage the development of an online instruction curriculum. It will also provide the opportunity for library spaces and facilities to be repurposed to support creative learning.

When the pandemic began, no one could have imagined that it would continue for such an extended period. The initial expectation was that the changes were temporary and only in place until a return to normal life. Instead, the pandemic has ushered in a new era, one which holds exciting possibilities for collection management, approaches to instruction, and the dissemination of information. Libraries should embrace this period of change and consider introducing innovative approaches that would chart a new direction for instruction and service delivery in what will become the new normal in a post-pandemic era.

REFERENCES

American Library Association. (2000). ACRL standards. Information literacy competency standards for higher education. *College & Research Libraries News*, *61*(3), 207–215. https://doi.org/10.5860/crln.61.3.207

Barbados Government. (2020). Emergency Management Act Cap 160 A SI 2020 no 27.

Cox, C., (2020, June). Academic libraries will change in significant ways as a result of the pandemic (opinion). *Inside Hired*.

Cox, C., & Butler, E. (2020, December 16). Visions of success: Academic libraries in a post COVID-19 world (News section). *Library Journal*.

International Monetary Fund (IMF). (2021, July). *Policy Responses to COVID-19*. IMF. https://www.imf.org/en/Topics/imf-and-covid19/Policy-Responses-to-COVID-19

Iton, I. (2006). *Breaking into unexplored Territory: A case study of the Information Literacy initiative at the Cave Hill Campus of the University of the West Indies*. Paper presented at the 72nd IFLA General Conference and Council, Seoul Korea.

Iton, I. (2008, June). First year information literacy competencies: Librarians perspective. *The Main Library*. Unpublished.

Iton, I. (2016, June). Learning outcomes for the library session. *Main Library*. Unpublished

Martzoukou, K. (2021). Academic libraries in COVID-19: A renewed mission for digital literacy. *Library Management Online, 42*(4/5).

Toppin, J., & Lewis, J. (2013). *Library orientation for new students at the Cave Hill Campus of the University of the West Indies. An Analysis*. UWI. unpublished.

Two cases confirmed. (2020, March 18). The Barbados Advocate.

United Nations (2022). Human development report. *Country Profile, Barbados*. Retrieved from https://hdr.undp.org/en/countries/profiles/BRB

University of West Indies (UWI) (2020a, February 28). The UWI establishes COVID-19 Task Force [Press release]. https://www.cavehill.uwi.edu/covid19/uwi-news -releases/the-uwi-establishes-covid-19-task-force.aspx

University of West Indies (UWI) (2020b, March 9). COVID-19 protocols and procedures. https://www.cavehill.uwi.edu/covid19/campus-updates/uwi,-cave-hill -covid-19-protocols-procedures.aspx

University of West Indies (UWI) (2020c, March 16). Letter to staff re. online teaching. https://www.cavehill.uwi.edu/covid19/staff-notices/letter-to-staff-re-online -teaching.aspx

University of West Indies (UWI) (2020d, March 20). Changes to the hours of the Sidney Martin Library and the Law Library. https://www.cavehill.uwi.edu /covid19/campus-updates/changes-to-the-hours-of-the-sidney-martin-library .aspx

University of West Indies (UWI) (2020e, March 23). Campus closure due to COVID-19. https://www.cavehill.uwi.edu/covid19/campus-updates/campus-closure-due -to-covid-19.aspx

University of West Indies (UWI) (2020f, March 24). Update on library services offered during the COVID-19 pandemic. https://www.cavehill.uwi.edu/covid19 /campus-updates/update-on-library-services-offered-during-the-covi.aspx

University of West Indies (UWI) (2020g). *Statistics 2019/20.* Cave Hill Campus, Barbados. Retrieved from https://www.cavehill.uwi.edu/about/resources/reports/cavehill-statistics-2019-2020.pdf

World Health Organization (WHO) (2020a, January 05). *Emergencies preparedness, response. Pneumonia of unknown cause—China* [Press release]. https://www.who.int/emergencies/disease-outbreak-news/item/2020-DON229

World Health Organization (WHO) (2020b, March 11). *WHO Director-General's opening remarks at the media briefing on COVID-19* [Press release]. https://www.who.int/director-general/speeches/detail/who-director-general-s-opening-remarks-at-the-media-briefing-on-covid-19—11-march-2020

APPENDIX

Sample of Research Worksheet Used with Information Literacy Instruction

Research Worksheet

Developing an Effective Search Strategy

This worksheet is designed to help you develop a strategy to search for information. It also includes exercises for you to practice searching the library's catalog, UWILinC, and the electronic databases. Before you begin, take a few minutes to think about your topic. This will help you to find what you are looking for quickly and easily.

Plan Your Search

State what you are looking for in one sentence, e.g., "I want to find information on *the effect of global warming on the economic development of island states.*

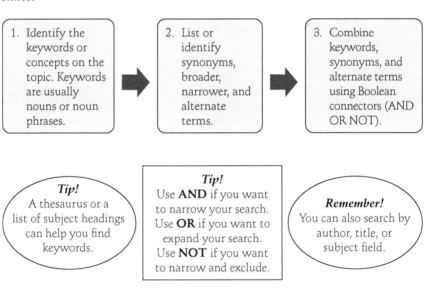

1. Identify the keywords or concepts on the topic. Keywords are usually nouns or noun phrases.

2. List or identify synonyms, broader, narrower, and alternate terms.

3. Combine keywords, synonyms, and alternate terms using Boolean connectors (AND OR NOT).

Tip!
A thesaurus or a list of subject headings can help you find keywords.

Tip!
Use **AND** if you want to narrow your search. Use **OR** if you want to expand your search. Use **NOT** if you want to narrow and exclude.

Remember!
You can also search by author, title, or subject field.

Worksheet designed and created by J. Toppin, Information Literacy Coordinator, SML

| **State Your Topic:** |
| **List Keywords:** |
| **Connect Keywords/Phrases:** |
| **Enter Search Terms into UWILinC.** |

Exercises

| 1. Use UWILinC to find a book written or edited by V. Eudine Barriteau.

What is the title of the book? _____

What year was it published? _____ Add the book to your e-shelf? |
| 2. Go to **Find Databases** and select **EBSCOHost** from the Databases A–Z list.

Select **Academic Search Complete** and **Business Source Complete**.

Conduct a search for a scholarly peer-reviewed article on your topic.

Open the article in full text and e-mail it to yourself. Include the MLA citation for the article. |
| 3. Go to **Find EJournals** in **UWILinC**.

Search for the journal **Social and Economic Studies**.

What is the earliest issue available in electronic format?

Search for an article on your topic. |
| 4. Use UWILinC to search for an audiovisual resource (**DVD, Video, Record,** etc.) on Psychology.

Where is it located—which library or unit? |
| 5. Select **Find Ebooks in UWLIinC**

Search for an e-book on tourism.

List the title of the e-book. _____

Select a chapter from the book for download. |

Worksheet designed and created by J. Toppin, Information Literacy Coordinator, SML

About the Editors and Contributors

EDITORS

MOU CHAKRABORTY is the director of External Library Services at Salisbury University Libraries. She is a liaison to several departments and oversees distance library services. Her professional interests include but are not limited to distance learning, information literacy, open educational resources, copyright, customer service training and issues, international students and education, etc. An active member in multiple library associations, Mou has presented at many conferences nationally and regionally, conducted interactive workshops on customer service, and published articles as well as a previous book with ABC-CLIO.

SAMANTHA HARLOW has been working with libraries, instructional technology, and online learning for over 10 years. She is currently the Online Learning Librarian at the University of North Carolina at Greensboro (UNC Greensboro, or UNCG) in Greensboro, North Carolina, and she serves as a liaison to the Community and Therapeutic Recreation, Kinesiology, and Public Health Education Departments. In her job at UNC Greensboro, she works with the Research, Outreach, and Instruction (ROI) Department of the UNCG University Libraries to train and assist liaison librarians with online learning, including creating accessible digital objects, managing the UNCG Libraries Research Tutorials, integrating the library into the Canvas learning management system (LMS), and hosting a variety of online and face-to-face events for students and instructors.

HEATHER MOOREFIELD-LANG is an associate professor for the Department of Library and Information Science at the University of North Carolina at Greensboro. She has long been interested in how technologies can enhance instruction in face-to-face and online learning in libraries and classrooms. Heather has a wide variety of journal publications as well the book *School Library Makerspaces in Action* with ABC-CLIO. To hear more about her work, follow her on Twitter @actinginthelib.

CONTRIBUTORS

PATRICIA E. ANDERSEN is an assistant librarian at the Colorado School of Mines. Over the last 20 years, she has worked on access services, assessment of user services, and space planning. Patricia is interested in how students use the library and plays a part in designing new student and staff space in the library. Patricia has published and presented on assessment and user services.

BEATRIZ BETANCOURT HARDY is Dean of Libraries and Instructional Resources at Salisbury University. She is active in statewide library diversity efforts and has twice chaired the Council of Library Directors of the University System of Maryland and Affiliated Institutions Library Consortium, serving as its acting director for nearly a year. Her presentation and publication interests tend to be whatever issues her libraries are facing, particularly diversity, instruction, and special collections. She also continues to be an active scholar in colonial Maryland history and Chesapeake studies.

HEATHER BLICHER, MLIS, is a community college library coordinator and formerly an Online Learning Librarian. Heather's professional interests include online librarianship and the intersection of open educational resources with diversity, equity, and inclusion. Heather is a recipient of the ACRL Distance Librarianship Award and an alumni of the ALA Leadership Institute.

BRIANNA B. BULJUNG is the Teaching and Learning Librarian at the Colorado School of Mines. She collaborates with classroom faculty to integrate information literacy instruction into the curriculum, teaches sessions, develops policy, and supports the efforts of other instruction librarians. Prior to joining Mines in 2016, she was the Engineering and Computer Science Librarian at the U.S. Naval Academy and a contract reference librarian at the National Defense University. She earned her master's in Library and Information Science from the University of Denver in 2011.

JONATHAN CORNFORTH is currently the Student Success Librarian for Pollak Library at California State University, Fullerton. He works with a range of learners, but first-year students in particular. He holds two master's degrees: an MA in English from California State University, Fullerton, and an MLIS degree from San José State University.

COTTON COSLETT is the Online Learning Librarian at California State University, Fullerton. His research interests include online pedagogy, library instruction, and the health sciences.

TRACY COYNE is the Distance Learning and Professional Studies Librarian at Northwestern University Libraries. She is the liaison to the School of Professional Studies and supports a number of undergraduate, graduate, and continuing studies programs. Her responsibilities include providing online and in-person research instruction and assisting students and faculty in locating materials and navigating information resources. Prior to becoming a librarian, she spent over 20 years as a researcher and writer in the international business field.

JENNY DALE (she/her/hers) is the information literacy coordinator of the UNCG University Libraries. In this role, she supervises two instruction librarians who coordinate the Libraries' first-year instruction program, which includes information literacy support for the basic communication course. She also serves as a liaison to a number of academic programs at UNCG, including Communication Studies. She holds a BA in English and an MS in Library Science from UNC-Chapel Hill.

GYASI EVANS is the Outreach and Engagement Librarian at the Arthur Lakes Library. As the Outreach and Engagement Librarian, he works across campus to connect with the Mines and Golden community members through events and programming. He also shares information regarding library services and information resources. Gyasi also comanages all the communication efforts in the library, including digital, social media, and physical advertising. Gyasi is available for reference/research consultations as well as tours of the library.

SUELI MARA FERREIRA has published and given dozens of works, lectures, and workshops in different countries inside and outside the Latin American and Caribbean region. Sueli is a senior professor at the University of São Paulo (USP), in the Postgraduate Program in Information Science and Documentation. She has long been interested in how technologies can enhance instruction in face-to-face and online learning in libraries and classrooms. Since 1995, she has been actively involved in various national and international associative movements, especially at the International Federation of Library Associations and Institutions, or IFLA (since 2000), in different positions and functions. She is currently president of the Brazilian Copyright and Open Access Commission of the Brazilian Federation of Associations of Librarians, Information Scientists and Associates (FEBAB, 2016–2023).

LAUREN M. FLETCHER, MLIS, MA, is the Medical Education and Clinical Engagement Librarian at Brown University. She has applied for and held library positions across the United States since she graduated with her MLIS from the University of Pittsburgh. Her research interests include digital pedagogy, medical education, and evidence synthesis.

MEGAN GRAEWINGHOLT is the Social Sciences and Government Documents Librarian for Pollak Library at California State University, Fullerton. Megan supports the History, American Studies, and Political Science Departments as a library liaison and subject specialist. She serves as the Dean's Fellow for Reference Services and Coordinator of the Government Documents Depository Collection. Megan is a feature columnist for *DttP: Documents to the People*, the journal of the American Library Association's Government Documents Round Table. Her research interests include the development of academic library reference services and the impact of primary sources in library instruction.

ROSLYN GRANDY, MLIS, MS, is the Pharmacy Librarian at the University of Connecticut. She has applied for hundreds and interviewed for dozens of library and information science (LIS) jobs throughout her career and is passionate about creating a positive hiring experience for both job candidates and employers. Her research interests include academic publishing, bibliometrics, hiring in LIS, and library anxiety.

COLLEEN ROBLEDO GREENE is the Digital Literacy Librarian for Pollak Library at California State University, Fullerton (CSUF). Her work focuses on helping faculty and students integrate more digital tools and strategies into their curriculum, research, and scholarship. Prior to this, she was the Systems Librarian and then Marketing Librarian for CSUF. She also has worked in newsroom and public libraries. Colleen is an instructor for the School of Information at San José State University, where she has taught an online asynchronous genealogy research methods and librarianship course since 2016. She is a nationally recognized presenter specializing in Mexican and Hispanic genealogy.

JULIE N. HORNICK is an Instructional Services Librarian at Florida Southern College, where she provides instructional and research support to a number of schools and departments. She earned her MA in French from Penn State University and her MLIS from the University of South Carolina's School of Library and Information Science. Her research interests include incorporating new technologies into instruction and instructional design.

JOY HOWARD is presently an associate professor of Teacher Education at the University of Southern Indiana. Her work utilizes critical race and intersectional frameworks to examine issues of educational inequities. To follow her work, please connect on ResearchGate at https://www.researchgate.net/profile/Joy-Howard.

AMY M. JONES is Head of Circulation for the Salisbury University (SU) Libraries, where she works with a great team of Access Services professionals who offer responsive service in Circulation, Course Reserves, and Interlibrary Loan. She is active on the SU Libraries' Diversity and Inclusion Committee and serves as an adjunct French instructor at the University.

ERIC KARKHOFF is a Research and Instruction Librarian at California State University, Fullerton. He holds an MLIS degree from San José State University and has worked in public and academic libraries for nearly 20 years.

DIANE G. KLARE is the associate dean and library director of the McDermott Library at the United States Air Force Academy. She was previously the Associate University Librarian for Research and Access Services at Wesleyan University and served twice as the interim university librarian. Her research interests include leadership, effective change management practices, and library space design to enhance user experiences. Diane earned a bachelor of arts in French and a a master of business administration from the University of Connecticut, a master of library science from Southern Connecticut State University, and a certificate of advanced study from Wesleyan University.

EMILY LEACHMAN is the Senior Librarian for Public Services at Central Piedmont Community College, a role she has held since 2015. Emily serves as the chair of the library's training committee and has long held an interest in staff training and development. When not at work, Emily is an avid quilter.

NOAH LENSTRA, MLIS, PhD, is an assistant professor of Library and Information Science and an affiliated faculty member in the Gerontology program at the University of North Carolina at Greensboro. He earned his PhD in Library and Information Science from the University of Illinois. His interests center around the diffusion of new models of community partnership in public librarianship, with a particular focus on public health partnerships. His work on these topics has been funded by the Institute of Museum and Library Services, the South Carolina Center for Rural and Primary Healthcare, and the State Library of North Carolina.

A. GARRISON LIBBY is the assistant director of Instructional and Research Services at Central Piedmont Community College. His research interests include instructional design and open educational resources. His non-research interests include running, mantis shrimp, and eating doughnuts.

RANDALL M. MacDONALD is Director of the Library at Florida Southern College, where he has served since 1986. He earned an MSLS from Florida State University, and he received a BA from the University of Alabama. He has published on diverse topics, such as the role of the Internet in school libraries, hiring in academic libraries, the architecture of Frank Lloyd Wright, and local history.

KIMBERLY MacKENZIE, MLIS, PhD, is a medical writer at OPEN Health and a former Research Data and Scholarly Communications Librarian at a Massachusetts medical school and research university. Her experiences applying and training for a position during the COVID-19 pandemic led to her interest in the process and experiences of other librarians. Her research interests include open science and medical/science communication.

MARINA MORGAN is the Metadata Librarian at Florida Southern College. In her role, she supervises the operations of Technical Services, serves as the ILS and ProQuest ETD administrator, manages the Institutional Repository, and comanages Digital Collections. She earned her master of information studies from the University of Toronto and post-master's certificate in Library and Information Science from San José State University. Her research interests focus on scholarly communications, digital scholarship, and digital humanities.

REBECCA NEEL, MLS, is the assistant director of Resource Management and User Experience at the University of Southern Indiana. As a former Online Learning Librarian, she works to adapt systems and technical services workflows to meet distance and online learning (DOL) user needs and expectations. Rebecca is also pursuing a doctoral degree in education, focusing on high school to college information literacy transitions.

LISA S. NICKUM is the Systems Discovery Librarian at the Colorado School of Mines. She is responsible for library systems that facilitate search, discovery, and delivery of library services and resources in both the physical and digital realms as systems administrator for a library management system and related products. Prior to the Systems position, Lisa was the Government Publications Librarian for over 20 years at Mines. She earned her master of science in Library Science from the University of North Carolina in 1993.

FATIH OGUZ, PhD, is an associate professor of Library and Information Science at the University of North Carolina at Greensboro. Dr. Oguz received his PhD in Library and Information Sciences at the University of North Texas. His research focuses on the interactions between people and technology, with an emphasis on the impact of information technologies on human communication behavior and social life.

RACHEL OLSEN (she/her/hers) is the First-Year Communication and Social Sciences Librarian at UNCG University Libraries. In this role, she is responsible for coordinating library instruction and research support for the Communication Studies 105 program. She is also the librarian for a number of different academic departments and programs on campus. She holds a BA in History from UNCG and an MSLS from UNC-Chapel Hill.

DAVID PALMQUIST has been an analyst/programmer with California State University, Fullerton, for over 20 years and has been on the Pollak Library's systems team for the last 5 years. He has been a volunteer instructor with Carpentries.org for over 2 years and is passionate about their mission for building a "global capacity in essential data and computational skills for conducting efficient, open, and reproducible research."

LAURA PASSOS SANTANA is a librarian from Latin America who holds a master's degree in Information Science from the University of São Paulo, Brazil. She is a researcher in the field of Information and Culture and a specialist in digital learning. She has been advising educational and governmental institutions across the Americas for 10 years under international organizations in the areas of technology and health care. Currently, she oversees digital skills educational programs across Latin America and supports the library of the UNESCO Institute for Lifelong Learning through literacy programs for emerging countries.

JAHALA SIMUEL was Head, Access Services, and Medical Librarian at the Louis Stokes Health Sciences Library at Howard University but is currently a High School Library Media Specialist with the District of Columbia Public Schools. She is skilled in creating LibGuides; giving reference assistance to faculty, staff, and students; and providing database training. She manages the day-to-day function of the Access Services desk and supervises staff and student workers. Jahala has been in the library profession for 18 years, with 5 of those years as a Health Sciences Librarian. She is a member of the American Library Association (ALA), the Black Caucus of the American Library Association (BCALA), and the Medical Library Association (MLA), and is currently on ALA Council.

SOPHIA SOTILLEO is an associate professor and the interim library director of Langston Hughes Memorial Library at Lincoln University in Pennsylvania. In this capacity, she has the privilege to teach information literacy sessions for all disciplines, First Year Experience and the African Experience course, and work with the Library Team to support and ensure that the Library is a part of the Lincoln University curriculum and cocurricular strategic plans for student success. Her current area of research and interest is embedded librarianship, with a focus on access, advocacy, and leadership in the field of librarianship.

KELLY STORMKING is a librarian in the Biomedical Library at St. Jude Children's Research Hospital in Memphis, Tennessee. Thanks to time spent with the fantastic team in the Library Experience and Access Department of Oregon State University's Valley Library, Kelly has developed a great enthusiasm for board gaming and joy curation in libraries. This is their first publication, and Kelly would like to acknowledge support from Beth Filar-Williams, Steve Weber, Rima Reeves, and Matthew Schuck in the development of this chapter, with an extra special round of applause to Mom.

DAVID SYE is a Research and Instruction Librarian and assistant professor at Murray State University, where he is the subject librarian for history, political science, sociology, and psychology. Much of his research focuses on digital archival literacy and how researchers use digital archives and repositories.

FAYTHE THURMAN, MLIS, MA, is the Scholarly Engagement Librarian at the West Virginia University Health Sciences Library. Her experiences job searching and working in academic libraries during the COVID-19 pandemic increased her interest in analyzing the ways libraries can utilize technology to create more equitable services and processes for people that use the library as well as current and prospective library employees. To learn more about her research and publications, visit Faythe's ORCiD page.

JUDITH TOPPIN is the Officer in Charge of the Sidney Martin Library at the Cave Hill campus of the University of the West Indies. She is also the coordinator of information literacy instruction and was instrumental in incorporating interactive software into library instruction. She has also written and researched on Caribbean heritage and the issues that have shaped Caribbean society.

STEVEN WADE is an Instructional Services Librarian at Florida Southern College in Lakeland, Florida. He earned his BA from Western Kentucky University in 2011, and his MLIS from Louisiana State University in 2015. Steven's research interests include combating misinformation online and creating engaging information literacy programs for students.

ZACH WELHOUSE is an Online Learning Librarian at Oregon State University. His research interests include information literacy instruction, game design, and the undergraduate experience. He holds an MLIS from the University of Washington and an MA in English with a specialization in cultural studies from Kansas State University. His Zoom bookshelf is divided between unplayed role-playing games and oversized comics.

RACHEL WHITNEY, MLIS, AHIP, is a Research and Education Informationist at the Medical University of South Carolina (MUSC) Libraries. Her experience applying and onboarding as an early career librarian during the COVID-19 pandemic fueled her interest in exploring the hiring experiences of other librarians. Her areas of interest are evidence-based librarianship, epidemiology, scholarly communication, and data management and visualization.

JOSEPH WINBERRY is a PhD candidate at the University of Tennessee's College of Communication and Information. His current research examines the roles and interactions of information, technology, and social justice in an aging society, often focusing on action-based methodologies and justice for marginalized elder populations. Winberry's research has been published in *The International Journal of Information, Diversity, and Inclusion, The Journal of Librarianship and Information Science*, and *The Library Quarterly*, among others. Joseph has received funding and awards from the American Library Association, the Association for Information Science and Technology, and the Association for Library and Information Science Education.

ANDREA M. WRIGHT brings her enthusiasm for library services to the United States Air Force Academy's McDermott Library as Associate Director for Public Services. Her work focuses on increasing student success through effective information literacy instruction, improving access to library resources and services, and connecting with students, faculty, staff, and administrators across campus to help them meet their information needs and achieve their goals.

Index

Page numbers followed by *f* or *t* indicate figures or tables, respectively.